Vocabulary Workshop
First Course

- **Words in Context**
- **Analogies**
- **Multiple Meanings**
- **Synonyms, Antonyms**
- **Prefixes, Suffixes, Roots**
- **Word Origins**

HOLT, RINEHART AND WINSTON

A Harcourt Classroom Education Company

Austin · New York · Orlando · Atlanta · San Francisco · Boston · Dallas · Toronto · London

Consultant

Norbert Elliot, the general editor of *Vocabulary Workshop,* has a Ph.D. in English from The University of Tennessee. He is a professor of English at New Jersey Institute of Technology. A former site director for the National Writing Project, he has directed summer language arts institutes for kindergarten through twelfth-grade teachers in the public schools. A specialist in test development and evaluation of writing, Norbert Elliot has written books and articles on writing assessment, communication, and critical thinking. Dr. Elliot is the father of five children and is married to Lorna Jean Elliot, under whose care, he says, "everything thrives."

Contents

Changes

MAKING NEW WORDS YOUR OWN 1

SKILLS AND STRATEGIES
- Context Clues
- Word Structure
- Sound Clues
- Dictionary Definition
- Like and Opposite Meanings

CONTEXT: Change in Arts and Literature

CONTEXT: Change in Individuals and Communities

CONTEXT: Change in Science and Technology

UNDERSTANDING NEW WORDS AND THEIR USES

SKILLS AND STRATEGIES
- Multimeaning
- Word Analysis
    Prefixes
    Suffixes
    Word Origins

CONTEXT: Change in Arts and Literature

CONTEXT: Change in Individuals and Communities

CONTEXT: Change in Science and Technology

CONNECTING NEW WORDS AND PATTERNS 155

SKILLS AND STRATEGIES
- Understanding Analogies
- Types of Analogies
- Solving Analogies

READING NEW WORDS IN CONTEXT 173

SKILLS AND STRATEGIES
- Reading Longer Passages
- Reading Strategically

CONTEXT: Change in Arts and Literature

CONTEXT: Change in Individuals and Communities

CONTEXT: Change in Science and Technology

COMMON ROOTS, PREFIXES, AND SUFFIXES

The following tables list some common roots, prefixes, and suffixes. Use these tables to help you determine the meaning of a word by examining its structure.

ROOTS		
BASE	**MEANING**	**EXAMPLES**
act	to do, drive	**act**ion, **act**or, re**act**, trans**act**, en**act**
alt	high	**alt**itude, **alt**imeter
ann, enn	year	**ann**ual, per**enn**ial, bicent**enn**ial
aqua	water	**aqua**rium, **aqua**marine, **aqua**naut
aster, astro	star	**astro**nomy, **astro**nomical, **aster**isk
aud	to hear	**aud**ience, **aud**itorium, **aud**ible
biblio, bibli	book	**bibli**ographer, **biblio**mania, **bibli**cal
bio	life	**bio**logy, **bio**chemistry, **bio**degradable
cede	to go; to yield	inter**cede**, super**cede**, con**cede**
cent	one hundred	per**cent**, bi**cent**ennial, **cent**ennial
chrono	time	**chrono**logy, **chrono**meter, **chrono**scope
circ, circum	around	**circum**ference, **circ**le, **circ**ular
cred	to believe, trust	**cred**ibility, in**cred**ible, **cred**it, **cred**ential
dem	people	**dem**ocracy, **dem**agogue, epi**dem**ic
dent	tooth	**dent**ist, **dent**al, **dent**ifrice
dic, dict	to say, to speak; to assert	**dict**ion, **dict**ionary, **dict**ate
dur	hard, lasting	**dur**ation, **dur**able, en**dur**e
fin	end, limit	**fin**ish, **fin**ite, in**fin**ite, **fin**al
gen	race, family, kind	**gen**ealogy, **gen**eral, **gen**eration
geo	earth	**geo**logy, **geo**centric, **geo**dynamics
graph, gram	to write, draw, record	auto**graph**, tele**gram**, para**graph**
hab	to have, to hold; to dwell	**hab**it, **hab**itat, in**hab**it
hydro	water	**hydro**gen, **hydro**dynamics, **hydro**plane
hypo	under, below	**hypo**dermic, **hypo**tension, **hypo**thermia
jur, jus, judic	law, right, judgment	**jur**ist, **jus**tify, **judic**ial
leg	law	**leg**al, **leg**islator, **leg**itimate
loc	place	**loc**al, **loc**alize, re**loc**ate, dis**loc**ate

ROOTS (continued)		
BASE	**MEANING**	**EXAMPLES**
logue, logo	idea, word, speech, reason	dia**logue**, mono**logue**, epi**logue**, **log**ical
manu	hand	**manu**al, **manu**facture
med, medi	middle	**med**iate, **medi**eval, **medi**ocre
meter, metr	measure	dia**meter**, **metr**ic, milli**meter**
morph	form	pseudo**morph**, meso**morph**, meta**morph**osis
micro	small	**micro**scope, **micro**rganism
mono	one	**mono**logue, **mono**gamy, **mono**graph
mov, mob, mot	to move	**mob**, **mob**ile, re**mov**e, **mot**ion
noc, nox	night	equi**nox**, **noc**turnal, **noc**turne
ped	foot	**ped**estal, **ped**estrian, **ped**al
peri	around	**peri**meter, **peri**scope, **peri**phery
petr	rock	**petr**ify, **petr**oleum, **petr**oglyph
phon	sound, voice	**phon**etics, **phon**ics, tele**phon**e
photo	light	**photo**graphy, **photo**flash, **photo**genic
port	to carry	im**port**, ex**port**, **port**able
pyr	fire	**pyr**omania, **pyr**otechnic
sci	to know	con**sci**ence, **sci**ence, **sci**entist
scope	to see	kaleido**scope**, tele**scope**, micro**scope**
scrib, script	to write	in**scrib**e, sub**script**ion, **script**
sign	mark	**sign**al, **sign**ature, in**sign**ia
spec, spect, spic	to see, look at, behold	in**spect**, re**spect**, **spect**acle, **spec**ies
syn, sym	together	**sym**phony, **syn**thesize
techn	art, skill	**techn**ical, **techn**ology, **techn**ique
temp	time	**temp**orary, **temp**er
therm	heat	**therm**ometer, **therm**onuclear
tract	to pull, draw	at**tract**, re**tract**, **tract**ion
vis, vid	to see, look	re**vis**ion, **vid**eo, **vis**ible
volve	roll	in**volve**, re**volve**, re**volu**tion

PREFIXES

PREFIX	MEANING	EXAMPLES
ab–	from; away from	**ab**normal, **ab**duct, **ab**sent, **ab**hor
ad–	to; motion toward; addition to	**ad**apt, **ad**dict, **ad**here, **ad**mit
aero–	air	**aero**bic, **aero**biology, **aero**space
amphi–	both, around	**amphi**bian, **amphi**theater
an–	not	**an**archy, **an**esthesia, **an**onymous
ante–	before	**ante**bellum, **ante**cede, **ante**date
anti–	against; opposite; reverse	**anti**aircraft, **anti**freeze, **anti**biotics
ap–	to; nearness to	**ap**proximate, **ap**point, **ap**proach
auto–	self	**auto**matic, **auto**graph, **auto**biography
bene–	good	**bene**diction, **bene**factor, **bene**volent
bi–	two	**bi**facial, **bi**focal, **bi**ennial
circum–	around	**circum**navigate, **circum**ference
co–, con–	together	**co**author, **co**operate, **con**front, **con**found
contra–	against	**contra**dict, **contra**distinguish, **contra**ry
de–	opposite of; away from; undo	**de**activate, **de**form, **de**grade, **de**plete, **de**scend
dis–	opposite	**dis**agree, **dis**arm, **dis**continue, **dis**honest
ex–	out; beyond; away from; former	**ex**cel, **ex**clude, **ex**hale, **ex**ile
extra–	outside; beyond; besides	**extra**ordinary, **extra**curricular
for–	not	**for**bid, **for**get, **for**go
fore–	before	**fore**cast, **fore**word, **fore**stall, **fore**thought
hyper–	more than normal; too much	**hyper**active, **hyper**critical, **hyper**tension
il–	not	**il**legal, **il**legible, **il**literate, **il**logical
im–	into	**im**mediate, **im**merse, **im**migrate, **im**port
im–	not	**im**balance, **im**mature, **im**mobilize
in–	not; go into	**in**accurate, **in**active, **in**habit
inter–	among; between	**inter**action, **inter**cede, **inter**change
intra–	within	**intra**mural, **intra**state, **intra**venous
ir–	not	**ir**redeemable, **ir**regular, **ir**responsible
mal–	wrong; bad	**mal**adjusted, **mal**function, **mal**ice
mis–	wrong; bad; no; not	**mis**fire, **mis**behave, **mis**conduct
non–	not; opposite of	**non**committal, **non**conductor, **non**partisan
ob–	against	**ob**stacle, **ob**stinate, **ob**struct, **ob**ject

PREFIXES (continued)		
PREFIX	**MEANING**	**EXAMPLES**
per–	through	percolate, perceive
post–	after	postglacial, postgraduate, posterior
pre–	before	preamble, prearrange, precaution
pro–	before; for; in support of	prognosis, program, prologue, prophet
pro–	forward	proceed, produce, proficient, progress
re–	back; again	recall, recede, reflect, repay
retro–	backward	retroactive, retrospect, retrocede
se–	apart	secure, secede, secession
self–	of the self	self-taught, self-worth, self-respect, selfish
semi–	half; partly	semicircle, semiformal, semitrailer
sub–	under; beneath	subcontract, subject, submarine, submerge
super–	over	superabound, superabundant, superhuman
sur–	over; above	surcharge, surface, surmount, surpass
trans–	across; over	transatlantic, transcend, transcribe, transfer
ultra–	extremely	ultraliberal, ultramodern, ultrasonic
un–	not	unable, uncomfortable, uncertain, unhappy

SUFFIXES

SUFFIX	MEANING	EXAMPLES
–able, ible	able to be; capable of being	intelligible, probable, inevitable
–ade	action or process	blockade, escapade, parade
–age	action or process	marriage, pilgrimage, voyage
–al, –ial	of; like; relating to; suitable for	potential, musical, national
–ance	act; process; quality; state of being	tolerance, alliance, acceptance
–ant	one who	assistant, immigrant, merchant
–ary	of; like; relating to	customary, honorary, obituary
–ate	characteristic of; to become	officiate, consecrate, activate
–cle, –icle	small	corpuscle, cubicle, particle
–cy	fact or state of being	diplomacy, privacy, relevancy
–dom	state or quality of	boredom, freedom, martyrdom
–ence	act or state of being	occurrence, conference
–ent	doing; having; showing	fraudulent, dependent, negligent
–er	one who; that which	boxer, rancher, employer
–ery	place for; act, practice of	surgery, robbery, nursery
–esque	like	picturesque, statuesque
–ess	female	goddess, heiress, princess
–ful	full of	careful, fearful, joyful, thoughtful
–ible	capable of being	collectible, legible, divisible
–ic	relating to; characteristic of	comic, historic, poetic, public
–ify	to make; to cause to be	modify, glorify, beautify, pacify
–ion	act, condition, or result of	calculation, action, confederation
–ish	of or belonging to; characterized by	tallish, amateurish, selfish
–ism	act, practice, or result of; example	barbarism, heroism, cyncism
–ity	condition; state of being	integrity, sincerity, calamity, purity
–ive	of; relating to; belonging to; tending to	inquisitive, active, creative
–ize	make; cause to be; subject to	jeopardize, standardize, computerize
–less	without	ageless, careless, thoughtless, tireless
–let	small	islet, leaflet, owlet, rivulet, starlet
–like	like; characteristic of	childlike, waiflike
–logy	study or theory of	biology, ecology, geology

SUFFIXES (continued)		
SUFFIX	**MEANING**	**EXAMPLES**
–ly	every	daily, weekly, monthly, yearly
–ly	like; characteristic of	fatherly, queenly, deadly
–ly	resembling	officially, sincerely, kindly
–ment	action or process	development, government
–ment	state or quality of	amusement, amazement, predicament
–ment	product or thing	fragment, instrument, ornament
–ness	state or quality of being	kindness, abruptness, happiness
–or	one who	actor, auditor, doctor, donor
–ous	having; full of; characterized by	riotous, courageous, advantageous
–ship	state or quality of being	censorship, ownership, governorship
–some	like; tending to be	meddlesome, bothersome, noisome
–tude	state or quality of being	solitude, multitude, aptitude
–y	characterized by	thrifty, jealousy, frequency, sticky

KINDS OF CONTEXT CLUES

CONTEXT

The words, phrases, or sentences around an unfamiliar word often provide clues about the word's meaning. In some cases, *signal words* can act as clues. See pp. 173–174 for further discussion of context clues.

Restatement Clues

Look for words and phrases that define an unfamiliar word or restate its meaning in familiar terms.

EXAMPLE The dried rose was as *fragile* as a butterfly's wing. **In other words,** its delicate petals can be damaged easily.

From the context, readers can tell that *fragile* means "damaged easily." The phrase *in other words* signals that the words *easily damaged* restate the meaning of the word *fragile.*

Restatement Signal Words		
in other words	that is	these

Example Clues

Examples sometimes give us hints to a word's meaning. If an unfamiliar word means a certain type of thing, action, or characteristic, examples of the type can be excellent clues to the word's meaning.

EXAMPLE When our neighbors travel, they always look for comfortable *accommodations,* **such as** a beach cottage, hotel suite, or mountain cabin.

From the context, readers can tell that the word *accommodations* means "a place to stay." The words *such as* signal that the list of places to stay provides examples of *accommodations.*

Example Signal Words		
for example	such as	in that
likewise	especially	

Contrast/Antonym Clues

Look for words or phrases that are the opposite of a word's meaning.

EXAMPLE Knowledge is a *remedy* for many environmental problems, **but** knowledge without action cannot cure the ills.

From the context, readers can tell that *remedy* means "cure." The word **but** signals that *remedy* contrasts with the phrase "cannot cure."

Contrast/Antonym Signal Words			
but	not	in contrast	on the other hand
however	still	although	some . . . but others

Keyword Clues

Look for words or phrases that modify or are related to the unfamiliar word.

EXAMPLE The two characters in my story believe it is their *destiny* to be enemies. Their elders have taught them that this is **meant to be.**

From the context, readers can tell that *destiny* means "something that necessarily happens to a person." The words *meant to be* signal the meaning of the word.

Definition/Explanation Clues

A sentence may actually define or explain an unfamiliar word.

EXAMPLE Alan will help the woman once she **escapes** and becomes a *fugitive* from her troubled country.

From the context, readers can tell that *fugitive* means "runaway." The word *escapes* signals the meaning of the word.

How We Make New Words Our Own

Use the **Context Structure Sound Dictionary (CSSD)** strategy to improve your vocabulary, to make new words your own. Use one or more of the strategies to determine the meanings of each word you do not know. The exercises that follow will show you how to go about making new words your own.

HOW TO DO EXERCISE 1 *Wordbusting*

In these exercises, you will read the Vocabulary Word in a sentence. You will figure out the word's meaning by looking at its **context**, its **structure**, and its **sound**. Then you will look up the word in a **dictionary** and write its meaning *as it is used in the sentence*.

Here is an example of the Wordbusting strategy, using the word *manuscript*.

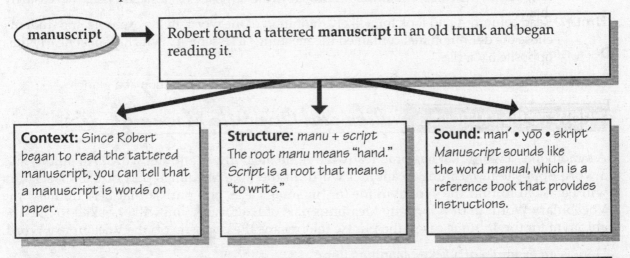

manuscript → Robert found a tattered **manuscript** in an old trunk and began reading it.

Context: Since Robert began to read the tattered manuscript, you can tell that a manuscript is words on paper.

Structure: manu + script
The root *manu* means "hand."
Script is a root that means "to write."

Sound: man′ • yo͞o • skript′
Manuscript sounds like the word *manual*, which is a reference book that provides instructions.

Dictionary: "a handwritten or typewritten document or paper, especially a copy of an author's work"

Hint #1   **Context:** Look for clues to the meaning of the word in the sentence. For example, "reading" is a keyword that helps reveal the meaning of *manuscript*.

Hint #2   **Structure:** Examine the word parts for roots, prefixes, and suffixes that you know. Consult the word-part tables on pages ix–xiv for meanings of parts you do not know.

Hint #3   **Sound:** Say the word aloud and listen for any word parts you know.

Hint #4   **Dictionary:** If you cannot determine a word's meaning from applying context, structure, and sound strategies, look up the unfamiliar word in a dictionary. Read all the definitions, and choose one that best fits the given sentence.

In this exercise, you will again see the new word used in a sentence. This exercise gives you the word's definition, and you must match the word in the sentence with its meaning. The word may be used in the same way as it was used in Wordbusting, or it may be used in a new way.

Here's an example of a Context Clues exercise:

COLUMN A	COLUMN B
_D_ **1.** word: _decrease_ *v.* to become smaller; to lessen; *n.* a lessening	(D) Recent years have seen a steady rise in the number of cat owners. On the other hand, there has been a **decrease** in the number of dog owners.

Hint #1 First, scan the definitions in Column A. Then, read Column B and look for clues to the meaning of the word. Here, the words "on the other hand" tell us that the sentence containing the word **decrease** contrasts with the sentence containing the words "a steady rise." Thus, the correct definition is probably the opposite of "a steady rise."

Hint #2 Read column A and look for a likely definition of the word. In the example, the student chose the definition that contained the meaning "a lessening," which is most nearly the opposite of "a rise."

Hint #3 Write the word in the blank so that later you can find its definition at a glance.

A synonym is a word that has practically the same meaning as another word. An antonym is a word opposite in meaning to another word. In the Like Meanings part of Exercise 3, you will be asked to find the synonym for (or, in some cases, the phrase that best defines) the Vocabulary Word. In the Opposite Meanings part of Exercise 3, you will be asked to find the antonym for (or, in some cases, the phrase that means the opposite of) the Vocabulary Word.

Here is an example of a Like Meanings item:

21. decrease the shedding of fur

    (A) remove
    (B) make comfortable
    (C) add to
    (D) lessen

Hint #1 Don't be fooled by choices that are closely related to the Vocabulary Word. Choice A may be tempting, but the removal of shedding is more extreme than a **decrease** in shedding.

Hint #2 Don't be fooled by distantly related choices. An animal may be more comfortable when it sheds, but there is no direct link between **decrease** and Choice B.

Hint #3 Don't be fooled by the opposite of the Vocabulary Word. Choice C would be the correct choice if this were an Opposite Meanings exercise, but here you are looking for a similar meaning.

MAKING NEW WORDS YOUR OWN

Lesson 1 | CONTEXT: Change in Arts and Literature
Aliens from Another Planet

Millions of people around the world devour science fiction novels and short stories and see as many sci-fi films as they can. Some writers of science fiction, such as Ursula K. LeGuin, Isaac Asimov, and Frank Herbert, are among the most popular authors ever. Sci-fi films like the Star Wars series and *Close Encounters of the Third Kind* are landmarks in film history.

In the following exercises, you will have the opportunity to expand your vocabulary by reading about science fiction. These ten Vocabulary Words will be used.

alien	galaxy	humane	planetary	tranquil
diplomatic	ghastly	mortal	satellite	velocity

EXERCISE 1 *Wordbusting* ☞

Directions. Follow these instructions for this word and the nine words on the next page.
- Figure out the word's meaning by looking at its **context,** its **structure,** and its **sound.** Fill in at least one of the three **CSS** boxes. Alternate which boxes you complete.
- Then, look up the word in a dictionary, read all of its meanings, and write the meaning of the word as it is used in the sentence.
- Follow this same process for each of the Vocabulary Words on the next page. You will need to draw your own map for each word. Use a separate sheet of paper.

1.

(alien) ➡ Of course, not all science fiction is about **alien** beings, but hundreds of these films have featured beings from another planet.

Context:

Structure:

Sound:

Dictionary:

2.

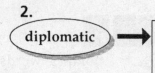

Sometimes the visitors from outer space are on a **diplomatic** mission to Earth; they hope to establish friendly relations between their people and Earthlings.

3.

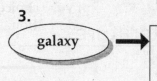

It is not always evident which **galaxy** the beings are from, but they definitely come from some other group of stars in space.

4.

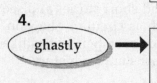

In other films the space creatures are horrible, **ghastly** beings on a mission to destroy Earthlings.

5.

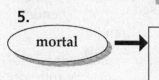

In some sci-fi films the visitor from space isn't **mortal,** but some advanced form of technology, often a robot.

6.

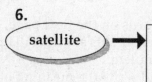

One sci-fi film features a **satellite** that was launched into Earth's orbit in the early 1960s. It is taken over by creatures from another planet and used as a station from which to observe Earthlings.

7.

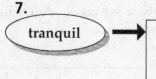

Science fiction can be fairly predictable. For example, creatures from outer space are likely to show up in a **tranquil** place, like a peaceful meadow in the country.

8.

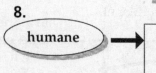

Often, the moral of sci-fi films is that people should learn to be more kind, or **humane**.

9.

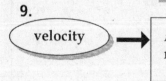

A familiar theme in science fiction is time travel, but nothing can really move at the **velocity** required to match the speed of light.

10.

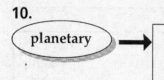

Jules Verne is considered the originator of modern science fiction. In the 1800s, he correctly predicted the development of airplanes, submarines, and space satellites. The idea of artificial **planetary** objects must have seemed absurd to readers then.

EXERCISE 2 Context Clues

Directions. Scan the definitions in Column A. Then think about how the boldface words are used in the sentences in Column B. To complete the exercise, match each definition in Column A with the correct Vocabulary Word from Column B. Write the letter of your choice on the line provided. Finally, write the Vocabulary Word on the line before the definition.

COLUMN A	COLUMN B
_____ **11.** word: _____ *adj.* possessing the best qualities of human beings; kind, sympathetic	(A) The idea of a woman playing a key role in a science fiction film or television series was **alien** only a short time ago but quite familiar today.
_____ **12.** word: _____ *adj.* certain to die eventually; causing death; to the death; very intense; *n.* a being who will die, especially a human	(B) In early sci-fi films and TV series women were **satellites** of men, that is, dependent on them.
_____ **13.** word: _____ *adj.* referring to a planet or planets; global; wandering; moving in an orbit	(C) Even though a **galaxy** of female stars was available, they were rarely used as authority figures.
_____ **14.** word: _____ *n.* a planet, moon, or artificial object that orbits a planet; a dependent person, company, or state	(D) However, women did take part in **planetary** adventures, visiting various parts of the solar system as assistants to the male crew or as visitors.
_____ **15.** word: _____ *n.* separate system of stars; group of well-known people	(E) The pilot episode of *Star Trek* cast actor Majel Barrett as Number One, but test audiences did not respond well to her in this key role. Barrett later appeared occasionally as the sympathetic, or **humane,** Nurse Chapel.
_____ **16.** word: _____ *adj.* foreign; strange; *n.* a foreigner; a stranger; a being from outer space	(F) In early *Star Trek* films, women remain in the **tranquil** areas of the ship, far from the action. Only Uhura, the communications officer, has a visible position on the bridge.
_____ **17.** word: _____ *adj.* having to do with official relationships between countries or governments; tactful	(G) In *Star Trek: The Next Generation,* however, the **diplomatic** Deanna Troi uses her tactful manner to deal with conflicts on and off the ship.
_____ **18.** word: _____ *adj.* undisturbed; calm; serene; quiet	(H) Guinan, the wise manager of the ship's lounge, is a mysterious being; she seems to be ageless, so many people believe she is not **mortal**.
_____ **19.** word: _____ *adj.* horrid; ghostlike; very unpleasant	(I) *Star Trek: The Next Generation* also gave key roles to aliens and androids. At first sight, Worf is a **ghastly** being. But fans love his frightful appearance.
_____ **20.** word: _____ *n.* rapidity of motion; rate of speed	(J) The U.S.S. *Enterprise* can travel at warp speed—faster than the **velocity** of light.

EXERCISE 3 *Like Meanings and Opposite Meanings* 👌

Directions. For each item below, circle the letter of the choice that means the same, or about the same, as the boldface word.

21. a **ghastly** mistake
   (A) surprising
   (B) horrible
   (C) pale
   (D) original

22. a **planetary** problem
   (A) technical
   (B) unsolvable
   (C) world-wide
   (D) social

23. a **galaxy** of movie stars
   (A) constellation
   (B) studio
   (C) group
   (D) photographer

24. a **satellite** state
   (A) poor
   (B) flying
   (C) dependent
   (D) organized

25. the **velocity** of the rocket
   (A) path
   (B) size
   (C) strength
   (D) speed

Directions. For each item below, circle the letter of the choice that means the opposite, or about the opposite, of the boldface word.

26. an **alien** idea
   (A) strange
   (B) familiar
   (C) distant
   (D) near

27. a **diplomatic** approach
   (A) ordinary
   (B) unusual
   (C) friendly
   (D) rude

28. a **humane** person
   (A) jailed
   (B) free
   (C) bad
   (D) unkind

29. a **mortal** blow
   (A) fatal
   (B) serious
   (C) minor
   (D) illegal

30. a **tranquil** moment
   (A) anchored
   (B) disturbed
   (C) lost
   (D) peaceful

MAKING NEW WORDS YOUR OWN

Lesson 2 | **CONTEXT:** Change in Arts and Literature
A Science Fiction Story

Many people who read science fiction have good ideas for science fiction stories of their own. Malcolm, a seventh-grade student at Dunbar Middle School, has written a sci-fi short story on one of the most common themes in science fiction—fear of change.

In the following exercises, you will have the opportunity to expand your vocabulary by reading about Malcolm's science fiction story. Below are ten Vocabulary Words that will be used in these exercises.

ally	destiny	fugitive	invade	overture
avert	fascinate	gesture	luminous	stellar

EXERCISE 1 *Wordbusting* ☞

Directions. Follow these instructions for this word and the nine words on the next page.
- Figure out the word's meaning by looking at its **context,** its **structure,** and its **sound.** Fill in at least one of the three **CSS** boxes. Alternate which boxes you complete.
- Then, look up the word in a dictionary, read all of its meanings, and write the meaning of the word as it is used in the sentence.
- Follow this same process for each of the Vocabulary Words on the next page. You will need to draw your own map for each word. Use a separate sheet of paper.

1.

⬭ **ally** ➔ Malcolm's science fiction story is about teenagers from the warring planets of Argon and Grimnan. These teenagers **ally,** or unite, themselves in an effort to find peace.

Context:	Structure:	Sound:

Dictionary:

2.

avert ➤ The teenagers hope to **avert** further destruction on both their planets by ending the war.

3.

destiny ➤ However, the adults on the planets think it is their **destiny** to fight. They believe fate has decided that the two planets should be enemies.

4.

fascinate ➤ The idea of peace continues to **fascinate** the teenagers, but the adults are not interested. They are determined not to accept a cease-fire, and they will not consider peace talks.

5.

fugitive ➤ Eventually, Phoebe, one of the teenagers, becomes a **fugitive**. She runs from her own people, the Argonians, who consider her a traitor.

6.

gesture ➤ She flees to the enemy planet, Grimnan, where she has a friend, and tries to disguise herself as one of its citizens. However, her costume, her accent, even her **gestures**—especially the motions she makes with her hands while talking—reveal that she is an Argonian.

7.

luminous ➤ Another problem is that her eyes are **luminous;** they glow in the dark, so she stays hidden after twilight.

8.

invade ➤ People from the planet Argon decide to **invade** the planet Grimnan. The young woman will be in grave danger during the Argonian attack.

9.

overture ➤ The teenagers decide it is best to warn the people of Grimnan that their enemies on planet Argon are planning an attack. However, their **overture** of friendship is rejected; their offer is turned down.

10.

stellar ➤ The teenagers led a **stellar** campaign for peace. It was frustrating for them to have their outstanding efforts rejected.

EXERCISE 2 *Context Clues*

Directions. Scan the definitions in Column A. Then think about how the boldface words are used in the sentences in Column B. To complete the exercise, match each definition in Column A with the correct Vocabulary Word from Column B. Write the letter of your choice on the line provided. Finally, write the Vocabulary Word on the line before the definition.

COLUMN A

_____ **11.** word: _____
adj. giving light; glowing in the dark; easily understood

_____ **12.** word: _____
v. to put under a spell; to bewitch; to hold motionless; to charm or captivate

_____ **13.** word: _____
v. to unite persons or groups; *n*. a country, person, or group joined for a common purpose; a plant, animal, or thing related to another; a helper

_____ **14.** word: _____
adj. fleeing from danger, justice, and so on; fleeting; *n*. a person who flees or has fled; a fleeting thing

_____ **15.** word: _____
n. the inevitable order of events; fate

_____ **16.** word: _____
v. to enter as an enemy; to intrude in

_____ **17.** word: _____
n. an offer; a show of willingness to deal; an introduction to an opera or other long musical work; any introductory section

_____ **18.** word: _____
v. to turn away; to keep from happening

_____ **19.** word: _____
n. movement of part of the body to express something; something said or done as a formality only; *v*. to express an idea or emotion with movement

_____ **20.** word: _____
adj. of stars; superior; leading

COLUMN B

(A) The two main characters, Phoebe and Cale, meet when they play in an intergalactic orchestra, rehearsing the **overture** that opens a symphony.

(B) It takes each of them a while to consider the other a friend, or **ally**.

(C) Phoebe makes the first **gesture** of friendship when she congratulates him on his solo.

(D) Cale has a **stellar** role in the symphony program; the solo was outstanding.

(E) Cale's musical ability—and his personality—**fascinate** Phoebe from the start. She becomes interested enough in Cale to break from her own culture.

(F) Of course, they are afraid that it is their **destiny** to be enemies. Their elders have taught them that this is meant to be.

(G) One night, when the stars seem especially **luminous,** or bright, they meet and plan how they can work together to save their planets.

(H) When Phoebe is forced to become a **fugitive,** Cale helps her escape from danger.

(I) They try very hard to **avert** disaster and save their planets.

(J) In the end, despite all of their attempts to prevent the attack, Argon **invades** Grimnan.

EXERCISE 3 — Like Meanings and Opposite Meanings ✍

Directions. For each item below, circle the letter of the choice that means the same, or about the same, as the boldface word.

21. to recognize her **destiny**
  (A) fate
  (B) desire
  (C) mistake
  (D) hope

22. a **luminous** picture
  (A) confusing
  (B) darkly colored
  (C) beautiful
  (D) filled with light

23. a **gesture** of contempt
  (A) motion
  (B) knowledge
  (C) variety
  (D) concern

24. the **overture** to the opera
  (A) boss
  (B) singer
  (C) introduction
  (D) instruments

25. a lonely **fugitive**
  (A) runaway
  (B) prisoner
  (C) animal
  (D) child

Directions. For each item below, circle the letter of the choice that means the opposite, or about the opposite, of the boldface word.

26. to find an **ally**
  (A) friend
  (B) enemy
  (C) pathway
  (D) place

27. to **avert** the danger
  (A) avoid
  (B) cause
  (C) prevent
  (D) describe

28. to **invade** the house
  (A) retreat from
  (B) build
  (C) burn down
  (D) enter

29. a **stellar** performance
  (A) demanding
  (B) weak
  (C) excellent
  (D) opening

30. to **fascinate** the crowd
  (A) bore
  (B) tease
  (C) interest
  (D) amuse

Name _____ Date _____ Class _____

MAKING NEW WORDS YOUR OWN

Lesson 3 | **CONTEXT: Change in Arts and Literature**
But Is It Dancing?

Every generation seems to enjoy criticizing the dances of other generations. Comments such as "Do you really call that 'dancing'?" have been heard in households throughout the country for generations.

In the following exercises, you will have the opportunity to expand your vocabulary by reading about dance and some of the changes that have occurred in dance styles. Below are ten Vocabulary Words that will be used in these exercises.

abstract	controversial	eventual	inferior	obsolete
absurd	defiant	grotesque	mere	technique

EXERCISE 1 *Wordbusting* ✍

Directions. Follow these instructions for this word and the nine words on the next page.
- Figure out the word's meaning by looking at its **context,** its **structure,** and its **sound.** Fill in at least one of the three **CSS** boxes. Alternate which boxes you complete.
- Then, look up the word in a dictionary, read all of its meanings, and write the meaning of the word as it is used in the sentence.
- Follow this same process for each of the Vocabulary Words on the next page. You will need to draw your own map for each word. Use a separate sheet of paper.

1.

(abstract) ⟶ We could talk about dance in **abstract** or general terms, but it's more interesting to talk about specific dances and dancers.

Context:	Structure:	Sound:

Dictionary:

2.

absurd ➡️ An older generation often thinks that a younger generation's dances are **absurd**. But, just as often, the younger generation thinks that their elders' dances are ridiculous.

3.

controversial ➡️ Dance styles change, but the arguments they cause stay around. The Charleston was just as **controversial** in the 1920s as break dancing was in the 1980s.

4.

grotesque ➡️ Today, few people would say that the Charleston, the Jitterbug, or the Twist are **grotesque,** but when these dances were popular with the young, many parents thought them bizarre.

5.

mere ➡️ To some people the difference in dance styles doesn't seem to be a **mere** question of taste. The issue isn't that simple to them.

6.

obsolete ➡️ No one likes to feel that his or her way of doing things has become old-fashioned, or **obsolete,** like a horse-drawn carriage.

7.

defiant ➡️ Each generation feels a little **defiant** when it hears its styles of dance criticized. Every generation resists the views of the previous generation.

8.

technique ➡️ One good **technique** for avoiding conflict is to ask parents whether they ever had this discussion with *their* parents.

9.

inferior ➡️ Actually, one generation's dances probably are neither **inferior** to nor better than another's. They're just different.

10.

eventual ➡️ The **eventual** result of time passing is that whatever dance style is "in" will soon become dated.

Name _____ Date _____ Class _____

EXERCISE 2 *Context Clues* ✍

Directions. Scan the definitions in Column A. Then think about how the boldface words are used in the sentences in Column B. To complete the exercise, match each definition in Column A with the correct Vocabulary Word from Column B. Write the letter of your choice on the line provided. Finally, write the Vocabulary Word on the line before the definition.

COLUMN A

____ **11.** word: _____
adj. happening at the end of, or as a result of, a series of events; ultimate, final

____ **12.** word: _____
adj. distorted; bizarre; absurd; *n.* a hideous or fantastic thing or quality

____ **13.** word: _____
adj. lower in importance, rank, order, or status

____ **14.** word: _____
adj. causing argument; debatable

____ **15.** word: _____
adj. nothing more or other than; only

____ **16.** word: _____
adj. openly and boldly resisting

____ **17.** word: _____
n. a way of using skills to achieve a task; a technical skill; a way of doing something

____ **18.** word: _____
adj. so untrue or unreasonable as to be ridiculous

____ **19.** word: _____
adj. out-of-date; no longer used

____ **20.** word: _____
adj. not concrete; theoretical; *n.* a summary; nonrepresentational schools of contemporary art; *v.* to summarize; to write an abstract

COLUMN B

(A) Classical ballet has not become **obsolete;** however, it has faced many competing styles in the world of serious dance.

(B) Some of the new forms of dance were as strange to lovers of classical dance as **abstract** art is to people who prefer representational art.

(C) These critics called the new dance forms ugly, even **grotesque**.

(D) They believed that modern dance could not begin to equal classical dance—that it was clearly **inferior**.

(E) When Isadora Duncan (1878–1927) was developing her free and expressive style in the 1920s, she was very **controversial**. Not everyone approved.

(F) Duncan's approach was unlike anything people had come to know as dance; they laughed at her style and called it **absurd**.

(G) Some critics thought Duncan was a **mere** upstart, that her dance style was nothing more than a passing fad. In reality, she made major contributions to the field of dance.

(H) While she used some of the **techniques** of classical ballet, she introduced new forms of movement.

(I) Duncan was **defiant**. She challenged her critics and won.

(J) The **eventual** popularity of today's modern-dance troupes is one of the results of her work.

EXERCISE 3 *Like Meanings and Opposite Meanings* ✍

Directions. For each item below, circle the letter of the choice that means the same, or about the same, as the boldface word.

21. mere excuses
   (A) only
   (B) similar
   (C) silly
   (D) unusual

22. an interesting **technique**
   (A) color
   (B) step
   (C) part
   (D) method

23. the **eventual** result
   (A) final
   (B) understandable
   (C) present
   (D) first

24. the **defiant** dance student
   (A) resisting
   (B) adopted
   (C) intelligent
   (D) talented

25. an **obsolete** dance
   (A) stupid
   (B) out-of-date
   (C) short-lived
   (D) fashionable

Directions. For each item below, circle the letter of the choice that means the opposite, or about the opposite, of the boldface word.

26. an **abstract** painting
   (A) representational
   (B) strange
   (C) interesting
   (D) boring

27. an **absurd** approach
   (A) ridiculous
   (B) sensible
   (C) old-fashioned
   (D) modern

28. a **controversial** dance instructor
   (A) well-trained
   (B) good-natured
   (C) extremely talented
   (D) widely accepted

29. a **grotesque** costume
   (A) beautiful
   (B) clever
   (C) ugly
   (D) earthy

30. an **inferior** style
   (A) unfortunate
   (B) lucky
   (C) superior
   (D) interior

Name _____ Date _____ Class _____

Lesson 4 | CONTEXT: Change in Arts and Literature
Television: An Instrument of Change

Television. Sometimes we love it; sometimes we hate it. Sometimes we don't even notice it. Many people argue that we have a dangerous addiction to TV that interferes with our real lives. Others say that television is an amazing medium that brings the world into our living rooms. They claim that we don't watch too much TV—we just don't watch the right things.

In the following exercises, you will have the opportunity to expand your vocabulary by reading about television. Below are ten Vocabulary Words that will be used.

conform	deliberate	excess	offend	reality
consequence	distort	impact	originality	recoil

EXERCISE 1 — *Wordbusting* ✍

Directions. Follow these instructions for this word and the nine words on the next page.
- Figure out the word's meaning by looking at its **context,** its **structure,** and its **sound.** Fill in at least one of the three **CSS** boxes. Alternate which boxes you complete.
- Then, look up the word in a dictionary, read all of its meanings, and write the meaning of the word as it is used in the sentence.
- Follow this same process for each of the Vocabulary Words on the next page. You will need to draw your own map for each word. Use a separate sheet of paper.

1.

(conform) → Television must **conform** to the changing times. Reruns, such as *I Love Lucy,* are fun to watch occasionally, but customs change, and people today want a different format in TV sitcoms.

Context:	Structure:	Sound:

Dictionary:

2.

consequence ➜ As a **consequence,** or result, sitcoms generally mirror what is happening in our everyday lives.

3.

deliberate ➜ Writers for TV must **deliberate** about what to include. Different age groups and time slots are among the considerations that must be carefully thought out.

4.

distort ➜ Some TV shows actually **distort** the truth. This can be fun and entertaining, as in science fiction programs, but at other times it gives wrong ideas about groups of people or events.

5.

reality ➜ Some critics claim that television is dangerous because it gives us a false view of **reality**. However, many educational programs not only reflect real life but also teach us many things that we might not learn otherwise.

6.

offend ➜ Television networks prefer not to **offend** the majority of their viewers. They try not to air programs that cause viewers to call the stations with complaints.

7.

originality ➜ TV programs are frequently dull and predictable, but some writers and directors are capable of great creativity and **originality**.

8.

impact ➜ Television has had a major **impact** on our lives. For example, large numbers of Americans now depend on television for news.

9.

excess ➜ Many parents and teachers are concerned about children watching TV to **excess**. They fear that too much time in front of the TV means not enough time reading.

10.

recoil ➜ Most of us **recoil** when we hear that American children spend more time watching TV than they spend in school. It's a rather scary thought.

EXERCISE 2 *Context Clues* 👈

Directions. Scan the definitions in Column A. Then think about how the boldface words are used in the sentences in Column B. To complete the exercise, match each definition in Column A with the correct Vocabulary Word from Column B. Write the letter of your choice on the line provided. Finally, write the Vocabulary Word on the line before the definition.

COLUMN A

_____ **11.** word: _____
adj. carefully thought out and formed; done on purpose or intentionally; *v.* to think or consider carefully

_____ **12.** word: _____
n. the quality of being new, unique, or earliest; the ability to be creative

_____ **13.** word: _____
v. to make similar; to bring into harmony; to become similar; to act in a conventional way

_____ **14.** word: _____
v. to hit with force; to produce change in; *n.* a collision; the power of an event to produce changes

_____ **15.** word: _____
v. to retreat; to shrink away out of fear, anger, surprise, or disgust

_____ **16.** word: _____
n. the result of an act or a decision; importance as a cause or influence

_____ **17.** word: _____
v. to twist out of shape; to misrepresent

_____ **18.** word: _____
n. the quality or fact of being real; the quality of being true to life

_____ **19.** word: _____
n. extra; an amount by which one thing is greater than another; *adj.* extra

_____ **20.** word: _____
v. to violate a law, custom, or religious commandment; to create anger

COLUMN B

(A) The **impact** of television is far reaching; billions of viewers around the world are influenced by TV every day.

(B) Some people make careful and **deliberate** choices about what they watch, while others watch anything that's on TV.

(C) Many people watch eight hours of television a day. Experts say that this amount is far in **excess** of what is healthy. In fact, they say that more than three hours is probably too much.

(D) One **consequence** of watching too much television may be eye strain.

(E) People may be disappointed when their lives do not **conform** to, or agree with, the happy standards of the world as it is shown on TV.

(F) Some television programs **offend** the values of viewers. Programs can also insult viewers by being dull or unrealistic.

(G) The violence on TV may cause some viewers to **recoil**. A dangerous result of watching too much violence is that eventually viewers no longer shrink from it. They just accept it.

(H) Many sitcoms use the same old plots and character types again and again. A few, however, show great **originality** and present us with new ideas.

(I) Television news sometimes **distorts**, or misrepresents, complicated stories because reports can only be a few minutes in length.

(J) It is possible for television to be a positive influence, but in **reality**, TV doesn't always live up to that possibility.

EXERCISE 3 *Like Meanings and Opposite Meanings* ✍

Directions. For each item below, circle the letter of the choice that means the same, or about the same, as the boldface word.

21. the **consequences** of an action
(A) complaint
(B) illness
(C) result
(D) thought

22. to **conform** to standards
(A) adapt
(B) ignore
(C) avoid
(D) disagree with

23. to **distort** her words
(A) listen to
(B) record
(C) laugh at
(D) twist

24. a moment of **originality**
(A) creativity
(B) loss
(C) joy
(D) hunger

25. events that **impact** daily life
(A) change
(B) delight
(C) confuse
(D) dignify

Directions. For each item below, circle the letter of the choice that means the opposite, or about the opposite, of the boldface word.

26. a **deliberate** choice
(A) accidental
(B) well thought out
(C) important
(D) unlucky

27. **excess** TV watching
(A) extra
(B) entertaining
(C) not enough
(D) supervised

28. to **offend** the audience
(A) upset
(B) worry
(C) please
(D) interest

29. an interest in **reality**
(A) life
(B) fantasy
(C) death
(D) property

30. to **recoil** suddenly
(A) advise
(B) run away from
(C) avoid
(D) come forward

MAKING NEW WORDS YOUR OWN

Lesson 5 | CONTEXT: Change in Arts and Literature

Television: The Early Days

Some of the first television shows were performed live. Since many were not recorded, we will never be able to view them. However, many of the shows from the early days of television do survive, and it is fun to watch them and think about how television has changed over the decades.

In the following exercises, you will have the opportunity to expand your vocabulary by reading about some of the major changes in television in the last half of the twentieth century. Below are ten Vocabulary Words that will be used in these exercises.

| congregate | hover | leash | maturity | signify |
| haunt | ignorance | loiter | motive | supervise |

EXERCISE 1   *Wordbusting* ☞

Directions. Follow these instructions for this word and the nine words on the next page.
- Figure out the word's meaning by looking at its **context,** its **structure,** and its **sound.** Fill in at least one of the three **CSS** boxes. Alternate which boxes you complete.
- Then, look up the word in a dictionary, read all of its meanings, and write the meaning of the word as it is used in the sentence.
- Follow this same process for each of the Vocabulary Words on the next page. You will need to draw your own map for each word. Use a separate sheet of paper.

1.

(congregate) → In the early days of television, neighbors would sometimes **congregate** in the home of the first family on the block to own a TV set, and they would watch the shows together.

| Context: | Structure: | Sound: |
| | | |

Dictionary:

2.

haunt ➡ People would also **haunt** furniture and hardware stores—if the managers didn't mind their hanging around—trying to get a glimpse of the new invention.

3.

hover ➡ Salespeople would **hover** in the background—like hawks waiting in midair to swoop down on their prey—if they thought there was any hope of interesting the viewers in buying a TV.

4.

ignorance ➡ **Ignorance** about how television worked was fairly common. Most people did not understand how pictures were broadcast.

5.

leash ➡ Few people could **leash** their enthusiasm for television. In fact, most didn't even try to hold back their excitement.

6.

loiter ➡ Before television, people tended to **loiter,** stopping to chat with neighbors on their way home from work. After television, however, many raced straight home to catch a favorite program.

7.

maturity ➡ Television was in its childhood in the late 1940s and early 1950s, and perhaps it has yet to reach its full **maturity**.

8.

motive ➡ Its future development may depend on our **motive** for watching: Do we watch to avoid thinking or to be challenged by new ideas?

9.

signify ➡ What does it **signify** that young people spend more time in front of the TV than they do in school? Can that possibly mean anything positive?

10.

supervise ➡ Supporters of television believe that the real problem is not TV; it's that children need someone to **supervise,** or direct, what they watch and for how long.

EXERCISE 2 Context Clues 👈

Directions. Scan the definitions in Column A. Then think about how the boldface words are used in the sentences in Column B. To complete the exercise, match each definition in Column A with the correct Vocabulary Word from Column B. Write the letter of your choice on the line provided. Finally, write the Vocabulary Word on the line before the definition.

COLUMN A	COLUMN B

COLUMN A

_____ **11.** word: _____
v. to visit often or continually; to appear or recur repeatedly; to fill the atmosphere of; n. a place often visited

_____ **12.** word: _____
n. a cord or strap used to hold a dog or some other animal in check; v. to control or check; to tie up

_____ **13.** word: _____
v. to oversee, direct, or manage

_____ **14.** word: _____
v. to gather in a mass or crowd; to assemble

_____ **15.** word: _____
v. to stay suspended or to flutter in the air near one place; to linger or wait close by, especially in an anxious way

_____ **16.** word: _____
v. to be a sign or indication of; to show or make known

_____ **17.** word: _____
n. an inner drive or impulse that causes a person to act in a certain way

_____ **18.** word: _____
n. the state of being fully grown or developed

_____ **19.** word: _____
v. to linger in an aimless way; to move slowly, stopping frequently

_____ **20.** word: _____
n. lacking knowledge; unawareness

COLUMN B

(A) When my mother was a child, all the kids in the neighborhood **congregated** at her house to watch television.

(B) My grandfather often **hovered** in the background. He pretended to be busy making breakfast, but he always seemed to be looking over the kids' shoulders.

(C) Grandfather said he was there to **supervise,** or oversee, what the kids watched.

(D) Mom says he had another **motive:** He enjoyed watching the shows.

(E) I don't know what this might **signify,** but it must mean something; my mom and grandfather still love to watch old reruns together.

(F) They are amazed at my **ignorance** of the early days of television. "How could you not know that?" they ask.

(G) They love to watch Dobie Gillis and Maynard G. Krebs **loiter** on their way home from school. These characters' frequent stops always led to one adventure or another.

(H) When they watch old programs, they also start to remember other things about the good old days. My mother always talks about her favorite **haunt,** the pizza place where she and all her friends used to get together.

(I) They say that when I reach **maturity,** I'll do the same thing.

(J) Not everyone in our family enjoys watching the old television shows. Actually, some of us would rather clean our rooms or walk the dog on his **leash.**

EXERCISE 3 *Like Meanings and Opposite Meanings* ☞

Directions. For each item below, circle the letter of the choice that means the same, or about the same, as the boldface word.

21. to **haunt** the mall
(A) frighten
(B) visit often
(C) stay away from
(D) look for

22. to **hover** above the trees
(A) flutter
(B) jump
(C) sing
(D) chop

23. a strange **motive**
(A) memory
(B) program
(C) reason
(D) idea

24. to **signify** his satisfaction
(A) believe
(B) understand
(C) hide
(D) make known

25. to **congregate** in front of the TV
(A) play
(B) gather
(C) race around
(D) ask questions

Directions. For each item below, circle the letter of the choice that means the opposite, or about the opposite, of the boldface word.

26. **ignorance** of the new program
(A) knowledge
(B) stupidity
(C) disgust
(D) innocence

27. having reached **maturity**
(A) adulthood
(B) childhood
(C) old age
(D) overly ripe

28. to **loiter** along the way
(A) stop often
(B) race
(C) gamble
(D) shout

29. to **supervise** the work
(A) oversee
(B) ignore
(C) put pressure on
(D) eliminate

30. to **leash** her anger
(A) release
(B) control
(C) recognize
(D) forget

MAKING NEW WORDS YOUR OWN

Lesson 6 | CONTEXT: Change in Arts and Literature
You Call That Music?

Attitudes toward music change with the times, but the arguments usually don't. "Turn it down; it's too loud!" and "That's not music; it's just noise!" have been familiar phrases in households for many generations.

In the following exercises, you will have the opportunity to expand your vocabulary by reading about individual tastes in music. Below are ten Vocabulary Words that will be used in these exercises.

audible	conspicuous	idle	modest	subtle
candid	diaphragm	lenient	notorious	threshold

EXERCISE 1   *Wordbusting* ☞

Directions. Follow these instructions for this word and the nine words on the next page.
- Figure out the word's meaning by looking at its **context,** its **structure,** and its **sound.** Fill in at least one of the three **CSS** boxes. Alternate which boxes you complete.
- Then, look up the word in a dictionary, read all of its meanings, and write the meaning of the word as it is used in the sentence.
- Follow this same process for each of the Vocabulary Words on the next page. You will need to draw your own map for each word. Use a separate sheet of paper.

1.

(audible) → Dad worries about my hearing. He wants me to turn the volume down so low that the music is barely **audible.**

Context:

Structure:

Sound:

Dictionary:

2.

candid ➞ To be **candid,** I'll have to admit that I do sometimes play music a bit too loudly.

3.

conspicuous ➞ Sometimes I turn it on extra loud so that when I have to turn it down, the volume is about where I want it. I guess this trick has become a bit **conspicuous** because Dad seems to catch on every time.

4.

diaphragm ➞ Dad always talks about the days when singers used their **diaphragms** and other lower-chest muscles to project their voices. Now, he says, they just scream into lots of electronic equipment.

5.

idle ➞ He also wants to know why I can't enjoy an **idle** moment in silence. He always asks what happened to the joys of sitting still and doing nothing.

6.

lenient ➞ Actually, my folks are fairly **lenient** about my music. My friend Clancy's parents, on the other hand, are quite strict.

7.

modest ➞ My parents helped me buy some excellent stereo equipment. The price was **modest,** but the quality is high.

8.

notorious ➞ Of course, my parents are **notorious** for their ability to find bargains. Store owners worry when they see my parents coming because they know my parents will talk them into a low price.

9.

subtle ➞ Dad tries to interest me in music he likes. He thinks he is being **subtle,** but I consider his giving me six CDs to be a plain, clear hint.

10.

threshold ➞ I may be at the **threshold** of sharing some of Dad's taste. I listened to his John Coltrane CD twice yesterday and three times today.

Name _____ Date _____ Class _____

EXERCISE 2   *Context Clues* 👈

Directions. Scan the definitions in Column A. Then think about how the boldface words are used in the sentences in Column B. To complete the exercise, match each definition in Column A with the correct Vocabulary Word from Column B. Write the letter of your choice on the line provided. Finally, write the Vocabulary Word on the line before the definition.

COLUMN A	COLUMN B
11. word: _____ *n.* a doorsill; the entrance or beginning point	(A) Before Toya enters the music store, she peeks through the door; then she crosses the **threshold**.
12. word: _____ *adj.* can be heard; loud enough to hear	(B) She is trying not to be **conspicuous**; that is, she doesn't want anyone to notice her.
13. word: _____ *adj.* requiring mental keenness; not open or direct; skillful; not obvious	(C) The clerk at the counter is **idle**. Toya sees that he is not busy and approaches him.
14. word: _____ *adj.* fair, just; honest, frank; unposed and informal	(D) Her voice is barely **audible** as she whispers the name of the compact disc she has come to buy.
15. word: _____ *adj.* well known; widely and unfavorably known or talked about	(E) The clerk compliments her on her taste, but she is **modest** and whispers a shy thank-you.
16. word: _____ *adj.* easy to see; attracting attention	(F) Toya looks up to see Carlotta entering the store. Carlotta is famous, even **notorious,** for teasing people.
17. word: _____ *adj.* not vain or boastful; shy, quiet; decent; reasonable, not extreme	(G) Toya believes that honesty is the best strategy; she decides to be **candid** with the clerk. "I don't want her to see what I'm buying," she whispers.
18. word: _____ *n.* the muscles between the chest cavity and the abdominal cavity; the midriff	(H) The clerk, however, is not very good at being **subtle**. "What's wrong with listening to Leontyne Price?" he shouts.
19. word: _____ *adj.* not harsh or strict when judging or disciplining; merciful	(I) "Buying opera?" says Carlotta. "Well, I'll be **lenient** and not tease you too much this time. After all, I'm here to buy Pavarotti!"
20. word: _____ *adj.* inactive; useless, pointless; without foundation; *v.* to waste; to be inactive; to operate an engine without engaging the gears that move machinery	(J) Soon the two are discussing vocal ranges, lung power, and the importance of the **diaphragm** in providing breath support to an opera singer.

EXERCISE 3 Like Meanings and Opposite Meanings ☞

Directions. For each item below, circle the letter of the choice that means the same, or about the same, as the boldface word.

21. an **audible** remark
    (A) easily heard
    (B) unheard
    (C) irritating
    (D) interesting

22. to strengthen the **diaphragm**
    (A) heart and its veins and arteries
    (B) pair of lungs
    (C) vocal cords
    (D) muscles below the chest

23. in **modest** clothing
    (A) costly
    (B) borrowed
    (C) proper
    (D) designer

24. a **notorious** character
    (A) disgusting
    (B) loud
    (C) interesting
    (D) famous

25. the **threshold** of life
    (A) pain
    (B) middle
    (C) beginning
    (D) end

Directions. For each item below, circle the letter of the choice that means the opposite, or about the opposite, of the boldface word.

26. a **candid** reply
    (A) sincere
    (B) sweet
    (C) dishonest
    (D) bitter

27. a **conspicuous** display
    (A) almost invisible
    (B) easily seen
    (C) very expensive
    (D) very cheap

28. to **idle** the hour away
    (A) spend wastefully
    (B) spend productively
    (C) spend frequently
    (D) spend playfully

29. a **lenient** approach
    (A) agreeable
    (B) loose
    (C) strict
    (D) silly

30. a **subtle** point
    (A) not direct
    (B) direct
    (C) soft
    (D) difficult

Name _____ Date _____ Class _____

| Lesson 7 | **CONTEXT:** Change in Arts and Literature |

Teens, Times, and Books

To a certain extent, television has changed people's attitudes toward reading. For example, many people expect their reading material to be as exciting and fast-paced as their favorite TV show and are disappointed when it is not. Of course, teenagers today read for enjoyment, just as their parents and grandparents did. In fact, they even read some of the same books. It's also true, though, that tastes in reading have changed somewhat.

In the following exercises, you will have the opportunity to expand your vocabulary by reading what one teenager has to say about her own reading habits. Below are ten Vocabulary Words that will be used in these exercises.

| aggravate | caliber | eloquent | maintain | placid |
| anticipate | distract | fulfill | phase | porcelain |

EXERCISE 1 *Wordbusting* ✍

Directions. Follow these instructions for this word and the nine words on the next page.
- Figure out the word's meaning by looking at its **context,** its **structure,** and its **sound.** Fill in at least one of the three **CSS** boxes. Alternate which boxes you complete.
- Then, look up the word in a dictionary, read all of its meanings, and write the meaning of the word as it is used in the sentence.
- Follow this same process for each of the Vocabulary Words on the next page. You will need to draw your own map for each word. Use a separate sheet of paper.

1.

(aggravate) → Sometimes my mother acts as though I choose books just to **aggravate** her. However, annoying her is the farthest thing from my mind.

| Context: | Structure: | Sound: |
| | | |

| Dictionary: |
| |

2.

(fulfill) ➤ She doesn't think the books I read **fulfill** her requirements for good literature. She doesn't believe they live up to the books she read as a girl.

3.

(maintain) ➤ I **maintain** that this is because she hasn't read any of my books. I claim that if she read them, she would see that they are excellent.

4.

(anticipate) ➤ One thing we do have in common is that I **anticipate,** or look forward to, a trip to the library just as much as she does.

5.

(caliber) ➤ We both also enjoy books of high **caliber,** so we both look for worthwhile reading material, even though we take home completely different books.

6.

(distract) ➤ Sometimes we choose books that are designed to **distract** us. For example, we occasionally like to read humorous books because they take our minds off our problems.

7.

(eloquent) ➤ My mother is quite **eloquent** when she speaks about the books she read as a girl. She describes the stories so well that I can picture all the characters.

8.

(phase) ➤ Another thing we have in common is that we both go through **phases** in our reading. Right now I'm reading detective fiction, while my mom has switched to historical fiction.

9.

(placid) ➤ We both love to while away a **placid,** peaceful Sunday afternoon with a good book.

10.

(porcelain) ➤ Last Sunday I finished an Agatha Christie novel. I don't remember what Mom read, but there was a woman on the cover who looked like the fragile **porcelain** figures my grandmother has on her mantelpiece.

EXERCISE 2   *Context Clues* ✍

Directions. Scan the definitions in Column A. Then think about how the boldface words are used in the sentences in Column B. To complete the exercise, match each definition in Column A with the correct Vocabulary Word from Column B. Write the letter of your choice on the line provided. Finally, write the Vocabulary Word on the line before the definition.

COLUMN A	COLUMN B

_____ **11.** word: _____
v. to look forward to; to expect; to foresee; to act in advance of

_____ **12.** word: _____
n. the diameter of a bullet, gun, or cylinder; quality; ability; worth

_____ **13.** word: _____
adj. speaking or writing gracefully; of forceful, persuasive communication; vividly expressive

_____ **14.** word: _____
v. to keep or keep up; to support; to uphold or defend; to declare or insist

_____ **15.** word: _____
n. any stage in a series of changes; *v.* to plan, carry out, or move in stages

_____ **16.** word: _____
v. to carry out; to perform or do; to satisfy a requirement; to finish

_____ **17.** word: _____
n. a white, nonporous, translucent type of ceramic ware; *adj.* made of this ceramic material

_____ **18.** word: _____
adj. undisturbed; tranquil, calm, quiet

_____ **19.** word: _____
v. to make worse or more unpleasant; to annoy

_____ **20.** word: _____
v. to draw attention away from; to confuse; to disturb

(A) I also enjoy nonfiction; last week I read a book about antique **porcelains**. I'd like to own a collection of fine ceramics one day.

(B) Reading outside of class helps me to **maintain** my grade-point average. It's easier to keep up my grades if I read more than is required.

(C) After finishing *Hatchet*, I had **fulfilled** the reading requirement in my English class. I then went beyond the requirement and read two more novels by Gary Paulsen.

(D) When I am **distracted** by some worry, I read to calm myself down and to focus my attention.

(E) I learn a lot from reading. I was feeling very **aggravated** with my dog until I read an article that explained her irritating behavior.

(F) I also read a book about the different stages of children's growth so I could understand each **phase** in my little nephew's development.

(G) I recently read a biography of Martin Luther King, Jr., who was an **eloquent** speaker. The biography suggests that he owed his powers of expression partly to his wide reading.

(H) My dad has read a lot about antique firearms. He can tell you the length of any gun's barrel and the **caliber** or size of the ammunition.

(I) My sister likes to read geography and travel books. Right now she is reading about the **placid** Lake District of northern England, where people go for a peaceful vacation.

(J) My sister is interested in so many different subjects that it is hard to **anticipate** what she will read next.

EXERCISE 3 — *Like Meanings and Opposite Meanings* ✍

Directions. For each item below, circle the letter of the choice that means the same, or about the same, as the boldface word.

21. to **anticipate** her remarks
(A) foresee
(B) avoid
(C) understand
(D) eliminate

22. a work of high **caliber**
(A) greeting
(B) taste
(C) shape
(D) quality

23. to **fulfill** his obligations
(A) understand
(B) overlook
(C) meet
(D) stuff

24. a new **phase**
(A) moon
(B) stage
(C) weapon
(D) vision

25. a **porcelain** vase
(A) expensive
(B) ceramic
(C) gold
(D) broken

Directions. For each item below, circle the letter of the choice that means the opposite, or about the opposite, of the boldface word.

26. to **aggravate** the child
(A) annoy
(B) calm
(C) hunt for
(D) lose

27. to be **distracted**
(A) confused
(B) attentive
(C) tired
(D) energetic

28. an **eloquent** defense
(A) unconvincing
(B) persuasive
(C) expensive
(D) cheap

29. to **maintain** the building
(A) sell
(B) buy
(C) keep up
(D) neglect

30. a **placid** face
(A) calm
(B) ugly
(C) disturbed
(D) beautiful

MAKING NEW WORDS YOUR OWN

Lesson 8 | CONTEXT: Change in Arts and Literature
Who Is a Star?

Actors have always had fans, but motion pictures brought actors a new popularity. Almost as soon as Hollywood began making movies, audiences began singling out particular performers to admire. These performers became stars who could demand enormous salaries for their work.

In the following exercises, you will have the opportunity to expand your vocabulary by reading about movie stars past and present. Below are ten Vocabulary Words that will be used in these exercises.

dashing	flaw	obligation	optional	spontaneous
dismal	frail	obstinate	principally	tiresome

EXERCISE 1   Wordbusting

Directions.   Follow these instructions for this word and the nine words on the next page.
- Figure out the word's meaning by looking at its **context,** its **structure,** and its **sound.** Fill in at least one of the three **CSS** boxes. Alternate which boxes you complete.
- Then, look up the word in a dictionary, read all of its meanings, and write the meaning of the word as it is used in the sentence.
- Follow this same process for each of the Vocabulary Words on the next page. You will need to draw your own map for each word. Use a separate sheet of paper.

1.

dashing → One of the earliest movie stars was Rudolph Valentino, who made a career playing the bold and **dashing** lover in films.

Context:

Structure:

Sound:

Dictionary:

2.

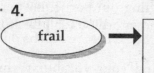
dismal

Like celebrities today, the early stars were admired and envied by many people. In reality, however, some of them lived **dismal,** unhappy lives.

3.

flaw

A number of them worried constantly about their looks. Even the tiniest **flaw,** such as a wrinkle or pimple, frightened and depressed them.

4.

frail

More than a few were quite insecure. Their self-esteem was so **frail** that the slightest criticism could damage it.

5.

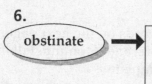
obligation

Often, stars felt an **obligation** to share their lives with their fans. To honor this duty, they usually had to give up much privacy.

6.

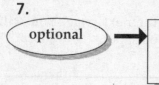
obstinate

Sometimes stars let their popularity go to their heads. When that happened, they would become stubborn, or **obstinate,** about getting their own way.

7.

optional

In Hollywood's early years, the studios controlled the stars' careers and lives. The stars were required to do what the studio demanded; few public appearances were **optional**.

8.

principally

Each star worked **principally** for one studio, although the studio might loan the star to another studio from time to time.

9.

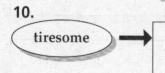
spontaneous

Little in the star's public life was **spontaneous**. Almost everything was carefully planned by studio executives.

10.

tiresome

It's easy to see how this lifestyle could become **tiresome**. It would be very annoying to have your life totally planned by someone else.

EXERCISE 2 *Context Clues* ✍

Directions. Scan the definitions in Column A. Then think about how the boldface words are used in the sentences in Column B. To complete the exercise, match each definition in Column A with the correct Vocabulary Word from Column B. Write the letter of your choice on the line provided. Finally, write the Vocabulary Word on the line before the definition.

COLUMN A

_____ **11.** word: _____
adj. full of spirit; bold; lively; stylish

_____ **12.** word: _____
adj. tiring; boring; annoying

_____ **13.** word: _____
adj. causing gloom or depression; dark and dreary; miserable

_____ **14.** word: _____
adj. acting from a natural impulse or tendency; not planned or forced

_____ **15.** word: _____
n. an imperfection; a defect

_____ **16.** word: _____
adv. mainly; chiefly; overall; for the most part

_____ **17.** word: _____
adj. easily broken or damaged; fragile

_____ **18.** word: _____
adj. left to one's choice; not required

_____ **19.** word: _____
n. a legal or moral responsibility or duty

_____ **20.** word: _____
adj. stubborn; unwilling to give in; hard to control

COLUMN B

(A) Media coverage of the stars' lives is so complete that even a star's **spontaneous,** or impulsive, decision to attend a benefit will be on the evening news.

(B) Most stars appreciate their fans, but it can be very **tiresome** to be recognized everywhere one goes. Most of us have no idea how irritating it would be never to be left alone.

(C) Some actors fear that their popularity is **frail**—that audiences could lose interest in them at any time.

(D) Fans should recognize that they have a duty, or **obligation,** to respect a star's privacy.

(E) Today, many public appearances are **optional** for stars. However, actors may have contracts that require them to do some publicity work.

(F) A few stars are quite **obstinate** about where they will appear, but most are not stubborn about appearing on talk shows.

(G) Of course, stars may be guests on TV talk shows for other reasons, but **principally** they come to let audiences know about their new films.

(H) The lives of some stars today may be as **dismal,** or unhappy, as those of the stars in the earlier days of Hollywood. However, many stars have found ways to live fairly normal, happy lives.

(I) Today's **dashing** leading man or leading woman may leap tall buildings in a single bound all day on the set and then go home to change diapers and feed the cat.

(J) Of course, the life of a star still has **flaws,** but no one's life is perfect.

EXERCISE 3 *Like Meanings and Opposite Meanings* 👈

Directions. For each item below, circle the letter of the choice that means the same, or about the same, as the boldface word.

21. a **dashing** young woman
- (A) bold
- (B) quick
- (C) running
- (D) bald

22. a **flaw** in his character
- (A) talent
- (B) imperfection
- (C) stage
- (D) action

23. a serious **obligation**
- (A) disease
- (B) discussion
- (C) responsibility
- (D) opportunity

24. an **obstinate** director
- (A) strict
- (B) popular
- (C) aged
- (D) stubborn

25. **principally** works for
- (A) sincerely
- (B) morally
- (C) kindly
- (D) mainly

Directions. For each item below, circle the letter of the choice that means the opposite, or about the opposite, of the boldface word.

26. a **dismal** mood
- (A) miserable
- (B) closing
- (C) stormy
- (D) pleasant

27. a **frail** creature
- (A) fragile
- (B) lost
- (C) angry
- (D) sturdy

28. an **optional** appearance
- (A) easy
- (B) difficult
- (C) required
- (D) chosen

29. a **spontaneous** event
- (A) unpredictable
- (B) planned
- (C) expensive
- (D) cheap

30. a **tiresome** experience
- (A) boring
- (B) interesting
- (C) exhausting
- (D) awakened

MAKING NEW WORDS YOUR OWN

Lesson 9 **CONTEXT: Change in Arts and Literature**

Alligators in the Sewers and Other Creepy Stories

In their English class, Zack and his friends are studying folk tales and legends. All the students agree that this is the most interesting unit they've read so far. For one thing, it is full of surprises. Everyone was amazed to find out how old some of the stories are. On the other hand, people create new folk tales all the time. Zack's class is especially interested in folk tales of city life in the United States. These stories have modern settings and characters, but they have much in common with older tales.

In the following exercises, you will have the opportunity to expand your vocabulary by reading about folk tales and legends. Below are ten Vocabulary Words that will be used.

authentic	contemplate	formal	interpret	myth
comparable	dual	immortal	legendary	profound

EXERCISE 1 *Wordbusting*

Directions. Follow these instructions for this word and the nine words on the next page.
- Figure out the word's meaning by looking at its **context,** its **structure,** and its **sound.** Fill in at least one of the three **CSS** boxes. Alternate which boxes you complete.
- Then, look up the word in a dictionary, read all of its meanings, and write the meaning of the word as it is used in the sentence.
- Follow this same process for each of the Vocabulary Words on the next page. You will need to draw your own map for each word. Use a separate sheet of paper.

1.

(authentic) → How can you tell whether a story is an **authentic** folk tale? It is probably real if it has been shared orally among many people.

Context:	Structure:	Sound:

Dictionary:

2.
comparable → Folk tales from one country are often **comparable** to those of another country. They may have many elements in common.

3.
contemplate → We don't often stop to **contemplate** what folk tales might mean, but it can be interesting to think about them seriously.

4.
interpret → Many scholars study and **interpret** folk tales. They tell us what they think the stories mean.

5.
dual → Most folk tales have a **dual** purpose. They serve both to entertain and to teach a lesson.

6.
formal → Most of us have heard many folk tales by the time we begin to study them in a **formal,** or orderly, way.

7.
immortal → Some folk tales seem to be **immortal**. They have been around for centuries, and they will continue to be popular for many more centuries.

8.
legendary → Many folk tales handed down through the generations tell of the **legendary** adventures of heroes such as Robin Hood, Davy Crockett, and Hiawatha.

9.
myth → A **myth** is a special form of folk tale. Usually, myths are stories about gods, and they are told to explain the beginnings of human life and the natural world.

10.
profound → Stories like these reveal **profound,** or deep, truths about the human condition.

EXERCISE 2 *Context Clues* ☞

Directions. Scan the definitions in Column A. Then think about how the boldface words are used in the sentences in Column B. To complete the exercise, match each definition in Column A with the correct Vocabulary Word from Column B. Write the letter of your choice on the line provided. Finally, write the Vocabulary Word on the line before the definition.

COLUMN A	COLUMN B

COLUMN A

_____ **11.** word: _____
adj. alike enough to be compared; worthy of comparison

_____ **12.** word: _____
adj. according to set rules or customs; stiff in manner; done or made in an orderly manner; of form, rather than content

_____ **13.** word: _____
adj. trustworthy, reliable; genuine, real

_____ **14.** word: _____
adj. living forever; having lasting fame

_____ **15.** word: _____
v. to look at very closely; to think carefully about; to consider

_____ **16.** word: _____
n. a traditional story used to explain the world or human behavior; such stories collectively; any unscientific account; a popular belief

_____ **17.** word: _____
adj. very deep; very serious

_____ **18.** word: _____
adj. based on legends or stories handed down from one generation to another; traditional; famous

_____ **19.** word: _____
v. to explain the meaning of; to translate; to show one's own understanding of

_____ **20.** word: _____
adj. consisting of two parts; double

COLUMN B

(A) Urban legends about alligators living in the sewers of major cities probably don't contain any **profound** truths. I certainly don't see any deep meaning there.

(B) Do these stories have a **dual** purpose? I think they are told to entertain, but what other role do they play?

(C) Perhaps if I **contemplate,** or think about, the stories a bit longer, I'll see something important.

(D) One story tells of a cat that crept into the engine of a jet and traveled five thousand miles, arriving unharmed at the jet's destination. People swear this story is true, but I haven't seen a **formal,** or proper, statement that supports it.

(E) Not only do many people believe this tale is **authentic,** they think it happened at their local airport.

(F) They don't realize that several communities have **comparable** stories. The stories are almost identical except for the name of the cat.

(G) I don't know how to **interpret** this information. I do, however, think there is some explanation for the similarities.

(H) I also think it is interesting that many figures in popular culture resemble the figures in ancient **myths.** For example, Superman seems to me to be a lot like the Greek god Apollo.

(I) Several comic-book heroes, such as Batman, Spider-Man, and Wonder Woman, have many of the features of **legendary** heroes.

(J) These superheroes aren't **immortal,** but from time to time one of them does seem to be indestructible.

EXERCISE 3 *Like Meanings and Opposite Meanings* ☞

Directions. For each item below, circle the letter of the choice that means the same, or about the same, as the boldface word.

21. at a **comparable** price
  - (A) costly
  - (B) reasonable
  - (C) similar
  - (D) unusual

22. to **contemplate** the question
  - (A) answer
  - (B) ask about
  - (C) think about
  - (D) color in

23. to **interpret** the speech
  - (A) explain
  - (B) confuse
  - (C) memorize
  - (D) forget

24. a **legendary** tale
  - (A) handed down from one generation to another
  - (B) ignored by one generation
  - (C) lost in time
  - (D) written down and then forgotten

25. to question the **myth**
  - (A) modern song
  - (B) scientific proof
  - (C) legendary monster
  - (D) popular belief

Directions. For each item below, circle the letter of the choice that means the opposite, or about the opposite, of the boldface word.

26. an **authentic** document
  - (A) legal
  - (B) genuine
  - (C) similar
  - (D) fake

27. a **formal** occasion
  - (A) serious
  - (B) frightening
  - (C) casual
  - (D) happy

28. the **immortal** movie star
  - (A) forgotten
  - (B) talented
  - (C) famous
  - (D) wealthy

29. a **dual** interest
  - (A) single
  - (B) double
  - (C) sincere
  - (D) cruel

30. a **profound** idea
  - (A) confusing
  - (B) deep
  - (C) lost
  - (D) shallow

Name _____ Date _____ Class _____

Lesson 10 | CONTEXT: Change in Arts and Literature

Reading Buddies

Charley Martin enjoys reading. It's a trait he shares with his grandmother. Charley and his grandmother often discuss their favorite books.

In the following exercises, you will have the opportunity to expand your vocabulary by reading about the relationship Charley and his grandmother have with books. Below are ten Vocabulary Words that will be used in these exercises.

cherish	crucial	gratify	mythology	versatile
consistent	designate	indispensable	resolve	vigor

EXERCISE 1   *Wordbusting* ☞

Directions. Follow these instructions for this word and the nine words on the next page.
- Figure out the word's meaning by looking at its **context,** its **structure,** and its **sound.** Fill in at least one of the three **CSS** boxes. Alternate which boxes you complete.
- Then, look up the word in a dictionary, read all of its meanings, and write the meaning of the word as it is used in the sentence.
- Follow this same process for each of the Vocabulary Words on the next page. You will need to draw your own map for each word. Use a separate sheet of paper.

1.

(cherish) → My grandmother taught me to **cherish** books by reading to me from the time I was a toddler. Now it is a love we both share.

Context:

Structure:

Sound:

Dictionary:

2.
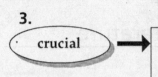 Sometimes my life seems confused and disorganized, but I can count on one thing to be **consistent**. On the weekends, I can always find my grandmother in her easy chair reading a book.

3.
 She considers reading a necessity of life, and I agree with her. It is **crucial** to the way we live.

4.
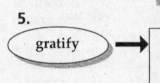 A long time ago we decided to **designate** Saturday afternoons as our time together. We named the time and the place—Saturday at noon at her place.

5.
 It is a time that **gratifies** both of us. We take a great deal of pleasure from each other's company.

6.
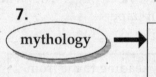 It is an **indispensable** part of my week. I could give up a lot of other things in my life if I had to, but not my time with her.

7.
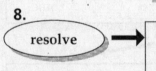 Grandmother knows a lot about **mythology,** especially the study of the stories and legends of Asian gods and goddesses, so we often discuss this subject.

8.
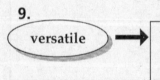 We also talk about how to **resolve** the problems of the world, as well as how to solve our own.

9.
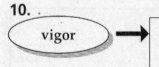 Reading has made my grandmother a **versatile** conversationalist. She can discuss many topics.

10.
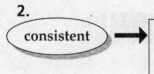 She approaches almost every subject with **vigor** and enthusiasm. She has an amazing amount of energy.

EXERCISE 2 · *Context Clues* ✍

Directions. Scan the definitions in Column A. Then think about how the boldface words are used in the sentences in Column B. To complete the exercise, match each definition in Column A with the correct Vocabulary Word from Column B. Write the letter of your choice on the line provided. Finally, write the Vocabulary Word on the line before the definition.

COLUMN A	COLUMN B
____ **11.** word: _____ *adj.* very important	(A) My grandmother **cherishes** the books she read when she was young. She has given many of them to me, and now I love them, too.
____ **12.** word: _____ *v.* to give pleasure or satisfaction; to give in to	(B) I have **resolved** to take good care of them so that someday I can pass them on to my grand-child. I told her about my decision.
____ **13.** word: _____ *adj.* absolutely essential; necessary	(C) She was **gratified** to learn that I would take good care of her prized books. She was also pleased to hear that I would read them aloud.
____ **14.** word: _____ *v.* to love or to hold dear; to take care of; to protect	(D) I agree with her that it is **crucial** to read some of the classics. They are very important to a good education.
____ **15.** word: _____ *n.* strength and energy of body or mind; strength of concentration; force or energy	(E) I think many of the modern books I read will be **designated** classics someday. Grandmother, on the other hand, doesn't think many of them will be singled out as masterpieces.
____ **16.** word: _____ *adj.* in agreement; able to coexist; holding regularly to the same rules	(F) She defends her position with **vigor**. Some-times she argues so powerfully that she almost shouts.
____ **17.** word: _____ *v.* to reach a definite decision; to find a solution; to explain or make clear; to change or transform; *n.* determination	(G) She agrees with me that Robert Cormier can be a great writer, but she says the quality of Cormier's books is not **consistent**. Some of the books are excellent and some are only fair.
____ **18.** word: _____ *adj.* able or skilled in many things; adaptable to many uses or situations	(H) She finds Isaac Asimov to be an extremely **versatile** writer. She is amazed not only at the number of books that Asimov wrote but also at the many different types of books.
____ **19.** word: _____ *v.* to point out; to specify; to name	(I) However, she doesn't find any of the writers I read to be **indispensable**. She says she can get along fine without them.
____ **20.** word: _____ *n.* a collection of myths or stories, usually about the gods and their relationships to human beings; the study of myths	(J) She reminds me to study the **mythology** of many different cultures. She says it is the basis of understanding literature.

EXERCISE 3 *Like Meanings and Opposite Meanings* ☞

Directions. For each item below, circle the letter of the choice that means the same, or about the same, as the boldface word.

21. an approach **consistent** with mine
(A) competing
(B) in agreement
(C) in disagreement
(D) terrible

22. to **designate** a captain
(A) obey
(B) select
(C) talk about
(D) report to

23. Asian **mythology**
(A) study
(B) group of myths
(C) legendary hero
(D) kingdom

24. to show **resolve**
(A) problems
(B) doubt
(C) determination
(D) fear

25. a **versatile** football player
(A) especially strong
(B) well-known
(C) confused
(D) well-rounded

Directions. For each item below, circle the letter of the choice that means the opposite, or about the opposite, of the boldface word.

26. to **cherish** the toys
(A) destroy
(B) hold dear
(C) buy
(D) polish

27. a **crucial** moment
(A) serious
(B) elegant
(C) cheap
(D) unimportant

28. to **gratify** his demands
(A) give in to
(B) ignore
(C) thank
(D) reveal

29. an **indispensable** part
(A) repaired
(B) broken
(C) important
(D) unnecessary

30. with **vigor**
(A) strength
(B) weakness
(C) money
(D) desire

MAKING NEW WORDS YOUR OWN

Lesson 11 | CONTEXT: Change in Individuals and Communities
Those with a Dream

A minority is a group of people who are different, either racially, ethnically, or religiously, from the majority of the overall community. Many needed changes in the twentieth-century United States were made by members of minority communities. Individual leaders played key roles in these struggles, but it was the people themselves who had the courage and determination to seek change.

In the following exercises, you will have the opportunity to expand your vocabulary by reading about how some minority groups have struggled to improve their lives. These ten Vocabulary Words will be used.

| discrimination | illustrious | legitimate | moderate | partial |
| guarantee | initial | merit | moral | unison |

EXERCISE 1 | *Wordbusting* ☞

Directions. Follow these instructions for this word and the nine words on the next page.
- Figure out the word's meaning by looking at its **context**, its **structure**, and its **sound**. Fill in at least one of the three **CSS** boxes. Alternate which boxes you complete.
- Then, look up the word in a dictionary, read all of its meanings, and write the meaning of the word as it is used in the sentence.
- Follow this same process for each of the Vocabulary Words on the next page. You will need to draw your own map for each word. Use a separate sheet of paper.

1.

(discrimination) → Any story about the civil rights movement should mention the number of people who were upset about receiving unfair treatment and who struggled to end **discrimination**.

| Context: | Structure: | Sound: |
| | | |

Dictionary:

2.
(guarantee) ➜ Over the years, many people have worked hard to make sure that the government would **guarantee** their rights and the rights of others. Making sure that the government would keep its promises was hard work.

3.
(illustrious) ➜ The list includes **illustrious** leaders such as Cesar Chavez, Russell Means, and Daisy Bates. Of course, many people who never became famous were also important.

4.
(initial) ➜ Leaders often take the **initial** steps, but the community has to be ready to work for change.

5.
(legitimate) ➜ In the twentieth century, many groups had **legitimate** complaints about the way they were treated by the people in power. For example, African Americans in the South were rightfully outraged that they could not vote.

6.
(merit) ➜ Members of minority groups have often had to struggle to get others to recognize the **merits** of their case. Eventually, most people have recognized the importance of what they were saying.

7.
(moderate) ➜ Some members of minority groups were conservative, or very cautious, in their approach; others were radical and demanded immediate, sweeping changes. Most were somewhere in between. They were **moderates**.

8.
(moral) ➜ People who struggled for equal rights had the satisfaction of knowing that their cause was just and **moral**. They knew that right was on their side.

9.
(partial) ➜ Some victories have been complete; others have been only **partial**.

10.
(unison) ➜ In any case, people have learned they can achieve more when they act in **unison**. Working together is important in bringing about change.

EXERCISE 2 *Context Clues* ✍

Directions. Scan the definitions in Column A. Then think about how the boldface words are used in the sentences in Column B. To complete the exercise, match each definition in Column A with the correct Vocabulary Word from Column B. Write the letter of your choice on the line provided. Finally, write the Vocabulary Word on the line before the definition.

COLUMN A	COLUMN B

COLUMN A

_____ **11.** word: _____
n. worth; state of deserving good or ill; award for excellence; *v.* to deserve

_____ **12.** word: _____
adj. famous; outstanding; distinguished

_____ **13.** word: _____
adj. first; occurring at the beginning; *n.* the first letter of a name

_____ **14.** word: _____
adj. lawful; rightful; reasonable

_____ **15.** word: _____
adj. not extreme in belief or action; mild; *n.* a person holding reasonable political or religious beliefs; *v.* to make less extreme; to preside over

_____ **16.** word: _____
n. unfair treatment of another; showing good judgment

_____ **17.** word : _____
n. agreement, harmony; producing the same sound at the same time

_____ **18.** word: _____
n. a promise that something will happen or that a product will be fixed if broken; *v.* to make such a promise

_____ **19.** word: _____
adj. dealing with distinctions between right and wrong; good, right, or ethical; *n.* a lesson taught by a fable or an event

_____ **20.** word: _____
adj. favoring one side; involving only a part; incomplete; unfair

COLUMN B

(A) "Of all the outstanding leaders, I don't think any is more **illustrious** than Cesar Chavez," remarks Delores. Her group is making a list of leaders in the civil rights movement.

(B) "He worked so hard. Before his death, he sought a **guarantee** that the needs of migrant farm workers would be met. Such a promise had never been made."

(C) "I agree with you totally. He **merits** our respect and admiration, but people who help the homeless also deserve credit," Terry said.

(D) "I don't know whether it is **legitimate** to put them on our list. Is it reasonable to call homeless Americans a minority group?"

(E) "I think so. I understand your **initial** reaction. But don't let your first response decide for you. Remember that Martin Luther King, Jr., believed that all poor people were the concern of the civil rights movement."

(F) "Okay, so we add those who help the homeless to our list, but it's still not complete. Do we want to hand in only a **partial** list?"

(G) "Well, I guess it's not exactly a matter of **morals,** but it does seem wrong not to do the best job we can."

(H) "Well, we have to find a **moderate** position. We have to settle somewhere between a list of three people and a list of everybody who ever helped organize minority communities."

(I) "It takes a lot of **discrimination** to decide who will be on our final list. What are our standards for deciding whom to include?"

(J) "Let's list our standards," Mike and Roberto said in **unison**.

EXERCISE 3 *Like Meanings and Opposite Meanings*

Directions. For each item below, circle the letter of the choice that means the same, or about the same, as the boldface word.

21. a solemn **guarantee**
(A) group
(B) price
(C) understanding
(D) promise

22. a **legitimate** concern
(A) reasonable
(B) serious
(C) criminal
(D) friendly

23. to **merit** attention
(A) get
(B) deserve
(C) end
(D) avoid

24. a **moderate** amount
(A) tiny
(B) extra
(C) modest
(D) additional

25. to act in **unison**
(A) separately
(B) legally
(C) together
(D) incorrectly

Directions. For each item below, circle the letter of the choice that means the opposite, or about the opposite, of the boldface word.

26. an **illustrious** leader
(A) unknown
(B) dignified
(C) remarkable
(D) intelligent

27. showing **discrimination** in dress
(A) changing taste
(B) poor taste
(C) good taste
(D) new styles

28. the **initial** request
(A) fair
(B) unfair
(C) first
(D) last

29. a **moral** person
(A) unimportant
(B) important
(C) evil
(D) good

30. **partial** to our cause
(A) favoring
(B) not favoring
(C) completely supporting
(D) remembering

Name _____ Date _____ Class _____

Lesson 12 | CONTEXT: Change in Individuals and Communities
The Women's Movement

Women made amazing progress in the world of politics during the twentieth century. At the beginning of the century, they did not even have the right to vote. Today women play a major role in local, state, and national politics, and the United States is stronger and more democratic as a result of the contributions of women.

In the following exercises, you will have the opportunity to expand your vocabulary by reading about women in politics. These ten Vocabulary Words will be used.

constitution	hypocrite	indirect	notable	segregation
elective	indefinite	judicial	prudent	veto

EXERCISE 1 *Wordbusting*

Directions. Follow these instructions for this word and the nine words on the next page.
- Figure out the word's meaning by looking at its **context,** its **structure,** and its **sound.** Fill in at least one of the three **CSS** boxes. Alternate which boxes you complete.
- Then, look up the word in a dictionary, read all of its meanings, and write the meaning of the word as it is used in the sentence.
- Follow this same process for each of the Vocabulary Words on the next page. You will need to draw your own map for each word. Use a separate sheet of paper.

1.

(constitution) → The United States **Constitution** was changed in 1920, giving women the right to vote.

Context:

Structure:

Sound:

Dictionary:

2.

(prudent) ➤ Not so long ago, many people did not believe women could be **prudent** leaders. They didn't believe a woman could make sound and sensible decisions under stressful circumstances.

3.

(segregation) ➤ In fact, it seems that there was a form of **segregation** being practiced in politics—women were excluded.

4.

(indefinite) ➤ Although members of Congress have limited terms, they often stay for an **indefinite** period of time; voters usually re-elect the same person.

5.

(elective) ➤ Today there are more women in **elective** offices than ever before. Voters have chosen women to serve as mayors, as members of Congress, and as state governors.

6.

(indirect) ➤ Citizens often try to change Congress in **indirect** ways, such as writing letters to newspapers. But in the late twentieth–century, many voters showed their disapproval of Congress directly by voting in new representatives, several of whom were women.

7.

(hypocrite) ➤ A politician who is a **hypocrite,** who says one thing and does another, eventually is exposed. Some voters hoped women would be honest.

8.

(judicial) ➤ More women are serving in the **judicial** branch of government, too. They serve as judges in city, county, state, and federal courts.

9.

(notable) ➤ One of the most **notable** advances that women have made in the United States is the appointment of women to the Supreme Court.

10.

(veto) ➤ Soon it may be common to hear comments like the following on the evening news: "The president met with congressional leaders today to explain why she decided to **veto** the proposed law. She rejected it for three reasons. . . ."

EXERCISE 2 *Context Clues* ✍

Directions. Scan the definitions in Column A. Then think about how the boldface words are used in the sentences in Column B. To complete the exercise, match each definition in Column A with the correct Vocabulary Word from Column B. Write the letter of your choice on the line provided. Finally, write the Vocabulary Word on the line before the definition.

COLUMN A	COLUMN B
_____ **11.** word: _____ *adj.* remarkable, outstanding; *n.* a person of distinction; a well-known person	(A) "I feel like a **hypocrite** if I don't say something when I hear people make negative remarks about women," says Mary.
_____ **12.** word: _____ *adj.* chosen by election; optional; *n.* an optional course in a curriculum	(B) "Me, too," says Elena. "How do you decide what is more **prudent**? Is it wiser to keep my temper or to show how angry I am?"
_____ **13.** word: _____ *n.* a basic set of laws and principles by which a country is organized; general physical or mental make-up of a person	(C) "If I don't say anything, it seems to indicate that women have **indefinite** opinions, that we are undecided about where we stand."
_____ **14.** word: _____ *adj.* not straight; roundabout; not straightforward; secondary	(D) "Yes, but if you give in to that sudden urge to make an angry remark, then they'll say that you don't have a strong **constitution**, that you are just too emotional."
_____ **15.** word: _____ *n.* a person who pretends to be something that he or she is not	(E) "Sometimes I try to be **indirect** in my response. I just make some roundabout comment that contains a strong hint."
_____ **16.** word: _____ *n.* the practice of forcing one group of people to live apart, and to use separate schools and facilities	(F) "Me, too. For example, I might mention several **notable**, or famous, women—anyone from Abigail Adams to Barbara Jordan."
_____ **17.** word: _____ *n.* an order or act forbidding some proposed action; *v.* to prevent; to prohibit	(G) "It is easy to do that these days since so many women hold **elective** offices. Our grandmothers didn't have many examples of female governors or mayors."
_____ **18.** word: _____ *adj.* uncertain; not clearly defined; without clear limits or boundaries	(H) "That's true. Isn't it strange to think that many people once believed women couldn't serve in **judicial** positions because they didn't have the fairness required to be judges?"
_____ **19.** word: _____ *adj.* sensible; practical; cautious; thrifty	(I) "Did you know that some of the advancements women have made are a result of the movement to end racial **segregation**, to give African Americans access to the same institutions as whites?"
_____ **20.** word: _____ *adj.* of or having to do with justice, judges, or courts of law	(J) "Yes, once most citizens rejected the idea that people were inferior because of their race, they also realized they should **veto** the notion that women were inferior to men."

EXERCISE 3 *Like Meanings and Opposite Meanings*

Directions. For each item below, circle the letter of the choice that means the same, or about the same, as the boldface word.

21. to behave like a **hypocrite**
(A) an insincere person
(B) an exceptionally honest person
(C) a medical specialist
(D) a circus performer

22. a **judicial** decision
(A) court
(B) foolish
(C) Congressional
(D) illegal

23. the issue of **segregation**
(A) opportunity
(B) education
(C) race
(D) separation

24. having a strong **constitution**
(A) belief system
(B) hunch
(C) opinion
(D) physical makeup

25. a **notable** cause
(A) lost
(B) written down
(C) invisible
(D) outstanding

Directions. For each item below, circle the letter of the choice that means the opposite, or about the opposite, of the boldface word.

26. an **elective** course
(A) chosen
(B) required
(C) popular
(D) unpopular

27. an **indefinite** answer
(A) vague
(B) specific
(C) lengthy
(D) short

28. an **indirect** route
(A) roundabout
(B) colorful
(C) straight
(D) false

29. to **veto** the idea
(A) vote on
(B) offer
(C) reject
(D) support

30. a **prudent** approach
(A) expensive
(B) cheap
(C) cautious
(D) foolish

MAKING NEW WORDS YOUR OWN

Lesson 13 | CONTEXT: Change in Individuals and Communities
The Writing Classroom

Some people love to write. Some people hate writing. Those people who don't enjoy writing shouldn't worry, however. Working in groups can change even the most unwilling student's attitude toward writing.

In the following exercises, you will have the opportunity to expand your vocabulary by reading about writing and about a group of students who are in the same writing class. Below are ten Vocabulary Words that will be used in these exercises.

credible	legible	mastery	refrain	tutor
grammatical	manuscript	participate	revise	usage

EXERCISE 1   *Wordbusting* ☞

Directions.   Follow these instructions for this word and the nine words on the next page.
- Figure out the word's meaning by looking at its **context,** its **structure,** and its **sound.** Fill in at least one of the three **CSS** boxes. Alternate which boxes you complete.
- Then, look up the word in a dictionary, read all of its meanings, and write the meaning of the word as it is used in the sentence.
- Follow this same process for each of the Vocabulary Words on the next page. You will need to draw your own map for each word. Use a separate sheet of paper.

1.

(credible) ➡️ At first, students may not find it **credible** that writing well can change their lives. They may not believe that skill in writing makes a difference in the real world.

Context:	Structure:	Sound:

Dictionary:

2.

grammatical → Of course, **grammatical** writing is important. We all need to learn to structure our words and sentences correctly.

3.

legible → **Legible** writing is important, too. What good is writing if people can't read it?

4.

manuscript → We all need to know how to produce a clean, correct, well-edited **manuscript**. We should treat our essays as if we plan to have them printed or published.

5.

mastery → **Mastery** of the rules and conventions of writing is important, but a high level of skill in these areas is only part of what it takes to be a good writer.

6.

participate → Students who **participate** with each other in the writing process— who work in pairs or groups and share ideas—really feel better about their writing.

7.

refrain → Although at first some students **refrain** from speaking in their groups, soon they can't hold back what they have to say.

8.

revise → Students can even become eager to **revise** their papers when they see someone else's reaction.

9.

tutor → After group members work together on two or three papers, they seem less like students and more like **tutors,** or writing coaches, who teach and advise.

10.

usage → These advisors not only help each other learn more about punctuation and **usage,** or the formal use of language, but they also help each other become more confident writers.

EXERCISE 2 Context Clues ✍

Directions. Scan the definitions in Column A. Then think about how the boldface words are used in the sentences in Column B. To complete the exercise, match each definition in Column A with the correct Vocabulary Word from Column B. Write the letter of your choice on the line provided. Finally, write the Vocabulary Word on the line before the definition.

COLUMN A

_____ **11.** word: _____
adj. believable; reliable

_____ **12.** word: _____
v. to correct or improve

_____ **13.** word: _____
adj. conforming to the rules of grammar

_____ **14.** word: _____
adj. that which can be read or deciphered

_____ **15.** word: _____
n. someone who gives individual instruction; *v.* to give individual instruction

_____ **16.** word: _____
n. a handwritten or typed copy of a book or other document that is to be printed or published

_____ **17.** word: _____
n. rule; control; expert skill or knowledge after much practice

_____ **18.** word: _____
v. to join or share with others

_____ **19.** word: _____
v. to hold back; to abstain; *n.* a phrase or verse repeated in a song or poem

_____ **20.** word: _____
n. use; established practice; customary manner of using the words in a language

COLUMN B

(A) "I sometimes have trouble making my papers **grammatical**," says Kwai. "That's because English is not my first language, and I am not used to these new rules."

(B) "I think I have **mastery** of the grammar," says Bonnie Lee, "but there are some other things I have trouble understanding."

(C) "Because my family uses a Southern dialect, I have some different **usages**. For example, I say 'y'all' and 'fixing to.' My teacher says these expressions are OK in some papers but not in others."

(D) "My handwriting is not very **legible**," says Leroi. "That's why I prefer to write my papers on a word processor—so they can be read."

(E) "On a word processor it's also much easier to **revise** papers. I can make changes and corrections by pushing a few keys."

(F) "Yes, a paper done on a word processor looks like a real **manuscript**, something you would send to be published."

(G) "'*It's my turn for the computer*,' is a familiar **refrain** at my house. It's repeated a dozen times a day. That's why I still handwrite some of my papers," says Nora.

(H) "Hey, Jamie, don't you want to **participate** in this discussion? Come over and join in."

(I) "I can't," says Jamie. "I promised to **tutor** Rosa. She wants me to help her with her brochure."

(J) "I don't find that very **credible**. Who would believe that Rosa would ask anyone for help?"

EXERCISE 3 *Like Meanings and Opposite Meanings* 👈

Directions. For each item below, circle the letter of the choice that means the same, or about the same, as the boldface word.

21. a **grammatical** sentence
    (A) correct
    (B) long
    (C) short
    (D) difficult

22. the word-processed **manuscript**
    (A) document intended to be thrown out
    (B) document intended to amuse
    (C) document intended to be published
    (D) document intended to teach

23. to **revise** a sentence
    (A) see
    (B) misunderstand
    (C) change
    (D) study

24. to **tutor** the student
    (A) look after
    (B) order
    (C) learn
    (D) teach

25. an interesting **usage**
    (A) topic
    (B) word
    (C) mistake
    (D) use

Directions. For each item below, circle the letter of the choice that means the opposite, or about the opposite, of the boldface word.

26. in order to **participate**
    (A) rapidly multiply
    (B) more than equal
    (C) take no part in
    (D) join in

27. a **credible** witness
    (A) in debt
    (B) wealthy
    (C) reliable
    (D) unbelievable

28. a **legible** word
    (A) clear
    (B) unreadable
    (C) honest
    (D) illegal

29. to demonstrate **mastery**
    (A) lack of control
    (B) control
    (C) understanding
    (D) disbelief

30. to **refrain** from speaking
    (A) join in
    (B) hold back
    (C) sing
    (D) listen

MAKING NEW WORDS YOUR OWN

Lesson 14 | **CONTEXT: Change in Individuals and Communities**
In the Office of The Lion's Roar *and* The Lion's Tales

The students in my school share their writings through a student newspaper and a student literary magazine. Educators support these publications to give students real-world experiences.

In the following exercises, you will have the opportunity to expand your vocabulary by reading about students who write for their community. Below are ten Vocabulary Words that will be used in these exercises.

dialogue	faculty	journal	narration	prose
editorial	forum	literary	persuasion	symbolic

EXERCISE 1 *Wordbusting*

Directions. Follow these instructions for this word and the nine words on the next page.
- Figure out the word's meaning by looking at its **context,** its **structure,** and its **sound.** Fill in at least one of the three **CSS** boxes. Alternate which boxes you complete.
- Then, look up the word in a dictionary, read all of its meanings, and write the meaning of the word as it is used in the sentence.
- Follow this same process for each of the Vocabulary Words on the next page. You will need to draw your own map for each word. Use a separate sheet of paper.

1.

(dialogue) ⟶ When I dropped by *The Lion's Roar* office, I overheard a **dialogue** between Latrice and Josh. Their conversation was about this week's edition of the school newspaper.

Context:	Structure:	Sound:

Dictionary:

2.

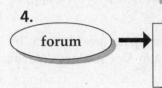

"I know we've never run an **editorial** on the front page before, but this is different," said Josh. "We have to let the school know the paper's opinion about the decision to appoint, rather than elect, the student council."

3.

"Well, you have a great **faculty** for getting along with Mr. Chin, but I don't think even you will be able to calm him down if we do this," responded Latrice.

4.

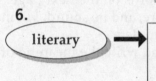

"You know as well as I do that Mr. Chin believes this newspaper provides the students with a **forum,** a place to discuss issues openly."

5.

"Josh, if you do this, the only place you'll be allowed to write is in English class—and in the private **journal** you keep under your pillow."

6.

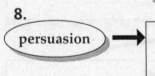

"Oh, I don't know. There's always the **literary** magazine. Maybe I'll give up news and try fiction—maybe short stories."

7.

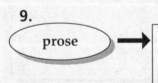

"Well, you ought to be good at **narration** at this point. You've written enough news stories," said Latrice.

8.

(persuasion)

"Don't forget that I have developed great powers of **persuasion**. I think I can convince Mr. Chin we are doing the right thing."

9.

(prose)

"You do have a way with all forms of **prose**. Have you ever tried poetry?"

10.

(symbolic)

"Let's get back to the original point. Will Mr. Chin understand why it is important to do this? Or will he see this as a **symbolic** act— maybe as a sign that we just want to rebel?"

EXERCISE 2 *Context Clues* ✍

Directions. Scan the definitions in Column A. Then think about how the boldface words are used in the sentences in Column B. To complete the exercise, match each definition in Column A with the correct Vocabulary Word from Column B. Write the letter of your choice on the line provided. Finally, write the Vocabulary Word on the line before the definition.

COLUMN A	COLUMN B
_____ **11.** word: _____ *n.* a place, an assembly, or a program for the discussion of public issues; an opportunity to discuss issues openly	(A) *The Lion's Roar* is not the only **forum** for students at Josh and Latrice's school. The school also holds regular discussion groups.
_____ **12.** word: _____ *n.* one of the five senses; special aptitude or skill; all of the teachers at a school, college, or university	(B) In general, members of the **faculty** encourage students to express their opinions. Most teachers no longer think that students should be seen and not heard.
_____ **13.** word: _____ *n.* ordinary language, not poetry; *adj.* written in ordinary language	(C) *The Lion's Roar* is an especially important publication—it is the only school **journal** that focuses on student activities and concerns.
_____ **14.** word: _____ *adj.* having to do with books or writing	(D) The **editorial** staff of the paper includes the two editors, Latrice and Josh, as well as Carlos, who is the features editor, and Jennifer, who is the sports editor.
_____ **15.** word: _____ *adj.* of or expressed by a sign, or something that represents another thing	(E) The newspaper staff shares an office with the staff of *The Lion's Tales,* the student **literary** magazine that publishes short stories and poetry.
_____ **16.** word: _____ *n.* storytelling; a story or account	(F) The newspaper staff is concerned with learning to write clear, lively **prose**—that is, ordinary language that is easily understood.
_____ **17.** word: _____ *n.* a conversation; the passages of speech in a literary work	(G) Both staffs rely heavily on good **narration**. Of course, the stories told in the newspaper are also supposed to be true and accurate.
_____ **18.** word: _____ *n.* being convinced by reasoning, urging, or force; a strong opinion or conviction	(H) *The Lion's Roar* staff has to use **persuasion**. Each member has to write a story or essay that will convince others of something.
_____ **19.** word: _____ *n.* a statement of opinion in the media by the editor; *adj.* characteristic of such a statement; of an editor	(I) *The Lion's Tales* staff agree that the most difficult task is writing **dialogue**. It's hard to make characters' speech believable.
_____ **20.** word: _____ *n.* a diary or personal record; a periodical; a record of a group's transactions	(J) The staff also has some interesting arguments about what is **symbolic**. Was the daisy in last month's short story just a flower, or did it stand for something else?

EXERCISE 3 *Like Meanings and Opposite Meanings* ✍

Directions. For each item below, circle the letter of the choice that means the same, or about the same, as the boldface word.

21. a serious **dialogue**
  (A) conversation
  (B) date
  (C) sermon
  (D) custom

22. a cloth-bound **journal**
  (A) dictionary
  (B) purse
  (C) diary
  (D) letter

23. in **literary** circles
  (A) having to do with travel
  (B) having to do with books
  (C) having to do with intelligence
  (D) having to do with paper

24. in the middle of the **narration**
  (A) opinion
  (B) argument
  (C) commercial
  (D) story

25. for **faculty** only
  (A) teachers
  (B) students
  (C) senses
  (D) abilities

Directions. For each item below, circle the letter of the choice that means the opposite, or about the opposite, of the boldface word.

26. an **editorial** comment
  (A) opinionated
  (B) stupid
  (C) disinterested
  (D) brilliant

27. the importance of **persuasion**
  (A) ignoring others
  (B) language
  (C) convincing others
  (D) including many

28. to discuss in a **forum**
  (A) public meeting
  (B) public hallway
  (C) private hospital
  (D) private conversation

29. in plain **prose**
  (A) book
  (B) dress
  (C) poetry
  (D) language

30. a **symbolic** act
  (A) representative
  (B) self-contained
  (C) artistic
  (D) important

Name _____ Date _____ Class _____

| Lesson 15 | **CONTEXT: Change in Individuals and Communities** |

Playing Together

Whether it's football, soccer, baseball, or basketball, most of us enjoy team sports, either as spectators or as participants. Sports provide a unique combination of cooperation and competition. Members of the same team cooperate, while teams compete with each other. This exciting mix makes us love to play or cheer for the team.

In the following exercises, you will have the opportunity to expand your vocabulary by reading about attitudes toward team sports. These ten Vocabulary Words will be used.

adhere	maneuver	opponent	penetrate	tactics
forbidding	minority	participant	recommend	yield

| EXERCISE 1 | *Wordbusting* 👉 |

Directions. Follow these instructions for this word and the nine words on the next page.
- Figure out the word's meaning by looking at its **context,** its **structure,** and its **sound.** Fill in at least one of the three **CSS** boxes. Alternate which boxes you complete.
- Then, look up the word in a dictionary, read all of its meanings, and write the meaning of the word as it is used in the sentence.
- Follow this same process for each of the Vocabulary Words on the next page. You will need to draw your own map for each word. Use a separate sheet of paper.

1.

(adhere) ➡️ Some people believe team sports are valuable because they teach players to **adhere** to rules. They believe it is important to learn to live by strict guidelines.

Context:	Structure:	Sound:

Dictionary:

2.

(forbidding) ➡ To some, though, contact sports are **forbidding,** so they choose something less dangerous, like golf.

3.

(maneuver) ➡ Some claim that learning to **maneuver** the basketball down the court will prepare the player to move through life with skill.

4.

(minority) ➡ The people who see sports as a sort of training field for life may be in the **minority**. The majority of us see sports as an opportunity for fun.

5.

(opponent) ➡ Of course, some people take sports too seriously. For example, some fans see their team as knights in shining armor and the **opponent** as the evil enemy.

6.

(participants) ➡ Some fans get so excited while watching sports that they act as if they are **participants**. They seem to forget that they are not actually taking part in the game.

7.

(penetrate) ➡ Trying to convince those people that a sport is just a game is like trying to **penetrate** a concrete wall with a butter knife. You won't be able to get through.

8.

(recommend) ➡ I **recommend** that you don't even try. I advise you to ignore them and go have fun.

9.

(tactics) ➡ Watching sports can be as much fun as playing. Comparing the **tactics** of different coaches is fun, too. It is interesting to see the different methods they use.

10.

(yield) ➡ Participating in team sports can **yield** many benefits. It gives you the opportunity to work with others to achieve a goal as well as a chance to learn to win and lose gracefully.

EXERCISE 2 *Context Clues* 👈

Directions. Scan the definitions in Column A. Then think about how the boldface words are used in the sentences in Column B. To complete the exercise, match each definition in Column A with the correct Vocabulary Word from Column B. Write the letter of your choice on the line provided. Finally, write the Vocabulary Word on the line before the definition.

COLUMN A	COLUMN B

COLUMN A

_____ **11.** word: _____
v. to stick fast; to follow closely

_____ **12.** word: _____
v. to force into or through; to see into; to move emotionally

_____ **13.** word: _____
adj. looking dangerous, uninviting, or stern; frightening

_____ **14.** word: _____
v. to suggest favorably; to advise

_____ **15.** word: _____
n. a planned military movement; a skillful or clever move; *v.* to conduct oneself or move something skillfully

_____ **16.** word: _____
n. [pl.] the science of employing military forces; method for reaching a goal

_____ **17.** word: _____
n. the lesser part or smaller number; a subgroup smaller than or different from the community as a whole

_____ **18.** word: _____
n. one who shares with others in some activity; one who takes part

_____ **19.** word: _____
n. a person who opposes; a competitor

_____ **20.** word: _____
v. to give up under pressure; to let or allow another; to produce; to return a profit; *n.* the amount produced

COLUMN B

(A) Jessie, Ellen, and Habib all play soccer. They are discussing the **tactics,** or strategies, they will use in tomorrow's game.

(B) The weather is **forbidding**. It's hurricane season, and the game may not take place.

(C) Ellen agrees that some players on the team don't **adhere** to the rules of good conduct. They don't obey the rules of common courtesy.

(D) Jessie points out that these players are the **minority**. Most members of the team are good sports.

(E) Sometimes, it is important for players to re-member why they became **participants** in the first place. There are many benefits to sharing an activity with other teammates.

(F) "The Whirlwinds are my favorite **opponents,**" he says. "Sometimes it is hard to think of them as foes. They seem more like friends."

(G) "They're nice kids, but don't forget they plan to beat us. They are really good at moving the ball. How can we stop their **maneuvers**?"

(H) "Do you have anything to **recommend,** Habib? You gave us good advice last time."

(I) "Remember that the best defense is a good of-fense. We need to **penetrate,** or push through, their defense to the goal."

(J) "Thanks, Habib. We won't **yield,** or surrender."

EXERCISE 3 _Like Meanings and Opposite Meanings_ ☞

Directions. For each item below, circle the letter of the choice that means the same, or about the same, as the boldface word.

21. a **forbidding** expression
  (A) pleasant
  (B) comical
  (C) serious
  (D) disagreeable

22. an interesting **maneuver**
  (A) move
  (B) request
  (C) game
  (D) organization

23. a **participant** in the race
  (A) one who drops out
  (B) an opponent
  (C) a teammate
  (D) one who takes part

24. the lost **yardage**
  (A) advantage
  (B) plans
  (C) players
  (D) yards

25. to **penetrate** the fog
  (A) cut through
  (B) predict
  (C) be trapped by
  (D) be blinded by

Directions. For each item below, circle the letter of the choice that means the opposite, or about the opposite, of the boldface word.

26. to **yield** to temptation
  (A) give in to
  (B) go over
  (C) inform about
  (D) resist

27. to **adhere** to the rules
  (A) confuse
  (B) understand
  (C) follow
  (D) disobey

28. the opinion of the **minority**
  (A) smallest number
  (B) more than half
  (C) people
  (D) government

29. a worthy **opponent**
  (A) foe
  (B) teammate
  (C) point
  (D) riddle

30. to **recommend** the action
  (A) begin
  (B) stop
  (C) disapprove of
  (D) fully support

MAKING NEW WORDS YOUR OWN

Lesson 16 | CONTEXT: Change in Individuals and Communities
Going to College

It's hard to believe now, but not so long ago colleges were closed to many people in the United States. Women and members of minority groups were not allowed to attend many universities. Little financial aid was available for those who couldn't afford college educations, but all that has changed.

In the following exercises, you will have the opportunity to expand your vocabulary by reading about opportunities for higher education. Below are ten Vocabulary Words that will be used in these exercises.

excel	fatigue	intellect	officially	pursue
expand	hardy	obstacle	opposition	scholarship

EXERCISE 1   *Wordbusting* 👈

Directions. Follow these instructions for this word and the nine words on the next page.

- Figure out the word's meaning by looking at its **context,** its **structure,** and its **sound.** Fill in at least one of the three **CSS** boxes. Alternate which boxes you complete.
- Then, look up the word in a dictionary, read all of its meanings, and write the meaning of the word as it is used in the sentence.
- Follow this same process for each of the Vocabulary Words on the next page. You will need to draw your own map for each word. Use a separate sheet of paper.

1.

(excel) → We all benefit when everyone is given the opportunity to **excel** in some chosen field. To go to college and become excellent at something gives each individual the chance to make a better life.

Context:	Structure:	Sound:

Dictionary:

2.

expand →

Recent government programs have worked to **expand** the number of people who attend college. Now, many high school graduates go on to two-year or four-year colleges.

3.

obstacle →

Most of us have the opportunity to attend college—almost any **obstacle** can be overcome. For example, a lack of money need not prevent someone from attending college.

4.

officially →

Almost every university helps its students find financial aid. This policy is usually stated **officially** in the college catalogue. In addition, government loans are available to many students.

5.

scholarship →

A student with good grades and high test scores can get a **scholarship**. Colleges also offer financial awards to talented athletes, musicians, and actors.

6.

opposition →

Once there was serious **opposition** to women and members of minority groups attending college, but now they are welcomed.

7.

pursue →

In fact, some schools actively **pursue** women and minorities. They seek them out and encourage them to attend.

8.

fatigue →

College students often complain of **fatigue;** they say that between their studies and their social lives, they are always worn out.

9.

hardy →

Only a **hardy** person can take a full load of courses and work at a parttime job.

10.

intellect →

Today, more and more employers value a worker's **intellect**. A good mind is the requirement for most jobs, and that usually means having a good education.

EXERCISE 2 · *Context Clues* ✍

Directions. Scan the definitions in Column A. Then think about how the boldface words are used in the sentences in Column B. To complete the exercise, match each definition in Column A with the correct Vocabulary Word from Column B. Write the letter of your choice on the line provided. Finally, write the Vocabulary Word on the line before the definition.

COLUMN A	COLUMN B
_____ **11.** word: _____ *adj.* by, from, or with an authority or official; formally	(A) "I'm so excited," says Georgia. "My sister just got a **scholarship** to go to Spelman College. It provides almost all the money she needs for her freshman year."
_____ **12.** word: _____ *n.* any person, group, or thing that is against; resistance	(B) "The college had hinted that she would probably be able to get the money, but we weren't told **officially** that she had it until yesterday."
_____ **13.** word: _____ *v.* to chase; to seek; to go on with	(C) "That's great. This will really **expand** her opportunities. It opens up a lot of possibilities," says Tish.
_____ **14.** word: _____ *adj.* strong; able to keep from tiring	(D) "My brother got a scholarship to college, too, but not for his **intellect**. He's smart enough, but the college wanted him for the gymnastics team," remarks Alvin.
_____ **15.** word: _____ *n.* a gift of money to help pay for a person's education; the knowledge of a learned person; the knowledge attained by scholars collectively	(E) "He's really strong and tough—very **hardy**. His best event is the parallel bars," Alvin continues.
_____ **16.** word: _____ *v.* to increase in size; to enlarge; to stretch out	(F) "Just thinking about all the work he has to do **fatigues** me. He has practice twice a day, plus he is taking five classes, and he works ten hours a week in the cafeteria."
_____ **17.** word: _____ *v.* to be superior at something; to be superior to another	(G) "I think I want to go on with my education after high school. Do you intend to **pursue** a college degree?" asks Georgia.
_____ **18.** word: _____ *n.* state of being tired, weary, or worn out; exhaustion; sturdy work clothing worn by soldiers; *v.* to make or become tired	(H) "Well, there is an **obstacle** in my way," says Tish. "My family doesn't have much money."
_____ **19.** word: _____ *n.* anything that gets in the way or hinders; a hindrance	(I) "Your family doesn't object to your going to college, do they? There isn't any real **opposition** to the idea, is there?"
_____ **20.** word: _____ *n.* the ability or power to think, reason, or understand; high intelligence	(J) "Oh, no. My family is very supportive. They realize that for me to **excel** in life, I need to become very good at something. I'll take courses at the community college and live at home."

EXERCISE 3 *Like Meanings and Opposite Meanings* ✍

Directions. For each item below, circle the letter of the choice that means the same, or about the same, as the boldface word.

21. an unusual **intellect**
(A) stupidity
(B) approach
(C) intelligence
(D) idea

22. a serious **obstacle**
(A) exercise
(B) method
(C) help
(D) block

23. to open **officially**
(A) with proper authority
(B) in an office building
(C) during business hours
(D) without doubt

24. with little **opposition**
(A) friendship
(B) resistance
(C) help
(D) understanding

25. an interest in **scholarship**
(A) work
(B) sports
(C) helping
(D) knowledge

Directions. For each item below, circle the letter of the choice that means the opposite, or about the opposite, of the boldface word.

26. to **expand** her opportunities
(A) borrow
(B) complete
(C) decrease
(D) increase

27. to feel **fatigue**
(A) lonely
(B) friendly
(C) tiredness
(D) energy

28. a **hardy** child
(A) weak
(B) strong
(C) intelligent
(D) silent

29. to **pursue** the enemy
(A) run after
(B) run toward
(C) run beside
(D) run away from

30. to **excel** in math
(A) make good grades
(B) do poorly
(C) do better than others
(D) work competitively

MAKING NEW WORDS YOUR OWN

| Lesson 17 | **CONTEXT:** Change in Individuals and Communities |

Teenagers and Change

The teenage years are a time of major change. In fact, it can sometimes seem as if almost everything changes. As a result, these years are difficult. It helps to remember that everyone goes through them.

In the following exercises, you will have the opportunity to expand your vocabulary by reading about some of the changes that teenagers face. Below are ten Vocabulary Words that will be used in these exercises.

adopt	blemish	immature	intolerable	rival
anguish	crisis	inhabit	maternal	self-conscious

EXERCISE 1 · *Wordbusting* ✍

Directions. Follow these instructions for this word and the nine words on the next page.
- Figure out the word's meaning by looking at its **context,** its **structure,** and its **sound.** Fill in at least one of the three **CSS** boxes. Alternate which boxes you complete.
- Then, look up the word in a dictionary, read all of its meanings, and write the meaning of the word as it is used in the sentence.
- Follow this same process for each of the Vocabulary Words on the next page. You will need to draw your own map for each word. Use a separate sheet of paper.

1.

(adopt) ⟶ Sometimes adults seem to **adopt** the attitude that the problems teenagers face are not important. You can bet they didn't have that attitude when they were thirteen!

Context:	Structure:	Sound:

Dictionary:

2.

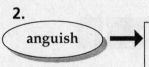

Teenagers sometimes have problems that can cause them great pain and **anguish**.

3.

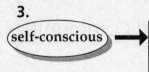

Changes in their bodies can make many teens feel **self-conscious**, embarrassed around others.

4.

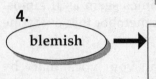

Teenagers are usually able to keep their problems in perspective. They know that a **blemish**, such as a pimple, is not the end of the world—although it can seem like it at the time.

5.

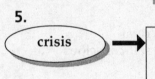

The teenage years can be a time of **crisis**, a turning point. Teenagers' attitudes and even their friendships may begin to change.

6.

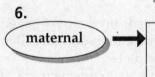

My aunt Lisa works with troubled teens, and she says it is important to respect teenagers. She is my **maternal** aunt, my aunt on my mother's side.

7.

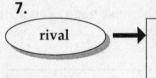

She says that most teens are dealing with **rival** desires. Their desire to have the freedom of adults conflicts with their desire to avoid adult responsibility.

8.

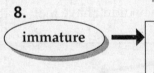

They realize that they are still **immature** in the sense that they aren't completely grown up, but they aren't children either.

9.

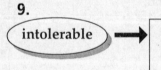

They find it **intolerable** to be treated as if they were children, but they also find it unbearable to be expected to behave like adults.

10.

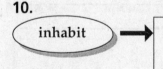

Most teens do not think only about themselves; many become concerned about the planet we **inhabit**.

EXERCISE 2 *Context Clues* ✍

Directions. Scan the definitions in Column A. Then think about how the boldface words are used in the sentences in Column B. To complete the exercise, match each definition in Column A with the correct Vocabulary Word from Column B. Write the letter of your choice on the line provided. Finally, write the Vocabulary Word on the line before the definition.

COLUMN A	COLUMN B

COLUMN A

_____ **11.** word: _____
adj. unbearable; too painful or cruel to be endured

_____ **12.** word: _____
adj. motherly; inherited from or related through one's mother

_____ **13.** word: _____
n. a person who tries to get the same thing as another; a competitor; *adj.* competing; *v.* to equal; to try to equal

_____ **14.** word: _____
n. the turning point; a decisive stage or event; a time of great danger or trouble

_____ **15.** word: _____
adj. awkward or embarrassed in the presence of others

_____ **16.** word: _____
v. to take up and use as one's own; to choose and follow; to vote to accept; to take into one's family

_____ **17.** word: _____
n. a mark or scar on the skin; a defect; *v.* to spoil; to make less perfect

_____ **18.** word: _____
n. great mental or physical suffering; *v.* to suffer; to cause to suffer

_____ **19.** word: _____
v. to dwell or live in

_____ **20.** word: _____
adj. not fully grown or developed

COLUMN B

(A) I felt **self-conscious** at the dance last Friday night. Now I know it was silly, but at the time I felt uncomfortable.

(B) I had a pimple on my nose. Mom told me it was just a **blemish** that no one would notice, but it felt as big as a grapefruit to me.

(C) My mom is something else. Sometimes I think she took a course in **maternal** love; she is really very motherly and loving.

(D) She tried very hard to talk me out of my **anguish** on Friday night, but I was determined to feel miserable.

(E) By the time I got out of the shower, I was having a major **crisis**—the time had come to make a decision. "I can't go out looking like this," I wailed, "but if I don't go, I'll miss all the fun."

(F) Either choice felt **intolerable**. Walking into the gym with the pimple on my face seemed unendurable, but so was staying home when all my friends were going.

(G) Finally, my sister Lisa lost her patience. "Don't be so **immature**. Stop acting like a child. Either go to the dance or stay home."

(H) Of course, I was furious. I didn't want to **inhabit** the same planet as Lisa, much less occupy the same house.

(I) I decided to **adopt** my mom's plan. She said that I should just pretend the pimple wasn't there. That's the plan I decided to accept.

(J) My feeling of embarrassment about my pimple was **rivaled** only by my excitement about the dance. Eventually, excitement won out. No one noticed the spot on my face, and I had a great time.

EXERCISE 3 *Like Meanings and Opposite Meanings* ✍

Directions. For each item below, circle the letter of the choice that means the same, or about the same, as the boldface word.

21. a former **rival**
- (A) friend
- (B) competitor
- (C) team
- (D) individual

22. a small **blemish**
- (A) mark
- (B) flower
- (C) scolding
- (D) regret

23. a major **crisis**
- (A) memory
- (B) belief
- (C) turning point
- (D) mood

24. to **inhabit** the cabin
- (A) sell
- (B) live in
- (C) build
- (D) buy

25. a **maternal** gesture
- (A) friendly
- (B) ugly
- (C) motherly
- (D) material

Directions. For each item below, circle the letter of the choice that means the opposite, or about the opposite, of the boldface word.

26. with great **anguish**
- (A) pain
- (B) joy
- (C) guilt
- (D) innocence

27. an **immature** attitude
- (A) adult
- (B) childish
- (C) silly
- (D) important

28. an **intolerable** situation
- (A) worried
- (B) confusing
- (C) bearable
- (D) unpleasant

29. to **adopt** the plan
- (A) create
- (B) abandon
- (C) understand
- (D) accept

30. a **self-conscious** glance
- (A) generous
- (B) selfish
- (C) embarrassed
- (D) confident

Name _____ Date _____ Class _____

MAKING NEW WORDS YOUR OWN

Lesson 18 | **CONTEXT:** Change in Individuals and Communities
When Grandfather Moved In

Advances in health care have resulted in people living much longer than they once did, so more and more young people have elderly family members to turn to for companionship and advice. Because some elderly people spend their later years with their children, later generations develop close relationships with grandparents and great-grandparents.

In the following exercises, you will have the opportunity to expand your vocabulary by reading about a boy's relationship with his grandfather. Below are ten Vocabulary Words that will be used in these exercises.

acute	hysterical	ridicule	timid	vague
hesitation	irritable	tendency	turmoil	wretched

EXERCISE 1 | *Wordbusting* 👆

Directions. Follow these instructions for this word and the nine words on the next page.
- Figure out the word's meaning by looking at its **context**, its **structure**, and its **sound**. Fill in at least one of the three **CSS** boxes. Alternate which boxes you complete.
- Then, look up the word in a dictionary, read all of its meanings, and write the meaning of the word as it is used in the sentence.
- Follow this same process for each of the Vocabulary Words on the next page. You will need to draw your own map for each word. Use a separate sheet of paper.

1.

(acute) ⟶ My grandfather lives with us. His thinking is **acute,** but some of his senses are not very sharp since he had a stroke.

Context:	Structure:	Sound:

Dictionary:

2.
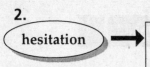 hesitation → He used to speak without **hesitation,** but now he sometimes has to pause as he tries to find the right words.

3.
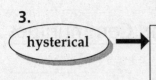 hysterical → He still has a great sense of humor. He tells jokes that make everyone laugh until they are practically **hysterical**.

4.
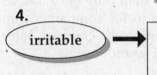 irritable → Despite the inconvenience of moving to a new place, he has been cheerful and patient with us, not **irritable**.

5.
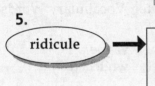 ridicule → One thing I like about my grandfather is that he never **ridicules** me for not knowing something. Instead of making fun of me, he patiently explains things to me.

6.
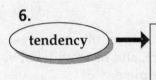 tendency → I have a **tendency** to be overly protective of my grandfather. Then again, he has always had a habit of watching out for me, too.

7.
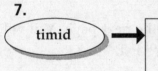 timid → I was a **timid** little kid, and I felt as though he truly understood my shyness.

8.
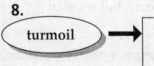 turmoil → Our house was always in **turmoil** because I have three sisters and four brothers. You can imagine the noise and confusion.

9.
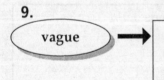 vague → Perhaps you have only a **vague** notion of what it is like to be a quiet child in a crowd of rowdy brothers and sisters, but my grandfather clearly understood.

10.
 wretched → I felt **wretched** when I was left out of things, but my grandfather always cheered me out of my misery. He still can cheer me up when I'm feeling down.

EXERCISE 2 *Context Clues* ✍

Directions. Scan the definitions in Column A. Then think about how the boldface words are used in the sentences in Column B. To complete the exercise, match each definition in Column A with the correct Vocabulary Word from Column B. Write the letter of your choice on the line provided. Finally, write the Vocabulary Word on the line before the definition.

COLUMN A	COLUMN B

COLUMN A

_____ **11.** word: _____
adj. shy or or easily frightened

_____ **12.** word: _____
n. uncertainty, indecision; a pause or delay; the act of searching for words

_____ **13.** word: _____
adj. very serious; mentally keen; very sensitive to physical stimulation; sharply pointed; severe but brief; in mathematics, of an angle that is less than 90°

_____ **14.** word: _____
adj. emotionally uncontrolled

_____ **15.** word: _____
adj. miserable; deeply unhappy; unfortunate; gloomy; of poor quality; deserving scorn

_____ **16.** word: _____
adj. easily annoyed; impatient

_____ **17.** word: _____
n. the act of making a person or thing seem foolish; *v.* to make fun of

_____ **18.** word: _____
n. a natural leaning to move or act in a particular way or direction

_____ **19.** word: _____
n. a great disturbance, uproar, commotion, or confusion

_____ **20.** word: _____
adj. not expressed clearly or exactly; unclear; not definite in shape or form

COLUMN B

(A) I sometimes feel **wretched** because I can tell that my grandfather is unhappy living away from his own home. I feel miserable when he is sad.

(B) However, his health problems are still **acute,** and he can't live alone as long as they are so serious.

(C) He has a **tendency** to become depressed when he can't do something he used to do. It's hard to accept because he used to always see the best in everything.

(D) I'm not always patient with him. I become **irritable** sometimes when he gets gloomy.

(E) He helps me with my schoolwork and never **ridicules** me for my mistakes. He would never say anything to mock me.

(F) When the baby becomes **hysterical,** Grandfather is the only one who can calm her.

(G) He almost seems to be **timid** about asking for assistance. Needing help is a little frightening for someone who has been independent for most of his life.

(H) All of our emotions have been in **turmoil** since Grandfather had a stroke. It was very disturbing to the whole family.

(I) The whole family seems to have a **vague** feeling of displacement since he came to live here. We're not sure why this is, but all our lives have changed.

(J) My parents showed no **hesitation** about having Grandfather move in with us. They were certain that it was the right thing to do.

EXERCISE 3　Like Meanings and Opposite Meanings ☜

Directions. For each item below, circle the letter of the choice that means the same, or about the same, as the boldface word.

21. an **acute** situation
- (A) serious
- (B) mild
- (C) childlike
- (D) adult

22. without any **hesitation**
- (A) problem
- (B) ideas
- (C) hint
- (D) uncertainty

23. an **irritable** child
- (A) pleasant
- (B) impatient
- (C) ignorant
- (D) frightened

24. a **tendency** to forget
- (A) sincere desire
- (B) natural leaning
- (C) situation
- (D) indication

25. in constant **turmoil**
- (A) memory
- (B) confusion
- (C) belief
- (D) action

Directions. For each item below, circle the letter of the choice that means the opposite, or about the opposite, of the boldface word.

26. a **hysterical** child
- (A) calm
- (B) upset
- (C) unpleasant
- (D) angry

27. to **ridicule** the plan
- (A) refuse to accept
- (B) laugh at
- (C) praise highly
- (D) quickly reject

28. a **timid** pet
- (A) unpleasant
- (B) homeless
- (C) shy
- (D) bold

29. a **vague** idea
- (A) interesting
- (B) unclear
- (C) definite
- (D) dull

30. a **wretched** experience
- (A) pleasant
- (B) miserable
- (C) twisted
- (D) straight

MAKING NEW WORDS YOUR OWN

Lesson 19 | CONTEXT: Change in Individuals and Communities
Learning About the Past

History is more than a collection of facts about the past. Studying history is like reading a continuing story of change over time. What do you think people in the future might learn from studying our era? To get an idea, think about the things you might learn from studying the past—for example, the Middle Ages. You might be surprised to discover that people in those times had many of the same concerns of people today.

In the following exercises, you will have the opportunity to expand your vocabulary by reading about a student's comments about her history class. Below are ten Vocabulary Words that will be used in these exercises.

barbarous	era	grandeur	pageant	serf
baron	fortress	monarchy	proclamation	tyrant

EXERCISE 1 · Wordbusting

Directions. Follow these instructions for this word and the nine words on the next page.
- Figure out the word's meaning by looking at its **context,** its **structure,** and its **sound.** Fill in at least one of the three **CSS** boxes. Alternate which boxes you complete.
- Then, look up the word in a dictionary, read all of its meanings, and write the meaning of the word as it is used in the sentence.
- Follow this same process for each of the Vocabulary Words on the next page. You will need to draw your own map for each word. Use a separate sheet of paper.

1.

barbarous → Our teacher, Mr. Pacino, tells us that the early Middle Ages used to be called the Dark Ages because **barbarous** warriors overran Europe. However, he says that this period was not really so uncivilized.

Context:	Structure:	Sound:

Dictionary:

2.

(era) →

I have to admit that this **era** fascinates me, but even though I love the time period, I don't want to study for the test Mr. Pacino is giving tomorrow.

3.

(monarchy) →

We're supposed to know something about the form of government in Europe at that time. In the Middle Ages, European nations were **monarchies** ruled by kings and queens.

4.

(tyrant) →

It is customary to think of kings and queens in the Middle Ages as **tyrants,** but those leaders were not always cruel and unfair.

5.

(baron) →

One type of person we learned about is the **baron**. A **baron** ranked lower than a king or queen but still had a lot of power.

6.

(serf) →

Serfs were low ranking and spent their lives working on the land.

7.

(fortress) →

We're supposed to be able to explain how a castle could be used as a **fortress**. Within the castle walls, people could protect themselves from outside enemies.

8.

(grandeur) →

Castles in the Middle Ages were cold, drafty, and dirty, yet they did have a sort of **grandeur**. From the pictures of them in our textbook, I can tell that they were quite majestic.

9.

(proclamation) →

Sometimes I daydream that I issue from my castle a **proclamation** that changes the world. Could any official announcement really do that, I wonder.

10.

(pageant) →

We are also supposed understand the purpose of the **pageants,** which sometimes consisted of weeks of feasts, plays, and contests.

EXERCISE 2   *Context Clues* ✍

Directions. Scan the definitions in Column A. Then think about how the boldface words are used in the sentences in Column B. To complete the exercise, match each definition in Column A with the correct Vocabulary Word from Column B. Write the letter of your choice on the line provided. Finally, write the Vocabulary Word on the line before the definition.

COLUMN A

_____ **11.** word: _____
n. a place that has been strengthened to resist attack; a fort

_____ **12.** word: _____
n. a period of time noted for certain characteristics or measured from some key event

_____ **13.** word: _____
adj. splendor; majesty; greatness

_____ **14.** word: _____
adj. uncivilized, savage, cruel; foreign; substandard

_____ **15.** word: _____
n. a government or a state headed by a king or a queen

_____ **16.** word: _____
n. a spectacular exhibition, show, or parade; a kind of detailed drama often staged outdoors

_____ **17.** word: _____
n. a person who is bound in servitude, forced to work a master's land

_____ **18.** word: _____
n. a person who uses his power in a cruel, overbearing manner

_____ **19.** word: _____
n. an official announcement

_____ **20.** word: _____
n. a nobleman; a man of great power

COLUMN B

(A) Mr. Pacino wants us to write and perform a play set in the Middle Ages. If we make the drama a **pageant,** Mr. Pacino will let us perform it outdoors.

(B) Our characters include a noble **baron** who is kind to the peasants working on his land.

(C) Our baron realizes that the **serfs** have no choice but to work his land, and he chooses to treat these workers kindly.

(D) We also have a harsh, brutal baron who does **barbarous** deeds.

(E) This savage baron is a true example of a **tyrant**. He is demanding and expects absolute obedience to any order he gives.

(F) He plots to attack the **fortress** of the good baron, but he can't break through the walls and defenses.

(G) Our play centers on the English **monarchy** during the period when King Richard the Lionhearted was on a crusade and his brother Prince John tried to steal the throne.

(H) Many people think of this time period as the **era** of Robin Hood, but this hero may never have existed in reality.

(I) Right now I am working on writing a key scene in which the evil Prince John has just issued a **proclamation**. The Prince's statement angers the good baron, and he gathers his armies together to rebel.

(J) We are still planning the set. It's a challenge to use simple materials to suggest the **grandeur,** or magnificence, of the period.

EXERCISE 3   *Like Meanings and Opposite Meanings* ✍

Directions. For each item below, circle the letter of the choice that means the same, or about the same, as the boldface word.

21. acting like a **tyrant**
- (A) confused person
- (B) madman
- (C) cruel ruler
- (D) king

22. the end of an **era**
- (A) journey
- (B) time period
- (C) drama
- (D) long story

23. to build a **fortress**
- (A) open field
- (B) house
- (C) fort
- (D) barn

24. a lively **pageant**
- (A) show
- (B) queen
- (C) history
- (D) fort

25. an unusual **proclamation**
- (A) throne
- (B) piece of advice
- (C) announcement
- (D) parade

Directions. For each item below, circle the letter of the choice that means the opposite, or about the opposite, of the boldface word.

26. a **barbarous** people
- (A) grand
- (B) silly
- (C) savage
- (D) civilized

27. the wise **baron**
- (A) nobleman
- (B) peasant
- (C) king
- (D) palace

28. government by **monarchy**
- (A) king or queen
- (B) nobles
- (C) the common people
- (D) presidents or prime ministers

29. the **grandeur** of the structure
- (A) splendor
- (B) outside
- (C) simpleness
- (D) inside

30. working like a **serf**
- (A) laborer
- (B) farmer
- (C) peasant
- (D) nobleman

Name _____ Date _____ Class _____

MAKING NEW WORDS YOUR OWN

Lesson 20 | **CONTEXT: Change in Individuals and Communities**
The Same Old Story

Have you ever heard the saying, "The more things change, the more they stay the same"? On the surface this expression may not make much sense. Yet anyone who has studied history— or who has a good memory—knows that the saying contains a grain of truth. People and communities are changing constantly, but they still have much in common with the past.

In the following exercises, you will have the opportunity to expand your vocabulary by reading about Cara and her grandmother. These ten Vocabulary Words will be used.

absolute	cultural	lure	status	valiant
banish	illusion	perilous	toil	vengeance

EXERCISE 1 *Wordbusting*

Directions. Follow these instructions for this word and the nine words on the next page.
- Figure out the word's meaning by looking at its **context,** its **structure,** and its **sound.** Fill in at least one of the three **CSS** boxes. Alternate which boxes you complete.
- Then, look up the word in a dictionary, read all of its meanings, and write the meaning of the word as it is used in the sentence.
- Follow this same process for each of the Vocabulary Words on the next page. You will need to draw your own map for each word. Use a separate sheet of paper.

1.

(absolute) → "It is true, Cara, that people have not changed as much as you think," says Mrs. Fuentes, with **absolute,** or total, conviction.

Context:	Structure:	Sound:

Dictionary:

2.
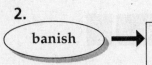

"Just **banish** that notion from your head, and don't let it come back," she tells her granddaughter.

3.

"By remembering the past, we can keep a sense of our **cultural** heritage. It is important for each new generation to have some tie to the customs of its particular people."

4.
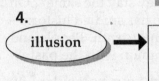

"To think that the past doesn't matter is an **illusion,** a false and sometimes dangerous belief."

5.
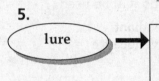

"For some reason, recent generations have let the idea that they are special tempt, or **lure,** them away from their pasts."

6.
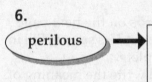

"It is a **perilous** thing, my dear, to forget your heritage. I want you to avoid this danger. Do you understand?" her grandmother asks.

7.
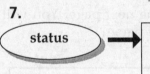

Cara respects her grandmother's position in the family as well as her grandmother's **status** in the community.

8.

Mrs. Fuentes has worked hard all her life, but years of **toil** have not weakened her spirit.

9.
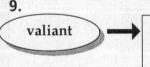

Cara believes that her grandmother is as **valiant** as any hero in a storybook—as brave and, in her own way, as strong.

10.

So when her grandmother speaks, Cara listens. From her grandmother she has learned many things about life and death, bravery and fear, **vengeance** and forgiveness.

EXERCISE 2 Context Clues

Directions. Scan the definitions in Column A. Then think about how the boldface words are used in the sentences in Column B. To complete the exercise, match each definition in Column A with the correct Vocabulary Word from Column B. Write the letter of your choice on the line provided. Finally, write the Vocabulary Word on the line before the definition.

COLUMN A	COLUMN B
_____ **11.** word: _____ *adj.* definite; unrestricted; total; pure; something that is pure or definite; *n.* something that cannot be compromised or questioned	(A) "People today have an interesting **illusion**," says Mrs. Fuentes. "They mistakenly think that the stories they make are new ones, with no connections to the stories of the past."
_____ **12.** word: _____ *adj.* dangerous, risky, or unsafe	(B) Just compare the old stories I've told you with those you see on TV. **Cultural** differences aren't as great as people think.
_____ **13.** word: _____ *v.* to exile; to force to leave; to get rid of	(C) "I once told you a story of a man who was **banished** from the village. Was that not the same as the TV show about the boy who was driven out of school?"
_____ **14.** word: _____ *v.* to attract or tempt; *n.* something that attracts or tempts; bait	(D) "Think of the story I told you of the mother who goes on a **perilous** journey through much danger to save her child. Was that not the same as the old movie we watched?"
_____ **15.** word: _____ *adj.* related to the appreciation of music, art, literature, etc., or to the customs and improvements of a certain people in a given period	(E) "You read a story of a man worrying about his **status** in the office. It's like the tale of the girl worrying about her rank in the village."
_____ **16.** word: _____ *n.* condition; position; rank	(F) "Remember that show about the girl who allowed her friend to **lure** her into wrongdoing? Doesn't she have something in common with the storybook boy who was tempted by the robbers?"
_____ **17.** word: _____ *n.* a false idea or belief; a misleading appearance or image	(G) "We told stories of bravery in the past, but today we have stories of **valiant** people, too."
_____ **18.** word: _____ *v.* to work hard and continuously; to advance or move with difficulty; *n.* hard, exhausting work or effort	(H) "We have stories of people who seek **vengeance,** only to learn that revenge may destroy them as well as their enemies."
_____ **19.** word: _____ *adj.* courageous, brave	(I) Cara listens to her grandmother with **absolute** devotion and total attention.
_____ **20.** word: _____ *n.* revenge; the desire for revenge	(J) "Since days of old," says Mrs. Fuentes, "people everywhere want to relax and be entertained after a day of **toil**."

EXERCISE 3 — *Like Meanings and Opposite Meanings*

Directions. For each item below, circle the letter of the choice that means the same, or about the same, as the boldface word.

21. with **absolute** silence
(A) ordinary
(B) unusual
(C) some
(D) total

22. a **cultural** event
(A) evening
(B) expensive
(C) recent
(D) artistic

23. tricked by an **illusion**
(A) warning
(B) attempt at revenge
(C) true story
(D) false belief

24. lacking in **status**
(A) height
(B) rank
(C) judgment
(D) experience

25. spoken with **vengeance**
(A) a sigh of relief
(B) complete understanding
(C) great authority
(D) the desire for revenge

Directions. For each item below, circle the letter of the choice that means the opposite, or about the opposite, of the boldface word.

26. a **valiant** prince
(A) cowardly
(B) brave
(C) kind
(D) hateful

27. to **toil** all day long
(A) work
(B) rest
(C) govern
(D) argue

28. a **perilous** road
(A) short
(B) long
(C) dangerous
(D) safe

29. an attempt to **lure**
(A) draw in
(B) loan
(C) drive off
(D) borrow

30. to **banish** the villain
(A) be amazed at
(B) bore
(C) send away
(D) invite in

Name _____ Date _____ Class _____

Lesson 21 CONTEXT: Change in Science and Technology
Modern Medicine and You

Many advances in science and technology have helped to improve the quality of health care for people and for animals. Because of the work of medical researchers, our lives have changed dramatically.

In the following exercises, you will have the opportunity to expand your vocabulary by reading about how some medical advances have affected human beings as well as their pets. Below are ten Vocabulary Words that will be used in these exercises.

antiseptic	endurance	immune	optical	parasite
edible	glucose	nutrition	organism	pigment

EXERCISE 1 *Wordbusting* ✍

Directions. Follow these instructions for this word and the nine words on the next page.
- Figure out the word's meaning by looking at its **context,** its **structure,** and its **sound.** Fill in at least one of the three **CSS** boxes. Alternate which boxes you complete.
- Then, look up the word in a dictionary, read all of its meanings, and write the meaning of the word as it is used in the sentence.
- Follow this same process for each of the Vocabulary Words on the next page. You will need to draw your own map for each word. Use a separate sheet of paper.

1.

(antiseptic) → "Imagine what it would have been like to live before there were **antiseptics**. Think of all the infections we can prevent now," remarks Eduardo.

Context:	Structure:	Sound:

Dictionary:

2.

(edible) ➤ "Yes, and imagine having to figure out by trial and error which foods were **edible**. You might accidentally eat something poisonous for dinner," says John.

3.

(endurance) ➤ "Now when people feel weak and tired, we often say that they need to build up their **endurance**. Doctors tell us that, to build up our strength, we should exercise, not rest," adds Tawanda.

4.

(glucose) ➤ "My sister has to check her **glucose** levels all the time because she has diabetes. That's a disease that has to do with blood sugar. Until fairly recently, doctors didn't know how to treat diabetes," Amy says.

5.

(immune) ➤ "Now we have shots that make us **immune** to viruses that once killed people. Today, lots of germs can no longer make us sick," Eduardo adds.

6.

(nutrition) ➤ "Yes, and we understand now how important **nutrition** is. We know that to be healthy we need to eat lots of grains, fruits, and vegetables," says Tawanda.

7.

(optical) ➤ "I'm thankful for the advances they have made in the **optical** field. I don't know what I'd do without my glasses," says John.

8.

(organism) ➤ "In some countries, health care still has a long way to go. For example, bacteria and other nasty little **organisms** in the water supply make people very sick," remarks Melissa.

9.

(parasite) ➤ "Some little children have worms and other **parasites** that live in them and rob them of their health," she adds.

10.

(pigment) ➤ John says, "It's funny how we don't always act on what we know. Tanning makes the **pigment** in our skin get darker and can cause cancer, yet a lot of us still lie out in the sun for hours."

EXERCISE 2 *Context Clues* ✍

Directions. Scan the definitions in Column A. Then think about how the boldface words are used in the sentences in Column B. To complete the exercise, match each definition in Column A with the correct Vocabulary Word from Column B. Write the letter of your choice on the line provided. Finally, write the Vocabulary Word on the line before the definition.

COLUMN A	COLUMN B

_____ **11.** word: _____
adj. related to the sense of sight; visual

_____ **12.** word: _____
adj. preventing infection; sterile; *n.* a substance that slows or stops germs

_____ **13.** word: _____
n. an animal or plant with organs that function together to maintain life; a living thing; anything that resembles a living thing in structure or function

_____ **14.** word: _____
adj. fit to eat

_____ **15.** word: _____
n. coloring matter in cells of plants and animals; coloring used in paints

_____ **16.** word: _____
n. strength to last or withstand hard wear; ability to put up with something

_____ **17.** word: _____
n. a plant or animal that gets food or protection from another living being without benefiting that other being

_____ **18.** word: _____
n. food or nourishment; the processes by which food is used for growth or energy

_____ **19.** word: _____
adj. protected from disease; free from

_____ **20.** word: _____
n. a type of sugar that occurs in fruits, honey, and so on

(A) I'm always concerned about the health of my pets. I try to make sure they have the right food to eat because **nutrition** is very important.

(B) My dogs probably wouldn't make very good choices about their diets. They chew almost anything that is **edible** and some things, such as house slippers and book covers, that are not.

(C) The veterinarian gives them shots to make sure that they are **immune** to certain diseases. For example, my dogs have been protected against parvo and distemper.

(D) She also checks them for **parasites** such as fleas, which live on the dogs without offering them any benefit in return.

(E) When my dog Ike was hurt, my vet prescribed an **antiseptic** cream. I put it on his wounds to keep them uninfected.

(F) My dogs are young, so they have a lot of energy and **endurance;** for example, they can run around much longer than I can.

(G) I think it is interesting that the **pigment** in a dog's skin can be pink with black and brown spots while the color of his fur is solid black.

(H) There is now some kind of medical treatment for almost any condition a dog can have. For example, we can give **glucose,** or sugar, solutions to a dog that is too ill to eat.

(I) Veterinarians have developed surgery for dogs with **optical** problems such as cataracts, but I have never seen a dog wearing glasses!

(J) I'm always surprised to learn that there are people who are cruel to dogs. These people don't seem to realize that dogs are living **organisms** just like human beings and that they feel pain and loneliness just as much as we do.

EXERCISE 3 *Like Meanings and Opposite Meanings*

Directions. For each item below, circle the letter of the choice that means the same, or about the same, as the boldface word.

21. a high level of **glucose**
(A) health
(B) sugar
(C) teeth
(D) experiment

22. good **nutrition**
(A) diet
(B) machine
(C) nurse
(D) attitude

23. an **optical** illusion
(A) hopeful
(B) disappointing
(C) visual
(D) make-believe

24. a small **organism**
(A) snail
(B) decision
(C) life form
(D) science project

25. brown **pigment**
(A) earth
(B) food
(C) animal
(D) color

Directions. For each item below, circle the letter of the choice that means the opposite, or about the opposite, of the boldface word.

26. an **antiseptic** environment
(A) hospital
(B) sterile
(C) dirty
(D) universal

27. an **edible** mushroom
(A) delicious
(B) special
(C) poisonous
(D) fit to eat

28. to have some **endurance**
(A) good luck
(B) bad luck
(C) weakness
(D) strength

29. to be **immune**
(A) free from
(B) unprotected
(C) confused
(D) lost

30. a new **parasite**
(A) being that lives off another
(B) office building
(C) life form
(D) being that lives freely

MAKING NEW WORDS YOUR OWN

Lesson 22 | CONTEXT: Change in Science and Technology

Eyeing Animals: Approaches to Studying the Animal World

Scientists have studied animal life for centuries, but recent decades have seen a major change in how they approach that study. While some scientists study animals in laboratories or in wildlife parks, many others go to live with the animals in their natural environment.

In the following exercises, you will have the opportunity to expand your vocabulary by reading about animal life and those who study it. These ten Vocabulary Words will be used.

camouflage	mammal	nocturnal	seasonal	undergrowth
habitat	naturalist	preservation	temperate	zoology

EXERCISE 1 | Wordbusting

Directions. Follow these instructions for this word and the nine words on the next page.
- Figure out the word's meaning by looking at its **context,** its **structure,** and its **sound.** Fill in at least one of the three **CSS** boxes. Alternate which boxes you complete.
- Then, look up the word in a dictionary, read all of its meanings, and write the meaning of the word as it is used in the sentence.
- Follow this same process for each of the Vocabulary Words on the next page. You will need to draw your own map for each word. Use a separate sheet of paper.

1.

(**camouflage**) → Some animals' coats change colors in the winter. For example, the fur of some weasels becomes a white **camouflage** that allows them to blend in with the snow.

Context:

Structure:

Sound:

Dictionary:

2.

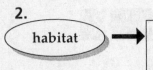 habitat → Animals have a special relationship with their **habitats**. An animal that can live successfully in the desert might not be able to survive in the jungle.

3.

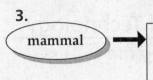 mammal → The duckbilled platypus can be considered a **mammal** because it is warmblooded and has vertebrae. Yet the platypus lays eggs just as birds and reptiles do.

4.

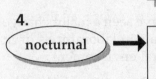 nocturnal → Hyenas are **nocturnal** animals. Anyone who wants to study them must be willing to work at night.

5.

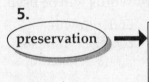 preservation → Today, many people are concerned about the **preservation** of plant and animal life. If we don't protect certain plants and animals from the dangers of the modern world, they could die out.

6.

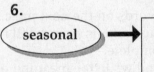 seasonal → Many birds have **seasonal** nesting places. They fly south to nest in winter and north to live in summer.

7.

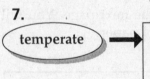 temperate → If the bird lives in a **temperate** climate, it may not need to migrate to avoid extreme heat or cold.

8.

 undergrowth → The **undergrowth** in a forest provides shelter to many small animals. These animals nest in the bushes and plants on the forest floor.

9.

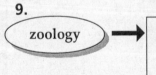 zoology → Biology, the study of life forms, has two major branches—botany, the study of plants, and **zoology,** the study of animals.

10.

 naturalist → Some **naturalists** are interested in plants; others are interested in animals. Some study both.

EXERCISE 2   Context Clues ✍

Directions. Scan the definitions in Column A. Then think about how the boldface words are used in the sentences in Column B. To complete the exercise, match each definition in Column A with the correct Vocabulary Word from Column B. Write the letter of your choice on the line provided. Finally, write the Vocabulary Word on the line before the definition.

COLUMN A	COLUMN B
_____ 11. word: _____ *n.* a disguise that lets beings or things blend in with their surroundings; *v.* to disguise or hide beings or things	(A) My mother wanted me to be a musician, so for a while I tried to **camouflage** my interest in science. Finally, I couldn't hide it from her any longer.
_____ 12. word: _____ *adj.* related to a season or seasons; dependent on a season	(B) As it turned out, my mom was happy to have a **naturalist** in the family. She bought me several books on plants and animals.
_____ 13. word: _____ *n.* a place where an animal or plant naturally lives; the place where a person or thing is ordinarily found	(C) When I began to neglect my other studies, my mom did advise me to be more **temperate** in my approach. "Don't overdo it!" she said.
_____ 14. word: _____ *n.* a warmblooded animal with vertebrae and offspring that nurse from the mammary glands of the mother	(D) She also advised me to get more sleep at night. Until summer, I have given up my **nocturnal** visits to the woods to observe owls.
_____ 15. word: _____ *adj.* not too hot or too cold; mild; not overdoing anything; self-controlled; having a balanced appetite	(E) Furthermore, she said I had better learn to mend my own clothes. There are a lot of brambles and thorns in the **undergrowth** of the woods, and I kept tearing my clothes on them.
_____ 16. word: _____ *n.* a person who studies nature	(F) I guess my work as a naturalist will have to be **seasonal**. I can work only during the summer and winter vacations.
_____ 17. word: _____ *n.* the branch of biology that deals with the study of animals	(G) I enjoy studying animals in their natural **habitat**. Animals behave differently in their own surroundings.
_____ 18. word: _____ *adj.* active at night; happening at night	(H) I am most interested in studying birds, but I am also interested in **mammals**—especially bears and wolves—as well as reptiles and fish.
_____ 19. word: _____ *n.* low-growing trees and bushes of a forest; underbrush	(I) When I go to college, I plan to continue my study of animals by taking classes in **zoology**.
_____ 20. word: _____ *n.* protection from change or damage	(J) I will also take some courses that deal with the **preservation** of the environment. I want to learn how forests and other natural areas can be guarded and saved.

EXERCISE 3 — *Like Meanings and Opposite Meanings* 👉

Directions. For each item below, circle the letter of the choice that means the same, or about the same, as the boldface word.

21. the monkey's **habitat**
    (A) surroundings
    (B) manners
    (C) clothing
    (D) experience

22. a wooly **mammal**
    (A) warmblooded animal
    (B) coldblooded animal
    (C) stuffed animal
    (D) intelligent animal

23. an amateur **naturalist**
    (A) a person who does not eat meat
    (B) a person who has musical ability
    (C) a person who studies plants and animals
    (D) a person who sells timber

24. hiding in the **undergrowth**
    (A) tall trees
    (B) low-growing plants
    (C) dense jungle
    (D) animal's natural surroundings

25. an interest in **zoology**
    (A) the study of rock formations
    (B) the study of zoos
    (C) the study of plants
    (D) the study of animals

Directions. For each item below, circle the letter of the choice that means the opposite, or about the opposite, of the boldface word.

26. to **camouflage** himself
    (A) hide
    (B) reveal
    (C) understand
    (D) misunderstand

27. a **nocturnal** event
    (A) casual
    (B) elegant
    (C) nighttime
    (D) daytime

28. the **preservation** of the plains
    (A) climate
    (B) mission
    (C) destruction
    (D) protection

29. a **seasonal** business
    (A) busy all year round
    (B) related to a season
    (C) very spicy
    (D) bland and boring

30. a **temperate** climate
    (A) mild
    (B) very hot or very cold
    (C) very hungry or very full
    (D) cheerful

MAKING NEW WORDS YOUR OWN

Lesson 23 | **CONTEXT: Change in Science and Technology**
Changing Technology, Changing Careers

Not so long ago, career options were much more limited than they are today. No one needed computer programmers before the invention of computers. No one needed MRI technicians before the invention of magnetic resonance imaging machines. There were no jet pilots before jets. Who knows what careers the next hundred years will bring?

In the following exercises, you will have the opportunity to expand your vocabulary by reading about careers. These ten Vocabulary Words will be used.

competent	efficiency	fundamental	percentage	relinquish
compute	exceed	futile	prestige	substantial

EXERCISE 1 *Wordbusting* ✍

Directions. Follow these instructions for this word and the nine words on the next page.
- Figure out the word's meaning by looking at its **context,** its **structure,** and its **sound.** Fill in at least one of the three **CSS** boxes. Alternate which boxes you complete.
- Then, look up the word in a dictionary, read all of its meanings, and write the meaning of the word as it is used in the sentence.
- Follow this same process for each of the Vocabulary Words on the next page. You will need to draw your own map for each word. Use a separate sheet of paper.

1.
(competent) ➙ "I'm **competent** at junior-high-level math, but I may not be good enough at college-level math to major in it," says Alicia.

Context:	Structure:	Sound:

Dictionary:

2.
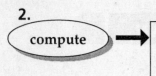
"Well, I can **compute** what twelve times twelve is, but I can't go much further than basic arithmetic. However, if I'm going to be a science major, I need to study more math," says Allan.

3.
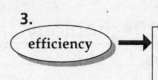
"If I don't become better organized, I'll never even finish middle school. **Efficiency** is not one of my talents," remarks Ricardo.

4.
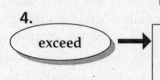
"What if I pick a career without realizing that many other people my age are choosing it, too? If there are a thousand workers but only a hundred jobs, the supply will **exceed** the demand!" Elizabeth says.

5.
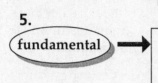
"These are some basic, or **fundamental,** problems with planning for the future," Ms. O'Rourke remarks.

6.
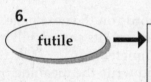
"My dad thinks it's **futile** to plan for a future career while we're in middle school. He thinks it's useless because the world will change so much before we even get to college," Ramone continues.

7.
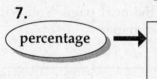
"He also says that a large **percentage** of us—almost all of us, in fact—will change careers several times."

8.
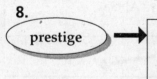
"My mom wants me to be a doctor because she thinks of it as a career with **prestige,** but I don't really care about impressing other people. I'd rather work to save wildlife," says Elizabeth.

9.
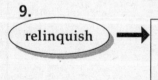
"Mom may have to **relinquish** her wish. She definitely wants me to be happy and, if that means giving up her dream, she will."

10.

"If you could save even one species from dying out, you would have made a **substantial** gift to the world. I'd like to do something just as important," she adds.

EXERCISE 2 *Context Clues* ✍

Directions. Scan the definitions in Column A. Then think about how the boldface words are used in the sentences in Column B. To complete the exercise, match each definition in Column A with the correct Vocabulary Word from Column B. Write the letter of your choice on the line provided. Finally, write the Vocabulary Word on the line before the definition.

COLUMN A	COLUMN B
_____ **11.** word: _____ *v.* to calculate; to reckon; to determine mathematically	(A) When thinking about a college and a career, consider areas in which you are **competent**. If you are skilled at handling technical equipment, you may want to think about becoming an engineer.
_____ **12.** word: _____ *v.* to be more or greater than; to go over the expected or allowed limits	(B) You might enjoy being a math teacher or an accountant if you like to work with numbers—that is, if you like to **compute**.
_____ **13.** word: _____ *v.* to give up an idea or a right	(C) One **fundamental** rule for choosing a career is to do something you enjoy. Following this key rule is usually necessary for success.
_____ **14.** word: _____ *n.* the ability to do something without wasting time or energy; effectiveness	(D) There are some careers you may have never heard of. For example, there are **efficiency** experts, people who show companies and workers how to work more productively.
_____ **15.** word: _____ *adj.* forming a basis; basic, necessary; primary, chief, most important; *n.* essential part; that which serves as a basis	(E) Unfortunately, some worthwhile careers don't get the respect, or **prestige,** they deserve.
_____ **16.** word: _____ *adj.* vain; hopeless; useless	(F) Some careers have more **substantial** financial rewards than others, but a big salary may not be as important as personal satisfaction.
_____ **17.** word: _____ *n.* a part or portion; a given part or amount of every hundred	(G) Most people prefer jobs that make them feel useful. In other words, people don't like to do things they consider **futile**.
_____ **18.** word: _____ *adj.* strong; solid; large; ample; of considerable size, weight, or value; important; actual	(H) Whatever you do, don't **relinquish** your true desires. Don't give up on the career that would make you the happiest.
_____ **19.** word: _____ *n.* a reputation based on ability, achievement, or associations; the power to impress; respect	(I) Most colleges want students who were willing to **exceed** the basic requirements in high school. Colleges are impressed with students who do more than they have to.
_____ **20.** word: _____ *adj.* capable; good enough	(J) Don't worry too much if you don't yet know what you want to do with your life. A high **percentage**—maybe more than 75 percent—of people don't decide until after high school graduation.

EXERCISE 3 *Like Meanings and Opposite Meanings*

Directions. For each item below, circle the letter of the choice that means the same, or about the same, as the boldface word.

21. to **compute** the cost
(A) ignore
(B) return to
(C) add up
(D) raise

22. to **relinquish** the belief
(A) stand by
(B) surrender
(C) discover
(D) restate

23. to **exceed** the limit
(A) deny
(B) go over
(C) almost meet
(D) completely avoid

24. **percentage** of the cost
(A) estimate
(B) limit
(C) all
(D) part

25. a **substantial** amount
(A) invisible
(B) visible
(C) small
(D) large

Directions. For each item below, circle the letter of the choice that means the opposite, or about the opposite, of the boldface word.

26. a person with **prestige**
(A) a bad reputation
(B) knowledge of a subject
(C) a large amount of money
(D) not enough energy

27. a **competent** lawyer
(A) capable
(B) careless
(C) special
(D) trial

28. work with **efficiency**
(A) no waste
(B) great waste
(C) a friendly way
(D) an enemy

29. a **futile** attempt
(A) dishonest
(B) honest
(C) useless
(D) successful

30. a **fundamental** principle
(A) basic
(B) unimportant
(C) interesting
(D) dull

MAKING NEW WORDS YOUR OWN

| Lesson 24 | **CONTEXT: Change in Science and Technology** |

More About Careers

Science and technology have changed the world of work in more ways than one. The film industry is a good example. The special effects in movies such as *Jurassic Park* and the *Star Wars* movies would be impossible without the advances in science and technology. These advances not only make new careers possible, they also add excitement to traditional careers, like teaching.

In the following exercises, you will have the opportunity to expand your vocabulary by reading about the career ideas of two teenagers. These ten Vocabulary Words will be used.

cancel	economical	logical	metropolitan	stationery
compensate	financial	memorandum	recognition	utility

| EXERCISE 1 | *Wordbusting* 👉 |

Directions. Follow these instructions for this word and the nine words on the next page.
- Figure out the word's meaning by looking at its **context,** its **structure,** and its **sound.** Fill in at least one of the three **CSS** boxes. Alternate which boxes you complete.
- Then, look up the word in a dictionary, read all of its meanings, and write the meaning of the word as it is used in the sentence.
- Follow this same process for each of the Vocabulary Words on the next page. You will need to draw your own map for each word. Use a separate sheet of paper.

1.

(cancel) ➡️ There are so many jobs in the fields of science and technology that I think I'll **cancel** my plans to become an accountant and work toward being an engineer for NASA.

Context:	Structure:	Sound:

Dictionary:

2.
compensate ➔ Of course, how much the job will **compensate** me is important. I want a career doing something that I enjoy and that also helps others, but it has to pay enough to live on.

3.
economical ➔ I'll have to be **economical**. Mom always says that you have to know how to save money in order to make money.

4.
financial ➔ There are all kinds of **financial** decisions in choosing a career. For example, some of the benefits companies offer, such as health care, retirement plans, and even the number of vacation days, are important.

5.
logical ➔ Becoming a glaciologist sounds interesting to me. A **logical** first step would be to research this career at the library before actually talking to people who study glaciers.

6.
memorandum ➔ I should write a **memorandum** about each career as I research it. It helps to keep notes to look over in the future.

7.
metropolitan ➔ Being in the city is more exciting to me than being in a smaller town. I think I will definitely begin my career job search in a **metropolitan** area.

8.
recognition ➔ It is important to me to have a career that earns me **recognition** for hard work. I want someone to appreciate what I do.

9.
stationery ➔ Next year, I am going to work part time in my uncle's **stationery** store. Selling writing paper and greeting cards will give me a little business experience.

10.
utility ➔ Besides, papers and cards have a certain **utility,** or usefulness. I'm glad to be able to sell people products they need.

EXERCISE 2 *Context Clues* ✍

Directions. Scan the definitions in Column A. Then think about how the boldface words are used in the sentences in Column B. To complete the exercise, match each definition in Column A with the correct Vocabulary Word from Column B. Write the letter of your choice on the line provided. Finally, write the Vocabulary Word on the line before the definition.

COLUMN A

_____ **11.** word: _____
adj. avoiding waste; thrifty

_____ **12.** word: _____
n. usefulness; something of use to the public, especially water, gas, or electricity

_____ **13.** word: _____
n. writing materials; papers and envelopes for correspondence

_____ **14.** word: _____
n. awareness of someone or something known before; gratitude; approval

_____ **15.** word: _____
adj. concerning the area or the population of a city and surrounding communities

_____ **16.** word: _____
v. to cross out; to do away with; to make ineffective; to neutralize or offset

_____ **17.** word: _____
v. to pay; to make up for

_____ **18.** word: _____
n. an informal written communication; a reminder in the form of a short note; a record of events for future use

_____ **19.** word: _____
adj. according to accurate reasoning

_____ **20.** word: _____
adj. having to do with money matters

COLUMN B

(A) I want to be a teacher. I don't care whether I teach at a large, **metropolitan** high school in the city or at a small school in the country.

(B) I know I won't get much **recognition**. Many people take the hard work of teachers for granted.

(C) I'll have to be very **economical** because I won't earn much money.

(D) Teachers do not usually get large **financial** rewards. Most of them say seeing students learn is what attracted them to the job, not the promise of high pay.

(E) Some teachers say that having extra time off in the summer **compensates** for the fact that they receive small salaries.

(F) Of course, many teachers **cancel** their summer vacation plans in order to teach summer classes or to attend classes themselves.

(G) It makes sense for teachers to keep up with advances in their areas. Not only is it **logical,** it's necessary.

(H) I really care about the **utility** of my career. I want to do something that is helpful and important to others.

(I) Teaching kids seems more important to me than sitting in an office writing a **memorandum** reporting the sales figures for the Topeka office.

(J) My business **stationery** will never say "chairman" under the letterhead.

EXERCISE 3 — *Like Meanings and Opposite Meanings*

Directions. For each item below, circle the letter of the choice that means the same, or about the same, as the boldface word.

21. to **compensate** him for his time
    (A) pay
    (B) fight
    (C) thank
    (D) promote

22. having **financial** difficulties
    (A) mathematical
    (B) serious
    (C) family
    (D) money

23. a short **memorandum**
    (A) event
    (B) envelope
    (C) memory
    (D) note

24. a **metropolitan** area
    (A) criminal
    (B) city
    (C) political
    (D) rural

25. a box of **stationery**
    (A) office supplies
    (B) pencils
    (C) writing paper
    (D) perfume

Directions. For each item below, circle the letter of the choice that means the opposite, or about the opposite, of the boldface word.

26. to have **utility**
    (A) usefulness
    (B) no purpose
    (C) silverware
    (D) water

27. the **recognition** of her work
    (A) praise
    (B) ignoring
    (C) reality
    (D) imagination

28. a **logical** statement
    (A) interesting
    (B) confused
    (C) boring
    (D) sensible

29. an **economical** meal
    (A) delicious
    (B) cheap
    (C) expensive
    (D) bad

30. to **cancel** the agreement
    (A) to lose
    (B) to read aloud
    (C) to create
    (D) to cross out

Name _____ Date _____ Class _____

Lesson 25 | CONTEXT: Change in Science and Technology

Shuttle to the Stars

The space program is no longer the concern of only scientists and astronauts. It affects everyone on Earth. You might not be able to watch your favorite television show without signals from satellites in space. Also, the technology used in space is eventually applied to make our lives better on Earth.

In the following exercises, you will have the opportunity to expand your vocabulary by reading about how one teenager feels about the space program. Below are ten Vocabulary Words that will be used in these exercises.

accord	chaos	debris	kernel	mechanism
approximate	coincide	elaborate	manual	surplus

EXERCISE 1 | *Wordbusting* ✍

Directions. Follow these instructions for this word and the nine words on the next page.
- Figure out the word's meaning by looking at its **context,** its **structure,** and its **sound.** Fill in at least one of the three **CSS** boxes. Alternate which boxes you complete.
- Then, look up the word in a dictionary, read all of its meanings, and write the meaning of the word as it is used in the sentence.
- Follow this same process for each of the Vocabulary Words on the next page. You will need to draw your own map for each word. Use a separate sheet of paper.

1.

(accord) → Most people have been in **accord** about the space program. They agree that it is both exciting and important.

Context:	Structure:	Sound:

Dictionary:

2.

approximate → Most of us will never get to travel into space, but we can enjoy rides at amusement parks that **approximate** the experience by giving us a momentary sense of space travel.

3.

coincide → My friend Marla's views on the space program don't exactly **coincide** with mine. She thinks it is interesting but unimportant. I think it is interesting and necessary.

4.

debris → My friend Arno thinks the space program is a complete waste of time and money. He says that all the stuff we've shot up into space is just **debris**, trash floating around in orbit.

5.

chaos → He thinks we should put our resources into dealing with the **chaos** here on Earth and explore space only when there is less confusion here.

6.

surplus → Arno believes that any **surplus** money the government has would be better spent on helping people on Earth. I see his point about the extra money, but I don't think he understands how much the space program has already helped us.

7.

elaborate → I have a good argument against that position, and I could **elaborate** on it for hours. However, Arno is unwilling to listen to my detailed explanations.

8.

kernel → I have learned to state the **kernel** of my argument without giving the less-important details.

9.

manual → Actually, Arno is an old-fashioned guy. He refuses to read the **manual** that came with his DVD player, so he doesn't even know how to program it.

10.

mechanism → I think he is afraid of any **mechanism** that is more complicated than a one-speed bicycle. Too many working parts scare him.

EXERCISE 2　Context Clues 👉

Directions. Scan the definitions in Column A. Then think about how the boldface words are used in the sentences in Column B. To complete the exercise, match each definition in Column A with the correct Vocabulary Word from Column B. Write the letter of your choice on the line provided. Finally, write the Vocabulary Word on the line before the definition.

COLUMN A	COLUMN B
_____ **11.** word: _____ *n.* harmony; an agreement; *v.* to grant	(A) I'm glad that nations have been able to reach some **accords** on space travel and exploration. These agreements will allow countries to work together to improve space technology.
_____ **12.** word: _____ *n.* bits and pieces of rubbish and litter; scattered fragments	(B) I am amazed by the **elaborate** preparations necessary for a successful launch. Launching a space shuttle is such a complex task.
_____ **13.** word: _____ *adj.* nearly correct or exact; *v.* to come close to	(C) When I watch the space center control room on TV during a launch, everything appears to be in **chaos**. It is hard to realize that the situation is being handled in an orderly manner.
_____ **14.** word: _____ *n.* much confusion or lack of order	(D) I think the **approximate** date for the next launch is the middle of March. The actual date is still uncertain.
_____ **15.** word: _____ *v.* to work out, or develop, carefully; to express at great length and in great detail; *adj.* complicated; highly ornamented; very detailed	(E) I hope it **coincides** with my birthday. If the two occasions are on the same day, I may have a space-travel theme for my party.
_____ **16.** word: _____ *adj.* made, done, or used by or with a hand or hands; *n.* a book of instructions	(F) Of course, many things can go wrong the day of the launch. A shuttle has many **mechanisms,** and if one working part fails, the whole mission has to be scratched.
_____ **17.** word: _____ *v.* to happen at the same time or place; to correspond exactly	(G) Many tasks that are done electronically can be done by **manual** methods if the computers fail.
_____ **18.** word: _____ *n.* the working parts of a machine or device; a system with parts that work together like those of a machine	(H) I've been especially interested in programs in which the astronauts take **kernels** into space to discover how the seeds are affected by space travel.
_____ **19.** word: _____ *n.* a grain or seed; the core; the central or most important part of something	(I) My friend Marla has a horrible idea. She thinks we should take all the **surplus** from the landfills and send that extra garbage into space.
_____ **20.** word: _____ *n.* a quantity over what is needed; left-over portion; *adj.* extra; excess	(J) I hate to think about all that **debris** cluttering the beautiful reaches of the universe.

EXERCISE 3 · Like Meanings and Opposite Meanings ☞

Directions. For each item below, circle the letter of the choice that means the same, or about the same, as the boldface word.

21. to **coincide** with the party
- (A) happen at the same time
- (B) happen at a different time
- (C) attend
- (D) leave

22. scattered **debris**
- (A) thoughts
- (B) trash
- (C) money
- (D) work

23. the **kernel** of the idea
- (A) approach
- (B) thought
- (C) core
- (D) discipline

24. a **manual** can opener
- (A) battery-operated
- (B) expensively built
- (C) electrically operated
- (D) hand-operated

25. a complicated **mechanism**
- (A) operating part
- (B) rocket booster
- (C) automobile
- (D) mechanic

Directions. For each item below, circle the letter of the choice that means the opposite, or about the opposite, of the boldface word.

26. a state of **chaos**
- (A) change
- (B) complete orderliness
- (C) extreme disorder
- (D) rebellion

27. an **elaborate** plan
- (A) foolish
- (B) reasonable
- (C) complicated
- (D) simple

28. the **approximate** amount
- (A) exact
- (B) historical
- (C) extra
- (D) nearly correct

29. to be in **accord**
- (A) agreement
- (B) set free
- (C) disagreement
- (D) tied up

30. to prevent a **surplus**
- (A) solution
- (B) shortage
- (C) problem
- (D) excess

MAKING NEW WORDS YOUR OWN

| Lesson 26 | **CONTEXT:** Change in Science and Technology |

Women in Science

Before Madame Marie Sklodowska Curie (1867–1934), who, with her husband Pierre, won a Nobel Prize for their work with radioactive elements, few women were known for their work in the sciences. In recent years, however, more and more women, like Nobel Prize-winning physicist Rosalyn Sussman Yalow, are becoming chemists, physicists, lab technicians, and computer scientists.

In the following exercises, you will have the opportunity to expand your vocabulary by reading about two students who are interested in science careers. Below are ten Vocabulary Words that will be used in these exercises.

abrupt	confirm	infinite	probability	random
commit	inert	magnitude	radiate	repel

EXERCISE 1   *Wordbusting*

Directions.   Follow these instructions for this word and the nine words on the next page.
- Figure out the word's meaning by looking at its **context,** its **structure,** and its **sound.** Fill in at least one of the three **CSS** boxes. Alternate which boxes you complete.
- Then, look up the word in a dictionary, read all of its meanings, and write the meaning of the word as it is used in the sentence.
- Follow this same process for each of the Vocabulary Words on the next page. You will need to draw your own map for each word. Use a separate sheet of paper.

1.

(abrupt) → The ringing of the bell brings an **abrupt,** or sudden, end to the discussion in Ms. Anderson's science class.

| Context: | Structure: | Sound: |

| Dictionary: |

2.

"You know, I wish I could **commit** myself to a career as a chemist," says Jennifer to Ella as they gather their books, "but I've decided to become a professional volleyball player."

3.

"Well," replies Ella, "this only **confirms,** or proves, that you have more than one talent. You could do both if you really wanted to."

4.

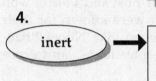

"I would certainly be busy—working in the lab and on the court. I wouldn't have any time to lie **inert** in front of the television, like my brother, the couch potato," says Jennifer.

5.

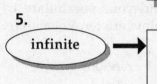

"Besides, you wouldn't have an **infinite** amount of time to play volleyball. Since you couldn't play forever, you could study chemistry after you retire," suggests Ella.

6.

Jennifer sighs, "I had no idea that choosing a career was a decision of such **magnitude;** it's so important that it scares me."

7.

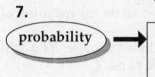

"In all **probability,** Jen, you won't be either a chemist or a volleyball player. You'll likely become an astronaut or a computer scientist instead."

8.

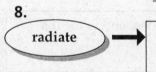

"It amazes me how you **radiate** such confidence, Ella. It comes from you the way light and heat come from the sun."

9.

"Well, I've always known that it won't be easy for me to settle down to one kind of science. I will have to take classes at **random** until I happen to find the area that really interests me," says Ella.

10.

"Maybe that's why I'm interested in sports—I like the rules and the orderliness. Confusion **repels** me; it makes me really uncomfortable."

EXERCISE 2 *Context Clues* ✍

Directions. Scan the definitions in Column A. Then think about how the boldface words are used in the sentences in Column B. To complete the exercise, match each definition in Column A with the correct Vocabulary Word from Column B. Write the letter of your choice on the line provided. Finally, write the Vocabulary Word on the line before the definition.

COLUMN A	COLUMN B

COLUMN A

____ **11.** word: _____
v. to establish; to make certain of; to verify; to approve or ratify

____ **12.** word: _____
adj. happening suddenly or unexpectedly; hasty; gruff; very steep

____ **13.** word: _____
n. likelihood; something likely to occur

____ **14.** word: _____
v. to force back; to drive away; to keep off or out; to cause to feel disgust

____ **15.** word: _____
adj. greatness in size, scope, or influence; the measurement of the brightness of a star

____ **16.** word: _____
v. to bind by promise or pledge; to make a position or opinion known; to give over for safekeeping; to do or perform an act, especially a crime

____ **17.** word: _____
adj. lacking aim or method; purposeless; not in any order; by chance

____ **18.** word: _____
v. to send out rays of light or heat; to branch out in lines or rays from a center

____ **19.** word: _____
adj. without limits or boundaries; endless; immense

____ **20.** word: _____
adj. unable to move or act; dull or slow

COLUMN B

(A) Ms. Anderson's science class is having a test on Tuesday. The **probability** is that Jennifer and Ella will do well on the test, as they always do.

(B) Because both students seem to enjoy figuring out problems, it would be an **abrupt,** or sudden, change for them not to do well on the test.

(C) Ms. Anderson reminded the students that they should be able to explain the difference between active and **inert** substances.

(D) She also told them to be able to explain why electrical charges of the same sign **repel,** or push away from, each other.

(E) They should also explain why some gases, such as neon, can be made to glow, while others never **radiate** light.

(F) They need to know something about the theory that the universe is **random** rather than ordered.

(G) They should be aware of the debate over whether the universe is **infinite** or whether it has boundaries.

(H) Finally, Ms. Anderson said, they should know how to judge the **magnitude,** or brightness, of a star.

(I) She knows that her best students will **commit** these formulas and problems to memory in order to remember them for the test.

(J) The high number of A's that Ms. Anderson has already given **confirms** her belief that her students are as bright as the stars.

EXERCISE 3 *Like Meanings and Opposite Meanings* 👉

Directions. For each item below, circle the letter of the choice that means the same, or about the same, as the boldface word.

21. to **commit** the deed
    (A) do
    (B) buy
    (C) sell
    (D) forget

22. of great **magnitude**
    (A) size
    (B) attraction
    (C) understanding
    (D) hope

23. with some **probability**
    (A) misunderstanding
    (B) grief
    (C) importance
    (D) likelihood

24. to **radiate** warmth
    (A) find
    (B) lose
    (C) take in
    (D) give off

25. to **repel** his friends
    (A) ignore
    (B) greet
    (C) disgust
    (D) invite

Directions. For each item below, circle the letter of the choice that means the opposite, or about the opposite, of the boldface word.

26. an **abrupt** departure
    (A) sudden
    (B) slow
    (C) sad
    (D) happy

27. to **confirm** the rumor
    (A) deny
    (B) support
    (C) spread
    (D) hear

28. an **inert** volcano
    (A) still
    (B) large
    (C) small
    (D) active

29. with **infinite** options
    (A) unusual
    (B) unlimited
    (C) ordinary
    (D) limited

30. a **random** approach
    (A) planned
    (B) rushed
    (C) forgotten
    (D) remembered

MAKING NEW WORDS YOUR OWN

Lesson 27 | CONTEXT: Change in Science and Technology

Animals and Humans: We Are the World

In recent years, we have begun to listen to the scientists who tell us that, in a way, animals are our brothers and sisters—or maybe our third or fourth cousins. In any case, this planet is a home not just for human beings but for an extended family of beings. Like all families, we are dependent on one another for survival.

In the following exercises, you will have the opportunity to expand your vocabulary by reading about some of the animals that share our planet. Below are ten Vocabulary Words that will be used in these exercises.

aerial	diversity	exotic	glacial	tributary
barren	ecosystem	geological	navigable	via

EXERCISE 1   *Wordbusting*

Directions. Follow these instructions for this word and the nine words on the next page.
- Figure out the word's meaning by looking at its **context,** its **structure,** and its **sound.** Fill in at least one of the three **CSS** boxes. Alternate which boxes you complete.
- Then, look up the word in a dictionary, read all of its meanings, and write the meaning of the word as it is used in the sentence.
- Follow this same process for each of the Vocabulary Words on the next page. You will need to draw your own map for each word. Use a separate sheet of paper.

1.

(aerial) ⟶ The eagle has an **aerial** view of the rabbit. From the sky, she swoops down and grabs him in her claws.

Context:	Structure:	Sound:

Dictionary:

2.

(barren) ➤ The desert may seem **barren**, but it is not totally without life. Lizards and cactuses think it is a fine home.

3.

(diversity) ➤ In fact, the desert has quite a **diversity** of living things. Many varieties of plants and animals can thrive there.

4.

(ecosystem) ➤ Each region has its own community of animals and plants that exist together in that particular place. This **ecosystem** is a delicate balance of nature that benefits all.

5.

(exotic) ➤ The rain forest is filled with strange, **exotic** creatures such as toucans and flying squirrels.

6.

(geological) ➤ **Geological** studies show that many life forms existed thousands of years ago. We see the fossils of their skeletons in the rocks.

7.

(glacial) ➤ Evidently, life can exist anywhere. Worms live in the ice of the **glacial** regions of Alaska and the Pacific Northwest.

8.

(navigable) ➤ Most parts of the Amazon River are **navigable,** and enormous knowledge has been gained by researchers exploring the area by boat.

9.

(tributary) ➤ In South America, piranhas live in almost every major river and any **tributary** that flows into one. Piranhas, by the way, do not necessarily eat humans.

10.

(via) ➤ Still, if you come to a river and discover a school of piranha swimming there, it is probably best to cross **via** bridge or by boat.

EXERCISE 2 *Context Clues* ✍

Directions. Scan the definitions in Column A. Then think about how the boldface words are used in the sentences in Column B. To complete the exercise, match each definition in Column A with the correct Vocabulary Word from Column B. Write the letter of your choice on the line provided. Finally, write the Vocabulary Word on the line before the definition.

COLUMN A

_____ **11.** word: _____
adj. foreign; strangely different

_____ **12.** word: _____
adj. concerned with geology, the science that deals with the physical nature of the earth

_____ **13.** word: _____
adj. of or like ice or glaciers; freezing; cold and unfriendly; moving as slowly as a glacier

_____ **14.** word: _____
n. the basic ecological unit; animals, plants, and bacteria living as one with the environment

_____ **15.** word: _____
adj. sterile; infertile; unable to reproduce; unproductive; empty; dull

_____ **16.** word: _____
n. difference; unlikeness; variety

_____ **17.** word: _____
adj. large enough and open enough to be traveled by ships; capable of being steered or directed

_____ **18.** word: _____
adj. of, in, or by the air; having to do with aircraft or flying; like air; not substantial; imaginary

_____ **19.** word: _____
prep. by way of; by means of

_____ **20.** word: _____
n. a small stream flowing into a larger one; owed or paid as tribute; contributory

COLUMN B

(A) Beavers can build dams that block an entire river so that it is no longer **navigable** by boats.

(B) A beaver might also build a dam where a **tributary** flows into a larger stream.

(C) Australia is home to many animals that seem **exotic,** or unusual, to people of the Northern Hemisphere.

(D) Scientists have used the **geological** record, the fossils found in the world's rocks, to determine that cockroaches have been around for about 300 million years.

(E) The emperor penguin lives in the **glacial** climate of Antarctica, where the temperature often drops to 70° below zero.

(F) To human beings the Antarctic looks like a **barren** wasteland empty of everything but snow. However, to the penguin this hostile land is home.

(G) There is such a **diversity** of creatures on the planet that it is hard to count them. In the shark family alone, there are about 250 different species.

(H) An **aerial** view of the earth, such as that seen from a balloon, reminds us that this planet is an amazing place.

(I) Sometimes human beings forget that their acts can negatively affect the **ecosystem** of the entire planet and upset this delicate balance of nature.

(J) We are now more careful about our environment than we once were because we are reminded of it **via** television, by our science teachers, and through people who work to protect the environment.

EXERCISE 3 *Like Meanings and Opposite Meanings* 👈

Directions. For each item below, circle the letter of the choice that means the same, or about the same, as the boldface word.

21. an **aerial** view
   (A) agreeable
   (B) interesting
   (C) from the air
   (D) from the ground

22. a **geological** formation
   (A) water
   (B) animal
   (C) plant
   (D) rock

23. safeguarding an **ecosystem**
   (A) local community
   (B) living organisms and their environment
   (C) planetary structure of the universe
   (D) water purity

24. a **tributary** flowing into the river
   (A) ship
   (B) ocean
   (C) stream
   (D) snowfall

25. to Rome **via** Venice
   (A) against
   (B) under
   (C) around
   (D) by way of

Directions. For each item below, circle the letter of the choice that means the opposite, or about the opposite, of the boldface word.

26. a **barren** room
   (A) large
   (B) small
   (C) full
   (D) empty

27. an **exotic** city
   (A) peaceful
   (B) familiar
   (C) troubled
   (D) strange

28. at a **glacial** pace
   (A) unreasonable
   (B) slow
   (C) rapid
   (D) reasonable

29. a river that is **navigable**
   (A) good for fishing
   (B) able to be traveled
   (C) polluted
   (D) dried up

30. a **diversity** of opinions
   (A) group
   (B) variety
   (C) similarity
   (D) combination

MAKING NEW WORDS YOUR OWN

| Lesson 28 | **CONTEXT:** Change in Science and Technology

More About Animals

As a result of interest in ecology and preserving endangered species, schools are providing students with more opportunities to learn about animal life. Of course, students have always studied animals, but because of our changing interest, the focus is now on the relationships between humans, other animals, and the environment.

In the following exercises, you will have the opportunity to expand your vocabulary by reading about animals and about some reports students are doing on animals. Below are ten Vocabulary Words that will be used in these exercises.

alternate	effect	inquisitive	propel	unpredictable
challenge	encounter	poach	universal	vital

| EXERCISE 1 | *Wordbusting* ✍

Directions. Follow these instructions for this word and the nine words on the next page.
- Figure out the word's meaning by looking at its **context,** its **structure,** and its **sound.** Fill in at least one of the three **CSS** boxes. Alternate which boxes you complete.
- Then, look up the word in a dictionary, read all of its meanings, and write the meaning of the word as it is used in the sentence.
- Follow this same process for each of the Vocabulary Words on the next page. You will need to draw your own map for each word. Use a separate sheet of paper.

1.

(alternate) ⟶ When an opossum is threatened, it usually puts on a display of fierceness. If it can't scare its opponent, it adopts an **alternate** approach: It pretends to be dead.

Context:	Structure:	Sound:

Dictionary:

Name _____ Date _____ Class _____

2.

 challenge → Animals have a built-in response to danger. If a kitten can't run away, it may **challenge** an opponent by raising its fur and hissing, as if to say "Come on, I dare you."

3.

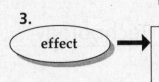 effect → The kitten's behavior is not likely to have much **effect,** but similar behavior in the kitten's cousin, the tiger, usually will produce instant results.

4.

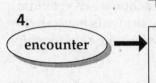 encounter → It is interesting to observe animals as they **encounter** humans or other animals. Different animals handle the chance meetings differently.

5.

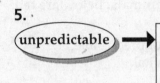 unpredictable → Researchers are careful around animals whose behavior can be **un-predictable**. No one wants to be chased by a rhinoceros that has suddenly become angry for no apparent reason.

6.

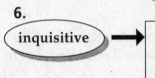 inquisitive → People who have observed chimpanzees report that many chimpanzees are as **inquisitive** about us as we are about them. They become curious about us and watch us with interest.

7.

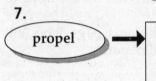 propel → Chimpanzees' curiosity definitely has not driven them to leave their homes to study us. However, interest in animals has **propelled** many naturalists to live in the wild for a while to observe chimps.

8.

 poach → Hunters continue to **poach** chimpanzees. Even famous ones have been killed illegally.

9.

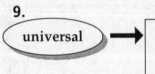 universal → Curiosity does seem to be a **universal** characteristic of mammals. Different mammals have different levels of curiosity about the world.

10.

 vital → The study of animals is **vital** for many reasons. It is essential to understanding our world and ourselves.

EXERCISE 2   *Context Clues* ✍

Directions. Scan the definitions in Column A. Then think about how the boldface words are used in the sentences in Column B. To complete the exercise, match each definition in Column A with the correct Vocabulary Word from Column B. Write the letter of your choice on the line provided. Finally, write the Vocabulary Word on the line before the definition.

COLUMN A	COLUMN B

COLUMN A

_____ **11.** word: _____
v. to meet, usually unexpectedly; to face in battle or conflict; *n.* a meeting

_____ **12.** word: _____
n. a demanding task; a dare; *v.* to call into question; to call to take part in a contest or duel

_____ **13.** word: _____
adj. surprising; not predictable; tending to act in unexpected ways

_____ **14.** word: _____
v. to cook in or over water; to enter another's property illegally; to interfere with another's property or rights; to steal

_____ **15.** word: _____
adj. essential; full of life and vigor; having to do with or manifesting life

_____ **16.** word: _____
adj. inclined to ask questions; curious

_____ **17.** word: _____
adj. present everywhere; unlimited; that can be used for many different kinds, sizes, and so on

_____ **18.** word: _____
v. to push or drive forward

_____ **19.** word: _____
v. to follow by turns; to take turns; *n.* a substitute; *adj.* substitute

_____ **20.** word: _____
n. results; a force which makes something happen; *v.* to cause

COLUMN B

(A) "I think I'll do my science report on the bifocal fish. It has two levels of vision so that it can **alternate** between seeing what is above the water and what is in the water," says Margaret.

(B) "I want to study the **effect** of global warming; I know it may have some serious results," says Ruth.

(C) "Yes, it certainly would have **universal** results, but such a big problem will be hard to research. You need to focus on something more limited," reminds Carla.

(D) Carla adds, "I'm going to write about the flying squirrel. It **propels** itself off one limb, glides to another, and lands."

(E) "I think it is **vital** to let people know that pandas are in danger, so that's the subject of my report. Maybe I can make other people see how terribly important it is to save them," says Pat.

(F) "I added statistics to show the number of pandas killed as a result of the hunters who **poach**," added Pat. "It needs to be known that pandas are being killed illegally."

(G) "I don't see how you did it. It's going to be a real **challenge** to get mine finished by Friday," Ruth notes.

(H) Margaret explains, "I did mine on bears. They're quite **inquisitive**, which just means that they're eager to learn and explore."

(I) "I've heard that an **encounter** between a bear and a human can be quite serious, but I forget what I'm supposed to do if I meet one by accident," Ruth says.

(J) "I read that you're not supposed to make any sudden, or **unpredictable**, motions and that you should make loud noises," Margaret replies.

EXERCISE 3 *Like Meanings and Opposite Meanings* ✍

Directions. For each item below, circle the letter of the choice that means the same, or about the same, as the boldface word.

21. an **alternate** selection
    (A) special
    (B) inferior
    (C) substitute
    (D) regular

22. a difficult **challenge**
    (A) task
    (B) war
    (C) story
    (D) belief

23. to **encounter** difficulty
    (A) overcome
    (B) create
    (C) avoid
    (D) meet with

24. to **effect** a change
    (A) misunderstand
    (B) understand
    (C) forget
    (D) cause

25. to **poach** an egg
    (A) eat
    (B) cook
    (C) drop
    (D) crack

Directions. For each item below, circle the letter of the choice that means the opposite, or about the opposite, of the boldface word.

26. a **universal** element
    (A) limited
    (B) difficult
    (C) occurring everywhere
    (D) simple

27. an **unpredictable** event
    (A) bitter
    (B) expected
    (C) amusing
    (D) surprising

28. an **inquisitive** child
    (A) mischievous
    (B) demanding
    (C) uninterested
    (D) curious

29. to **propel** the boat
    (A) start
    (B) stop
    (C) move
    (D) jump off

30. a **vital** truth
    (A) clear
    (B) confusing
    (C) unimportant
    (D) necessary

MAKING NEW WORDS YOUR OWN

| Lesson 29 | **CONTEXT: Change in Science and Technology**

A Technological Revolution

Technology means putting science to use. It's amazing to think of all the changes technology has made possible, from cars to bullet trains, from glider planes to space shuttles. It's certainly no exaggeration to say that we live in an age of technological revolution.

In the following exercises, you will have the opportunity to expand your vocabulary by reading about how some people react to the idea of further change. Below are ten Vocabulary Words that will be used in these exercises.

capacity	intermediate	minimum	prompt	speculate
digital	intricate	perpetual	reception	stability

EXERCISE 1 *Wordbusting* ✍

Directions. Follow these instructions for this word and the nine words on the next page.
- Figure out the word's meaning by looking at its **context,** its **structure,** and its **sound.** Fill in at least one of the three **CSS** boxes. Alternate which boxes you complete.
- Then, look up the word in a dictionary, read all of its meanings, and write the meaning of the word as it is used in the sentence.
- Follow this same process for each of the Vocabulary Words on the next page. You will need to draw your own map for each word. Use a separate sheet of paper.

1.

(capacity) ➔ | Science and technology have the **capacity** to change our lives in many ways. They alter the way we live in the fields of health, careers, and entertainment, to name only three.

Context:	Structure:	Sound:

Dictionary:

2.

Most of us are very attached to the new technology and wouldn't want to give it up. Who wouldn't prefer **digital** video to the old video-cassettes? This type of reproduction, in which electronic bits of information are stored in a magnetic medium, is superior in many ways.

3.
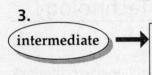

Televisions of today are better than the televisions of the 1950s, but they may be only an **intermediate** step. We are on the way toward television technology that is better still.

4.
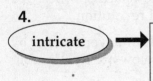

Advances in technology can be a problem. For example, some people found the instructions for using their videocassette recorders to be too **intricate,** or difficult, to follow.

5.
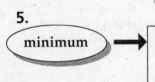

It really doesn't take a college degree in electronics to operate most of the new technology. Actually, the **minimum** requirement is just a willingness to read the directions.

6.
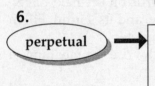

Confusion about how to deal with advances in technology may be a **perpetual** problem. On the other hand, with proper education, it may cease to be a continuing concern.

7.
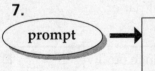

The younger generation has been **prompt** to accept changes in technology. They take to the changes quickly and enthusiastically.

8.
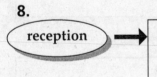

This warm **reception** is probably the result of having grown up in a high-tech society. It is easier to accept gadgets if one has been used to them from childhood.

9.
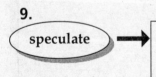

The older generation is more likely to **speculate** about the broad and longterm effects of new technologies.

10.

They understand that rapid change may threaten the **stability** of society—that some changes might cause disorder rather than progress.

EXERCISE 2 *Context Clues* ✍

Directions. Scan the definitions in Column A. Then think about how the boldface words are used in the sentences in Column B. To complete the exercise, match each definition in Column A with the correct Vocabulary Word from Column B. Write the letter of your choice on the line provided. Finally, write the Vocabulary Word on the line before the definition.

COLUMN A	COLUMN B
_____ **11.** word: _____ *n.* capability; the amount of space inside something; the ability to hold or contain	(A) Ms. Slavinsky has just asked her class to **speculate,** or reflect on, how scientific advances may change the future.
_____ **12.** word: _____ *adj.* complicated; elaborate	(B) Her request has **prompted** a lively discussion. Students need little urging to discuss this issue.
_____ **13.** word: _____ *adj.* permanent; continual	(C) Actually, we could spend all of our time imagining how many more uses might be found for **digital** recording alone. Already, this method of converting data is used in cameras and videos, to name a few.
_____ **14.** word: _____ *adj.* quick to act; on time; *v.* to urge to action; to remind; *n.* a reminder	(D) "I think television **reception** will improve. I think we'll receive broadcast TV from around the world," says Kerry.
_____ **15.** word: _____ *v.* to think about or consider; to guess; to buy and sell at a risk	(E) "I think we'll always have to go to school, that we'll have to be **perpetual** students just to keep up with the changes and advances," adds Joe.
_____ **16.** word: _____ *n.* steadiness; resistance to change; firmness of character or purpose	(F) "I had to struggle with basic and **intermediate** math; I wish we'd have been allowed to use calculators," Joe complains.
_____ **17.** word: _____ *n.* a receiving; the manner of being received; a function for welcoming guests	(G) "Do you think we are going to make machines that are so **intricate,** so complex, that we can no longer control them?" asks Ms. Slavinsky.
_____ **18.** word: _____ *adj.* performed with a finger; using a row of figures on a dial; a method of recording that changes sounds or pictures to bits that can be read electronically	(H) "It's a good plot for a science fiction movie. The Alamodome is filled to **capacity**—not a seat left in the house—and the machine that controls the scoreboard suddenly takes control of the stadium," she adds.
_____ **19.** word: _____ *n.* the smallest quantity or degree possible or allowed; *adj.* the smallest possible, permissible, or reached	(I) "Well, the machine doesn't have even the bare **minimum** of intelligence. Without humans, it's no smarter than a log," says Kevin.
_____ **20.** word: _____ *adj.* in the middle; *n.* anything in a middle position	(J) "No, technology need not be a great threat to the peace and **stability** of human beings. In fact, it can help us make the world more secure," says Ms. Slavinsky.

EXERCISE 3 *Like Meanings and Opposite Meanings* 👉

Directions. For each item below, circle the letter of the choice that means the same, or about the same, as the boldface word.

21. her intellectual **capacity**
- (A) desire
- (B) confusion
- (C) ability
- (D) worth

22. in the **intermediate** stages
- (A) first
- (B) last
- (C) in-between
- (D) most important

23. a **digital** switch
- (A) operated by fingers
- (B) operated by numbers
- (C) row of figures
- (D) difficult to operate

24. to **speculate** about the event
- (A) argue
- (B) write
- (C) worry
- (D) think

25. his emotional **stability**
- (A) loss
- (B) state
- (C) steadiness
- (D) welfare

Directions. For each item below, circle the letter of the choice that means the opposite, or about the opposite, of the boldface word.

26. a friendly **reception**
- (A) friend
- (B) enemy
- (C) goodbye
- (D) greeting

27. to be **prompt**
- (A) on time
- (B) late
- (C) lost
- (D) found

28. **perpetual** surprise
- (A) routine
- (B) infrequent
- (C) amazing
- (D) continual

29. a **minimum** of ten books
- (A) understanding
- (B) limit
- (C) maximum
- (D) list

30. an **intricate** explanation
- (A) elaborate
- (B) simple
- (C) strange
- (D) polite

MAKING NEW WORDS YOUR OWN

Lesson 30 | CONTEXT: Change in Science and Technology

The World of Plants

We have come to realize that plant life must be respected and protected. Plants are not only a source of beauty; they also keep our air clean. They provide food and medicine for humans and animals. We know now that plants help to regulate the climate.

In the following exercises, you will have the opportunity to expand your vocabulary by reading about the study of plant life. Below are ten Vocabulary Words that will be used in these exercises.

conifer	involuntary	precaution	preliminary	stationary
germinate	photosynthesis	precise	proportion	submerged

EXERCISE 1 *Wordbusting* ✐☞

Directions. Follow these instructions for this word and the nine words on the next page.
- Figure out the word's meaning by looking at its **context,** its **structure,** and its **sound.** Fill in at least one of the three **CSS** boxes. Alternate which boxes you complete.
- Then, look up the word in a dictionary, read all of its meanings, and write the meaning of the word as it is used in the sentence.
- Follow this same process for each of the Vocabulary Words on the next page. You will need to draw your own map for each word. Use a separate sheet of paper.

1.

conifer → One of the most attractive trees in the plant world is the spruce, a **conifer**. There are about 40 kinds of this cone-bearing evergreen in the Northern Hemisphere.

Context:	Structure:	Sound:

Dictionary:

2.

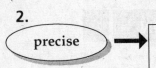

A sequoia tree named General Sherman is one of the tallest trees in the world. I don't know its **precise** measurements, but it is about 35 feet in diameter at its base and at least 295 feet tall.

3.

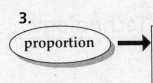

The banyan tree, which grows in Southeast Asia, can measure two thousand feet across the top. If you have never seen one, it is hard to imagine a tree of such **proportions.**

4.

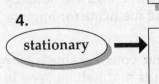

A group of mangroves looks as though it might start marching at any moment. Like all trees, however, mangroves are rooted and **stationary**.

5.

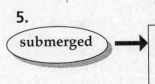

Their roots are **submerged** in sea water and anchored in mud. The trees look as if they are standing on stilts.

6.

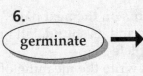

Any discussion of the sciences must include the study of botany. Understanding how plants **germinate**, develop, and grow is basic.

7.

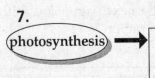

Learning how plants grow and use the sunlight to change water and carbon dioxide into carbohydrates is necessary to understanding **photosynthesis.**

8.

Scientists may have detected **involuntary** movement in plants. The plants seem to shudder and pull away from danger. Of course, this movement is not conscious, for plants have no brains.

9.

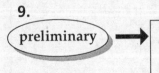

In its first, or **preliminary,** stages, the jack-in-the-pulpit is a male plant, but after three to five years it changes into a female plant.

10.

Some plants, such as the Venus' flytrap, actually eat meat. Insects that are not aware of the danger and so do not take **precautions** to protect themselves may end up as plant snacks.

EXERCISE 2 *Context Clues*

Directions. Scan the definitions in Column A. Then think about how the boldface words are used in the sentences in Column B. To complete the exercise, match each definition in Column A with the correct Vocabulary Word from Column B. Write the letter of your choice on the line provided. Finally, write the Vocabulary Word on the line before the definition.

COLUMN A	COLUMN B

COLUMN A

_____ **11.** word: _____
adj. not moving or movable; not increasing or decreasing; unchanging in condition, values, etc.

_____ **12.** word: _____
v. to begin to grow and develop; to take root

_____ **13.** word: _____
adj. underwater; covered or hidden; sunken; suppressed

_____ **14.** word: _____
n. any of the cone-bearing bushes or trees, mostly evergreens

_____ **15.** word: _____
n. process by which green plants produce organic substances by using sunlight on chlorophyll

_____ **16.** word: _____
adj. not done of one's free will; accidental; automatic

_____ **17.** word: _____
n. care taken beforehand; a measure taken against danger

_____ **18.** word: _____
n. a part or share in relation to the whole; ratio; *v.* to cause to be in proper balance

_____ **19.** word: _____
adj. accurately stated; minutely exact; communicated definitely and distinctly

_____ **20.** word: _____
adj. coming before; introductory; leading up to the main event

COLUMN B

(A) The students in Ms. Slavinsky's class are doing reports on plant life. Even though she has given them **precise** directions, they don't seem to know exactly what to do.

(B) The teacher seems to be **submerged** in work. Her desk is buried in papers.

(C) The students begin their **preliminary** investigations. Their first task is to decide what questions they would like to research.

(D) Ms. Slavinsky stops her paperwork and watches the class as the ideas **germinate** in the students' minds. She can see the ideas beginning to develop.

(E) "I wonder if plant and animal life have to be in a certain ratio for both to do well. If so, I wonder what the **proportion** might be," says Kerry.

(F) "Maybe some of us could do a demonstration of **photosynthesis**," suggests Kim. "We could find some way to show the class how plants make their food."

(G) "Well, if fish can walk, maybe plants can, too. I'm going to investigate whether all plants are **stationary**," says Joe.

(H) Susie reacts with an **involuntary** chuckle. "I'm sorry," she says. "I didn't mean to laugh, but plants walk only in science fiction."

(I) "I'm going to study what **precautions** are being taken to save plant life in the rain forests. It's important to plan carefully, or we may lose a valuable source of medicines," Kevin says.

(J) "Do **conifers** grow in the rain forests?" asks Arturo. "I've never noticed trees with cones in photos I've seen, but I'm not sure."

EXERCISE 3 *Like Meanings and Opposite Meanings* ✍

Directions. For each item below, circle the letter of the choice that means the same, or about the same, as the boldface word.

21. an unusual **precaution**
(A) rescue
(B) protection
(C) view
(D) meaning

22. out of **proportion**
(A) order
(B) proposal
(C) breath
(D) ratio

23. trees in the **conifer** class
(A) cone-bearing
(B) fruit-bearing
(C) flower-producing
(D) sap-producing

24. a study of **photosynthesis**
(A) animal life
(B) medical science
(C) a plant process
(D) agriculture

25. to be **submerged** in thought
(A) happy
(B) buried
(C) understood
(D) blended

Directions. For each item below, circle the letter of the choice that means the opposite, or about the opposite, of the boldface word.

26. the seeds **germinate**
(A) hibernate
(B) bloom
(C) dry up
(D) develop

27. an **involuntary** action
(A) accidental
(B) deliberate
(C) valuable
(D) worthless

28. a **precise** amount
(A) estimated
(B) exact
(C) intentional
(D) accidental

29. the **preliminary** question
(A) hardest
(B) easiest
(C) last
(D) first

30. a **stationary** device
(A) letter opener
(B) brilliant
(C) fixed in place
(D) movable

INTRODUCTION

UNDERSTANDING NEW WORDS AND THEIR USES

Building Your Vocabulary

One way to build your vocabulary is to learn the different meanings of a single word. Another way is to learn how to make new words by using prefixes and suffixes. A third way is to learn about the origins of words. Learning about the origins of words will help you remember the words' meanings. The following exercises will help you build on, and remember, vocabulary.

HOW TO DO EXERCISE 1 — *Multimeaning*

Words often have more than one meaning. In a Multimeaning exercise, you will read a boldface vocabulary word in a sentence. You will then read four more sentences that use the same vocabulary word. Your job is to choose the sentence that uses the vocabulary word in the same way as it is used in the first sentence. Here is an example of a Multimeaning exercise:

> The fog of nineteenth-century London was, in fact, **foul** air caused by pollution.
>
> **(A)** Soot from the city's many chimneys would also **foul** the air.
> **(B)** In this setting, Detective Sherlock Holmes tracks down **foul** murderers and other evil-doers.
> **(C)** Nothing keeps Holmes from the chase. He goes out into the streets of London even in a thunderstorm or other **foul** weather.
> **(D)** Waste dumped into London's river Thames had made the waterway **foul**.

In the first sentence, the air was **foul** because of pollution. Pollution makes things dirty or impure. **Foul** is used as an adjective to mean dirty or impure. How does this compare to the uses of the word in choices A, B, C, and D?

- In choice A, **foul** is a verb meaning to pollute or make dirty.
- In choice B, **foul** means evil, not dirty.
- In choice C, **foul** is used to describe weather, and it means unfavorable or stormy.
- In the correct choice, D, **foul** again describes something made dirty or impure.

HOW TO DO EXERCISE 2 — *Word Analysis*

Prefixes and Suffixes

The following items will give you practice in identifying the kinds of prefixes and suffixes that you will run into again and again as you read. In each of these items, you will read two words. Both words will contain the same prefix or suffix. You will be asked to identify the choice that describes the meaning of the prefix or suffix as it is used in both words. Here is an example of a prefix exercise:

> <u>re</u>adjust   <u>re</u>write
> (A) after
> (B) with
> (C) before
> (D) again

Hint #1 The second word will usually be a word that you already know well. For example, you probably already know that *rewrite* means "to write again."

Hint #2 The first word or its root (in this case, *adjust*) is a Vocabulary Word in this program. When you remember that *rewrite* means "to write again," you can guess that *readjust* means "to adjust again." That leads you to the correct choice, D.

Note: The tables in the front of this book list some common prefixes and suffixes. These tables will help you to complete the exercises on *Prefixes* and *Suffixes* in the lessons that follow.

Word Origins

Many words in the English language come from Greek, Latin, French, and other languages. Word Origins exercises will give you practice in learning the roots of Vocabulary Words. In these exercises, you will be asked to identify the choice that best completes the sentence.

Here is an example of a Word Origins exercise:

debt   decrease   definite   descriptive

The Latin word *crescere*, "to grow," combined with the prefix *de–*, "away," gives us the word _____.

Hint #1 Compare the Latin root to the list of words provided above the item. If you remove *de–* from all of the choices, the part of the word left that most resembles the Latin root would be *–crease,* from the word *decrease.*

Hint #2 The choices in Word Origins will be Vocabulary Words you studied in *Making New Words Your Own.* In the introduction to *Making New Words Your Own,* you learned that to decrease means "to grow smaller." *Decrease* is the correct response.

UNDERSTANDING NEW WORDS AND THEIR USES

Lesson 1 | CONTEXT: Change in Arts and Literature
Science Fiction: Modern Myths?

EXERCISE 1 *Multimeaning*

Directions. Read each numbered sentence below. Then, circle the letter of the choice that uses the boldface word in the same way as it is used in the numbered sentence.

1. In myth and folklore, the main character might not be a **mortal;** he or she could be a god.
   - (A) If a human hero suffers a **mortal** wound, he or she will die.
   - (B) Although a god in mythology may have the character of a **mortal,** he or she is more than human.
   - (C) A human who offends a god might live in **mortal** terror of the god's terrible revenge.
   - (D) No one wants to make a **mortal** enemy of a powerful being. That's why characters in myth fear making lifelong foes of the gods.

2. In science fiction stories, sometimes an **alien** has characteristics similar to the gods of myth and legend.
   - (A) Sometimes the myths and legends may be **alien,** or foreign, to us.
   - (B) The idea that myth and science fiction could be related may seem **alien** at first, but when you think about it, it may not seem so strange after all.
   - (C) An **alien** who came in friendship from another planet might decide to punish Earthlings who treated him badly.
   - (D) In some stories, violence is completely **alien** to the peaceful nature of another planet's culture.

EXERCISE 2 *Word Analysis*

Prefixes

Directions. Read each numbered pair of words below. Then, circle the letter of the choice that best describes the meaning of the underlined prefix as it is used in each pair.

3. <u>in</u>humane   <u>in</u>correct
   - (A) against
   - (B) around
   - (C) not
   - (D) outside

4. <u>un</u>allied   <u>un</u>comfortable
   - (A) with
   - (B) before
   - (C) against
   - (D) not

Suffixes

Directions. Read each numbered pair of words below. Then, circle the letter of the choice that best describes the meaning of the underlined suffix as it is used in each pair.

5. diploma**tic**   patrio**tic**
   (A) capable of being
   (B) not
   (C) characteristic of
   (D) one who

6. distort**ion**   prevent**ion**
   (A) act of
   (B) tending to
   (C) science of
   (D) full of

Word Origins

Directions. Read each of the following sentences. Then, from the vocabulary list below, choose the word that best completes the sentence. Write the word in the blank.

alien	fascinate	humane	planetary
ally	fugitive	invade	satellite
avert	galaxy	luminous	stellar
destiny	gesture	mortal	tranquil
diplomatic	ghastly	overture	velocity

7. The Middle English word *gasten*, meaning "to terrify," became the Modern English word _____.

8. We get a hint of the meaning of the word _____ when we learn that the Latin word *velox* means "swift."

9. Knowing that the prefix *in–* can mean "in" and that the Latin word *vadere* means "to go" can help you understand the meaning of the word _____.

10. The Latin word *fascinare*, meaning "to enchant," is related to our word _____.

UNDERSTANDING NEW WORDS AND THEIR USES

Lesson 2 | **CONTEXT:** Change in Arts and Literature
Books for Young Adults

EXERCISE 1 *Multimeaning*

Directions. Read each numbered sentence below. Then, circle the letter of the choice that uses the boldface word in the same way as it is used in the numbered sentence.

1. The author of this article about books for teenagers used some **abstract** terms that are hard to understand because they don't relate to material things.
   (A) Let me **abstract** the article for you; maybe if I try to summarize it I'll understand it better.
   (B) The author said that teens don't like to read about **abstract** subjects, that they would rather read about concrete situations.
   (C) I wasn't able to **abstract** any general ideas from the article.
   (D) Maybe I'd better read the article again before I write the **abstract;** I'm afraid my summary won't be very clear otherwise.

2. The author of this article said that many teenagers **deliberate** carefully before choosing a book.
   (A) They make **deliberate** choices because if they think carefully about what they want to read, they're more likely to be pleased with their selections.
   (B) Some teens read at a **deliberate,** or unhurried, pace, while others race through a book.
   (C) When a new book by a favorite author appears, teenagers have to **deliberate** over whether to buy the book or check it out of the library.
   (D) Libraries make **deliberate** decisions about what books to purchase. They buy young-adult books on purpose.

EXERCISE 2 *Word Analysis*

Prefixes

Directions. Read each numbered pair of words below. Then, circle the letter of the choice that best describes the meaning of the underlined prefix as it is used in each pair.

3. <u>non</u>conforming   <u>non</u>living
   (A) good
   (B) two
   (C) with
   (D) not

4. <u>re</u>coil   <u>re</u>turn
   (A) back
   (B) not
   (C) against
   (D) for

Suffixes

Directions. Read each numbered pair of words below. Then, circle the letter of the choice that best describes the meaning of the underlined suffix as it is used in each pair.

5. excess**ive**   product**ive**
   - (A) able
   - (B) of or tending to
   - (C) one who does
   - (D) condition of

6. defi**ant**   pleas**ant**
   - (A) one who is
   - (B) condition of
   - (C) belonging to
   - (D) suitable for

Word Origins

Directions. Read each of the following sentences. Then, from the vocabulary list below, choose the word that best completes the sentence. Write the word in the blank.

abstract	defiant	grotesque	offend
absurd	deliberate	impact	originality
conform	distort	inferior	reality
consequence	eventual	mere	recoil
controversial	excess	obsolete	technique

7. The Latin word *evinire*, meaning "to happen," is related to our word _____

8. We get a hint of the meaning of the word _____ when we learn that the Latin word *merus* means "pure."

9. You may recognize the Greek word *tekhne*, meaning "art," in the Modern English word _____.

10. We get a hint of the meaning of the word _____ when we learn that the Latin word *obsolescere* means "to wear out."

UNDERSTANDING NEW WORDS AND THEIR USES

Lesson 3 CONTEXT: Change in Arts and Literature
A Visit to an Art Exhibit

EXERCISE 1 *Multimeaning* ✍

Directions. Read each numbered sentence below. Then, circle the letter of the choice that uses the boldface word in the same way as it is used in the numbered sentence.

1. Carla and Andy are impatient to get to the art exhibit devoted to dogs. They can barely keep their excitement in **leash**.
   - (A) Their favorite work of art is a display titled *New* **Leash** *on Leif.* The title makes Andy imagine a dog named Leif with a new strap.
   - (B) The artist has a deep sympathy toward dogs; he hates to **leash** them, or tie them up.
   - (C) At this exhibit, the artist has chosen to place a diamond-studded **leash** and a food dish on a pedestal and call it a work of art.
   - (D) "Try to keep your urge to touch the exhibit in **leash**," Carla says. "I know it's hard, but you don't want to make the artist angry."

2. They make a quick tour of the exhibit, but when they are finished, they find themselves with some time to **idle** away.
   - (A) They can't go to a ballgame because the team is **idle** this week.
   - (B) Carla's mom **idles** the car engine as she waits for them to decide what they want to do.
   - (C) "This may be **idle** gossip," she says, "but I've heard that the artist hasn't been able to create anything all year."
   - (D) "All he could do was **idle** his time away watching television," she continues. "He just hasn't been able to call his creative powers together to produce new work."

EXERCISE 2 *Word Analysis* ✍

Prefixes

Directions. Read each numbered pair of words below. Then, circle the letter of the choice that best describes the meaning of the underlined prefix as it is used in each pair.

3. <u>in</u>audible   <u>in</u>capable
   - (A) between
   - (B) not
   - (C) across
   - (D) over

4. <u>pre</u>maturely   <u>pre</u>date
   - (A) around
   - (B) together
   - (C) against
   - (D) before

Suffixes

Directions. Read each numbered pair of words below. Then, circle the letter of the choice that best describes the meaning of the underlined suffix as it is used in each pair.

5. sign<u>ify</u>   beaut<u>ify</u>
   (A) make
   (B) becoming
   (C) state of
   (D) like

6. conspicuous<u>ness</u>   happi<u>ness</u>
   (A) suitable for
   (B) state of being
   (C) one who
   (D) in the direction of

Word Origins

Directions. Read each of the following sentences. Then, from the vocabulary list below, choose the word that best completes the sentence. Write the word in the blank.

audible	haunt	lenient	notorious
candid	hover	loiter	signify
congregate	idle	maturity	subtle
conspicuous	ignorance	modest	supervise
diaphragm	leash	motive	threshold

7. You may recognize the French word *motif*, meaning "causing motion," in the Modern English word _____.

8. The Latin word *notus*, meaning "known," is related to our word _____.

9. The Middle English word *haunten*, meaning "to frequent," became the Modern English word _____.

10. The Latin word *videre*, meaning "to see," and the prefix *super–*, meaning "over" or "above," combine to give us the English word _____.

UNDERSTANDING NEW WORDS AND THEIR USES

| Lesson 4 | **CONTEXT:** Change in Arts and Literature
Adventures in Books

| EXERCISE 1 | *Multimeaning* ✍

Directions. Read each numbered sentence below. Then, circle the letter of the choice that uses the boldface word in the same way as it is used in the numbered sentence.

1. Arlene has entered a new **phase** in her reading—suddenly she has started reading history books.
   (A) She is interested in every **phase** of the Civil War—from the early days to the war's conclusion.
   (B) She seems to have **phased** out all other interests; step by step, she has dropped all her other reading.
   (C) Her mother knows that, with time, Arlene will **phase** in other interests.
   (D) Her mother knows it would be a mistake to try to force her to read other subjects; it's best to allow other interests to **phase** in naturally.

2. Arlene wants to read about the **dashing,** or high-spirited, women who risked their lives to nurse soldiers near the battle sites.
   (A) Right now, she is **dashing** to the library to find a book on one of these women.
   (B) As she searches for a book to read, she knocks over a shelf, thus **dashing** books to the floor.
   (C) On the cover of one of the books is a drawing of a **dashing** young man. She is attracted by his lively appearance.
   (D) The cover illustration shows the man **dashing,** or running, across a meadow toward a castle. Arlene's reading interests suddenly take a new turn.

| EXERCISE 2 | *Word Analysis* ✍

Prefixes

Directions. Read each numbered pair of words below. Then, circle the letter of the choice that best describes the meaning of the underlined prefix as it is used in each pair.

3. <u>un</u>anticipated   <u>un</u>related
   (A) all
   (B) beneath
   (C) twice
   (D) not

4. <u>in</u>eloquent   <u>in</u>comparable
   (A) against
   (B) not
   (C) for
   (D) with

Suffixes

Directions. Read each numbered pair of words below. Then, circle the letter of the choice that best describes the meaning of the underlined suffix as it is used in each pair.

5. distrac<u>tion</u>   opera<u>tion</u>
   - (A) concerning
   - (B) act of
   - (C) that which belongs to
   - (D) becoming

6. obstina<u>cy</u>   priva<u>cy</u>
   - (A) location of
   - (B) away from
   - (C) against
   - (D) quality or state of

Word Origins

Directions. Read each of the following sentences. Then, from the vocabulary list below, choose the word that best completes the sentence. Write the word in the blank.

aggravate	distract	maintain	placid
anticipate	eloquent	obligation	porcelain
caliber	flaw	obstinate	principally
dashing	frail	optional	spontaneous
dismal	fulfill	phase	tiresome

7. The Modern English word _____ comes from the Middle English word *fraile*, which in turn came from the Latin word *frangere*, meaning "to break."

8. You may recognize the Old French word *obligier*, meaning "to bind," in the English word _____.

9. It's easy to see the English word _____ in the word *porcellana*, which is an Italian word for a type of shell.

10. The Middle English word *flaue*, meaning "splinter," became the Modern English word _____.

UNDERSTANDING NEW WORDS AND THEIR USES

Lesson 5   CONTEXT: Change in Arts and Literature
A Night at the Ballet

EXERCISE 1   Multimeaning ✍

Directions. Read each numbered sentence below. Then, circle the letter of the choice that uses the boldface word in the same way as it is used in the numbered sentence.

1. When my mother first attended the ballet, she had to wear **formal** clothes. The custom of the day required it.
   (A) Going to the ballet back then would have been too **formal** for me. I hate to feel stiff and uncomfortable in fancy clothes.
   (B) However, when my family got a **formal** invitation to a ballet, one that was officially signed by the ballet director, we all dressed in our best clothes.
   (C) I wore the **formal** dress that I bought for the Christmas dance—everybody had to dress up for that.
   (D) My mom is interested in the **formal** side of ballet—in how the dancers move and when they do this or that—but I just like the story the dance tells.

2. The ballet I saw was based on a Greek **myth**.
   (A) I had heard that Baryshnikov would be there, but it was probably just a **myth**.
   (B) I once saw a ballet that used a Native American **myth** as its source.
   (C) I'd like to be a dancer, but I have heard that if you don't start before you are six, you'll never be great. I wonder if that is a **myth**; there must be some professional dancers who started later than that.
   (D) Studying **myth**—all of the traditional stories of a culture or cultures—in school can help you understand dance, music, and art.

EXERCISE 2   Word Analysis ✍

Prefixes

Directions. Read each numbered pair of words below. Then, circle the letter of the choice that best describes the meaning of the underlined prefix as it is used in each pair.

3. <u>im</u>mortal   <u>im</u>proper
   (A) not
   (B) before
   (C) around
   (D) against

4. <u>re</u>interpret   <u>re</u>play
   (A) away
   (B) twice
   (C) again
   (D) across

Suffixes

Directions. Read each numbered pair of words below. Then, circle the letter of the choice that best describes the meaning of the underlined suffix as it is used in each pair.

5. mytho**logy**   bio**logy**
   (A) state of
   (B) becoming
   (C) science or theory of
   (D) that which

6. compar**able**   read**able**
   (A) like
   (B) able to be
   (C) concerning
   (D) in the direction of

Word Origins

Directions. Read each of the following sentences. Then, from the vocabulary list below, choose the word that best completes the sentence. Write the word in the blank.

authentic	crucial	immortal	mythology
cherish	designate	indispensable	profound
comparable	dual	interpret	resolve
consistent	formal	legendary	versatile
contemplate	gratify	myth	vigor

7. We get a hint of the meaning of the word _____ when we learn that the Latin word *cher* means "dear."

8. The Latin word *gratus,* meaning "pleasing," is related to our word

_____.

9. The Middle English word *resolven*, meaning "to dissolve," became the Modern English word _____.

10. We get a hint of the meaning of the word _____ when we learn that the prefix *de–* can mean "out" and the Latin word *signare* means "to mark."

Name _____ Date _____ Class _____

UNDERSTANDING NEW WORDS AND THEIR USES

Lesson 6 | **CONTEXT: Change in Individuals and Communities**
Career Choices

EXERCISE 1 *Multimeaning* ☞

Directions. Read each numbered sentence below. Then, circle the letter of the choice that uses the boldface word in the same way as it is used in the numbered sentence.

1. Once upon a time, if a man were a tailor, that would **guarantee** that his oldest son would become a tailor too.
   (A) There is no longer any **guarantee** that this will be the case.
   (B) The father taught the son how to **guarantee** that the son's work would be high quality.
   (C) In those days, people did not issue a **guarantee** with their products.
   (D) We would all like a **guarantee** of happiness when we choose our careers.

2. I'm going to **moderate** a panel discussion on careers and the economy. I'm in charge, so I have to make sure the panel members don't get out of control.
   (A) The panel is composed of people with different political approaches: a liberal, a conservative, and a **moderate**.
   (B) We are going to discuss how Americans can produce quality goods that can be sold at **moderate** prices.
   (C) I used to think that the minimum wage ought to be $25 per hour, but I have had to **moderate** my views.
   (D) Perhaps my parents will attend the discussion if Dad doesn't have to **moderate** a sales meeting in Toledo that day. He's looking for someone to preside in his place.

EXERCISE 2 *Word Analysis* ☞

Prefixes

Directions. Read each numbered pair of words below. Then, circle the letter of the choice that best describes the meaning of the underlined prefix as it is used in each pair.

3. <u>de</u>segregation <u>de</u>caffeinated
   (A) double
   (B) through
   (C) opposite of
   (D) around

4. <u>il</u>literate <u>il</u>legal
   (A) against
   (B) not
   (C) before
   (D) all

Suffixes

Directions. Read each numbered pair of words below. Then, circle the letter of the choice that best describes the meaning of the underlined suffix as it is used in each pair.

5. moment**ary**   compliment**ary**
   (A) a person who
   (B) relating to
   (C) total
   (D) suitable

6. judic**ial**   nation**al**
   (A) speech
   (B) study
   (C) of
   (D) act

Word Origins

Directions. Read each of the following sentences. Then, from the vocabulary list below, choose the word that best completes the sentence. Write the word in the blank.

constitution	illustrious	legitimate	partial
discrimination	indefinite	merit	prudent
elective	indirect	moderate	segregation
guarantee	initial	moral	unison
hypocrite	judicial	notable	veto

7. We get a hint of the meaning of the word _____ when we learn that the Latin word *moralis* means "of manners or customs."

8. The Latin word *eligere*, meaning "to pick out," is related to our word _____.

9. The Latin word *illustris*, meaning "distinguished," is related to our word _____.

10. The Middle English word *parcial*, meaning "biased," became the Modern English word _____.

UNDERSTANDING NEW WORDS AND THEIR USES

| Lesson 7 | **CONTEXT:** Change in Individuals and Communities |

Students Teaching Students

EXERCISE 1 *Multimeaning*

Directions. Read each numbered sentence below. Then, circle the letter of the choice that uses the boldface word in the same way as it is used in the numbered sentence.

1. Individuals have different talents; one person might have a **faculty** for art, while another is good at math.
   - (A) The entire **faculty** at our school knows how to make this work to students' advantage.
   - (B) The English **faculty** is especially good at it.
   - (C) Since I have a **faculty** for writing, I help students who are not quite as good at it as I am.
   - (D) Yesterday I worked with Barbara in the **faculty** lounge.

2. I **tutor** Barbara in English. Each week, I help her with her grammar and vocabulary.
   - (A) In England, a **tutor** is an official at a university who oversees the studies of the students, but in American schools, just about anyone who is good at a certain subject can help others with that subject.
   - (B) In return for my helping her, Barbara will **tutor** me in math.
   - (C) Her skill in math makes her a good **tutor**.
   - (D) She appreciates the help I give her as a **tutor**.

EXERCISE 2 *Word Analysis*

Prefixes

Directions. Read each numbered pair of words below. Then, circle the letter of the choice that best describes the meaning of the underlined prefix as it is used in each pair.

3. <u>in</u>credible   <u>in</u>complete
   - (A) not
   - (B) twice
   - (C) across
   - (D) from

4. <u>il</u>legible   <u>il</u>legal
   - (A) before
   - (B) not
   - (C) after
   - (D) again

Suffixes

Directions. Read each numbered pair of words below. Then, circle the letter of the choice that best describes the meaning of the underlined suffix as it is used in each pair.

5. dia**logue**   mono**logue**
   (A) study
   (B) speech
   (C) act of
   (D) one who

6. symbol**ic**   romant**ic**
   (A) relating to
   (B) against
   (C) beyond
   (D) becoming

Word Origins

Directions. Read each of the following sentences. Then, from the vocabulary list below, choose the word that best completes the sentence. Write the word in the blank.

credible	grammatical	mastery	refrain
dialogue	journal	narration	revise
editorial	legible	participate	symbolic
faculty	literary	persuasion	tutor
forum	manuscript	prose	usage

7. The Latin word *particeps,* meaning "partaker" or "partner," is related to our word

   _____.

8. The Middle English word *refryn,* meaning "echo," became the Modern English word

   _____.

9. You may recognize the Italian word *giornale,* meaning "daily," in the English word

   _____.

10. We get a hint of the meaning of the word _____ when we learn that the Latin word *prosa* means "straightforward."

UNDERSTANDING NEW WORDS AND THEIR USES

Lesson 8   **CONTEXT:** Change in Individuals and Communities

We're in the Army Now

EXERCISE 1 *Multimeaning* ✍

Directions. Read each numbered sentence below. Then, circle the letter of the choice that uses the boldface word in the same way as it is used in the numbered sentence.

1. In the army, individuals must learn to work together on any **maneuver**. The large-scale movement of troops requires total cooperation.
   (A) The tank commanders must be able to **maneuver** their vehicles into position.
   (B) There should be no underhanded **maneuvers,** no sly scheming on the part of individuals.
   (C) The men and women of the armed services must know how to **maneuver,** to move as a military unit, in the field.
   (D) The success of a military **maneuver** depends on the ability of individuals to act as a team.

2. The soldiers were tired, but they did not allow their **fatigue** to overcome them.
   (A) The captain ordered her troops to put on their **fatigue** clothing, a sure sign that they were in for hard, physical labor.
   (B) Over time, use and bad weather can **fatigue** the steel beams of a bridge. The soldiers' job was to replace the beams.
   (C) After forty-eight hours without sleep, the soldiers gave in to **fatigue** and went to sleep.
   (D) Hard work will **fatigue** anyone; the soldiers needed their rest.

EXERCISE 2 *Word Analysis* ✍

Prefixes

Directions. Read each numbered pair of words below. Then, circle the letter of the choice that best describes the meaning of the underlined prefix as it is used in each pair.

3. <u>ad</u>here   <u>ad</u>mire
   (A) half
   (B) for
   (C) against
   (D) to

4. <u>ob</u>stacle   <u>ob</u>long
   (A) before
   (B) against
   (C) again
   (D) two

Suffixes

Directions. Read each numbered pair of words below. Then, circle the letter of the choice that best describes the meaning of the underlined suffix as it is used in each pair.

5. scholar**ship**   apprentice**ship**
(A) nearness to
(B) away from
(C) state of being
(D) result of

6. official**ly**   sincere**ly**
(A) study of
(B) in the manner of one who is
(C) belonging to
(D) action or process

Word Origins

Directions. Read each of the following sentences. Then, from the vocabulary list below, choose the word that best completes the sentence. Write the word in the blank.

adhere	hardy	officially	pursue
excel	intellect	opponent	recommend
expand	maneuver	opposition	scholarship
fatigue	minority	participant	tactics
forbidding	obstacle	penetrate	yield

7. The Middle English word *yelden*, meaning "to pay," became the Modern English word
_____.

8. The Latin word *intellegere*, meaning "to perceive," is closely related to our English word _____.

9. The Middle English word *opposicioun*, meaning "a contradiction," became the Modern English word _____.

10. We get a hint of the meaning of the word _____ when we learn that the Latin word *pandere* means "to spread."

UNDERSTANDING NEW WORDS AND THEIR USES

Lesson 9 | **CONTEXT:** Change in Individuals and Communities
The Winning Team

EXERCISE 1 *Multimeaning*

Directions. Read each numbered sentence below. Then, circle the letter of the choice that uses the boldface word in the same way as it is used in the numbered sentence.

1. The Jefferson High School team will play against Duncan High School, their strongest **rival,** next Friday night.
   (A) Jefferson's team is the Wildcats, and their **rival** team is the Wolverines.
   (B) This year's Wildcat team **rivals** any other in the school's history.
   (C) If they can beat their **rival** on Friday night, they will go to the playoffs.
   (D) Nothing can **rival** the enthusiasm with which the students support the team.

2. Coach Pollard is in **anguish** over a decision about the team.
   (A) He must make a choice that **anguishes** him.
   (B) He knows that he may cause **anguish** to the rest of the school if his decision causes the team to lose.
   (C) He **anguishes** over the decisions for hours.
   (D) Finally, he announces that the star quarterback will not play on Friday, a decision that will **anguish** the quarterback, the team, and the school.

EXERCISE 2 *Word Analysis*

Prefixes

Directions. Read each numbered pair of words below. Then, circle the letter of the choice that best describes the meaning of the underlined prefix as it is used in each pair.

3. <u>in</u>tolerable   <u>in</u>complete
   (A) against
   (B) not
   (C) before
   (D) two

4. <u>im</u>mature   <u>im</u>possible
   (A) across
   (B) under
   (C) before
   (D) not

Suffixes

Directions. Read each numbered pair of words below. Then, circle the letter of the choice that best describes the meaning of the underlined suffix as it is used in each pair.

5. irrit**able**   believ**able**
(A) capable of being
(B) somewhat
(C) relating to
(D) like

6. hesitat**ion**   operat**ion**
(A) one who
(B) relating to
(C) act of
(D) in the direction of

Word Origins

Directions. Read each of the following sentences. Then, from the vocabulary list below, choose the word that best completes the sentence. Write the word in the blank.

acute	hesitation	irritable	tendency
adopt	hysterical	maternal	timid
anguish	immature	ridicule	turmoil
blemish	inhabit	rival	vague
crisis	intolerable	self-conscious	wretched

7. The Latin word *habitare,* meaning "to dwell," is related to the word

_____.

8. We get a hint of the meaning of the word _____ when we learn that the Latin word *mater* means "mother."

9. You may recognize the Latin word *ridiculum,* meaning "joke," in the English word

_____.

10. Many scholars believe that the word _____ comes from the Indo-European root *op–,* meaning "to choose." The prefix *ad–* was added later, by speakers of Latin.

UNDERSTANDING NEW WORDS AND THEIR USES

Lesson 10 | **CONTEXT:** Change in Individuals and Communities
Helping Out in the Community

EXERCISE 1 *Multimeaning*

Directions. Read each numbered sentence below. Then, circle the letter of the choice that uses the boldface word in the same way as it is used in the numbered sentence.

1. The Good Samaritans, a club that helps others, will **toil** all day Saturday to help the elderly make home repairs.
   (A) These senior citizens have worked hard all their lives, and the Good Samaritans believe they deserve a rest from their **toil**.
   (B) Besides, most eighty-year-olds cannot withstand the **toil** of reroofing a house.
   (C) With so much work to be done, the Good Samaritans sometimes feel it would be easier to **toil** up a mountain, but they always carry on.
   (D) They **toil** away, doing the best they can to help others.

2. Sometimes friends try to **lure** them from their tasks with promises of fun at the mall.
   (A) On the days that they are involved in working for the community, they resist the **lure** of the mall.
   (B) They prefer the **lure** of knowing that, at the end of the day, they have made a difference in the world.
   (C) Sometimes they do minor chores such as trying to **lure** a kitten down from a tree.
   (D) Some people take simple pleasure in dropping a **lure** in the water to catch a fish; others take pleasure in helping members of their community.

EXERCISE 2 *Word Analysis*

Prefixes

Directions. Read each numbered pair of words below. Then, circle the letter of the choice that best describes the meaning of the underlined prefix as it is used in each pair.

3. **dis**illusion   **dis**agreement
   (A) free from
   (B) opposite
   (C) around
   (D) with

4. **ab**solute   **ab**normal
   (A) again
   (B) with
   (C) away from
   (D) between

Suffixes

Directions. Read each numbered pair of words below. Then, circle the letter of the choice that best describes the meaning of the underlined suffix as it is used in each pair.

5. barbar<u>ous</u>   luxuri<u>ous</u>
   - (A) a person who
   - (B) full of
   - (C) study of
   - (D) similar to

6. vali<u>ant</u>   pleas<u>ant</u>
   - (A) in the direction of
   - (B) one who is
   - (C) study or theory of
   - (D) similar to

Word Origins

Directions. Read each of the following sentences. Then, from the vocabulary list below, choose the word that best completes the sentence. Write the word in the blank.

absolute	era	monarchy	status
banish	fortress	pageant	toil
barbarous	grandeur	perilous	tyrant
baron	illusion	proclamation	valiant
cultural	lure	serf	vengeance

7. The Old French word *venger*, meaning "to avenge," is related to our word

   _____.

8. The Latin word *fortis*, meaning "strong," is related to our word _____.

9. The Greek word *monarchia*, meaning "absolute rule," is related to our word

   _____.

10. We learn one meaning of the word _____ when we learn that the
    Middle English word *banischen* means "to exile."

UNDERSTANDING NEW WORDS AND THEIR USES

Lesson 11 | CONTEXT: Change in Science and Technology
Observing Animals in Their Habitats

EXERCISE 1   *Multimeaning*

Directions. Read each numbered sentence below. Then, circle the letter of the choice that uses the boldface word in the same way as it is used in the numbered sentence.

1. Many animals have a built-in ability to **camouflage** themselves in the wild.
   (A) An animal's coat can serve as **camouflage**.
   (B) A spotted fawn can **camouflage** itself by blending in with the leaves.
   (C) Humans who observe animals may buy special clothing for **camouflage**.
   (D) Even when wearing **camouflage**, humans may find it difficult to get close to wild animals.

2. It takes a patient and **temperate** person to be an observer of wild animals. A person who wants to observe wild animals must be willing to control his or her desire to reach out and touch them.
   (A) A **temperate,** or mild, climate makes observing animals more comfortable.
   (B) The climate in Antarctica is fiercely cold—anything but **temperate**.
   (C) The penguins that live there, however, seem to be fairly **temperate** animals. That is, they seem capable of exercising moderation.
   (D) Penguins can survive in more **temperate** surroundings, but most of them seem to prefer cold.

EXERCISE 2   *Word Analysis*

Prefixes

Directions. Read each numbered pair of words below. Then, circle the letter of the choice that best describes the meaning of the underlined prefix as it is used in each pair.

3. __anti__septic   __anti__slavery
   (A) against
   (B) before
   (C) with
   (D) beyond

4. __auto__immune   __auto__mobile
   (A) after
   (B) toward
   (C) self
   (D) between

Suffixes

Directions. Read each numbered pair of words below. Then, circle the letter of the choice that best describes the meaning of the underlined suffix as it is used in each pair.

5. season**al**   person**al**
  (A) of
  (B) state of being
  (C) becoming
  (D) one who does

6. preservat**ion**   conversat**ion**
  (A) act of
  (B) one who does
  (C) study of
  (D) similar to

Word Origins

Directions. Read each of the following sentences. Then, from the vocabulary list below, choose the word that best completes the sentence. Write the word in the blank.

antiseptic	habitat	nutrition	preservation
camouflage	immune	optical	seasonal
edible	mammal	organism	temperate
endurance	naturalist	parasite	undergrowth
glucose	nocturnal	pigment	zoology

7. We get a hint of the meaning of the word _____ when we learn that the Latin word *pingere* means "to paint."

8. The Greek word *ops*, meaning "eye," is the root of our word _____.

9. You may recognize the Latin word *nutrire*, meaning "to feed," in the English word _____.

10. We get a hint of the meaning of the word _____ when we learn that the Latin word *edere* means "to eat."

UNDERSTANDING NEW WORDS AND THEIR USES

Lesson 12 **CONTEXT:** Change in Science and Technology
The Importance of Being Scientific

EXERCISE 1 *Multimeaning*

Directions. Read each numbered sentence below. Then, circle the letter of the choice that uses the boldface word in the same way as it is used in the numbered sentence.

1. Understanding science is **fundamental,** a necessary basis, for understanding today's world.
   (A) Students should learn the **fundamental** principles of science.
   (B) Science is a basic, or **fundamental,** subject, like reading and math.
   (C) It is important to have a **fundamental** background in science.
   (D) Students sometimes don't realize that science is a **fundamental,** but when they graduate, many students discover science's key importance.

2. Sometimes the members of school boards don't recognize the importance of modern technology; our school board just decided to **cancel** two computer-science classes.
   (A) Computers are great for writing papers—if you make a mistake, you just push a key to **cancel** it. You won't have to deal with erasers ever again!
   (B) I am happy to be taking computer-science classes, but that does not **cancel** out my desire to take math, too.
   (C) I hope the school board doesn't **cancel** advanced math classes.
   (D) Computers do so much these days. They are used to **cancel** checks at the bank and stamps at the post office—jobs that once were done by hand.

EXERCISE 2 *Word Analysis*

Prefixes

Directions. Read each numbered pair of words below. Then, circle the letter of the choice that best describes the meaning of the underlined prefix as it is used in each pair.

3. <u>re</u>cognition   <u>re</u>call
   (A) back; again
   (B) beyond
   (C) before
   (D) after

4. <u>ex</u>ceed   <u>ex</u>hale
   (A) against
   (B) with
   (C) out; beyond
   (D) twice

Suffixes

Directions. Read each numbered pair of words below. Then, circle the letter of the choice that best describes the meaning of the underlined suffix as it is used in each pair.

5. util<u>ity</u>   possibil<u>ity</u>
   (A) becoming
   (B) concerning
   (C) total
   (D) state of being

6. economi<u>cal</u>   histori<u>cal</u>
   (A) of; relating to
   (B) the study of
   (C) away from
   (D) able

Word Origins

Directions. Read each of the following sentences. Then, from the vocabulary list below, choose the word that best completes the sentence. Write the word in the blank.

cancel	efficiency	logical	recognition
compensate	exceed	memorandum	relinquish
competent	financial	metropolitan	stationery
compute	fundamental	percentage	substantial
economical	futile	prestige	utility

7. You may recognize the Middle English word *finaunce*, meaning "money supply," in the Modern English word _____.

8. The Greek word *logos*, meaning "word, reason, or thought," is related to our word _____.

9. You may recognize the Latin word *substantia*, meaning "substance," in our word _____.

10. We get a hint of the meaning of the word _____ when we learn that the Latin word *per centum* means "by the hundred."

UNDERSTANDING NEW WORDS AND THEIR USES

Lesson 13 | CONTEXT: Change in Science and Technology
The Science Project

EXERCISE 1 Multimeaning ✍

Directions. Read each numbered sentence below. Then, circle the letter of the choice that uses the boldface word in the same way as it is used in the numbered sentence.

1. Matthew and Heather are in **accord**; they have agreed that they will do their science project together.
   - (A) The other students **accord** them respect because they know that Matthew and Heather are good at science.
   - (B) Matthew and Heather **accord** their schedules so they can work together.
   - (C) They want to make sure that Ms. Oppenheimer is in **accord** with their project. They will only go ahead with it if she agrees with their plan.
   - (D) Eventually, she **accords** them a good grade.

2. First, Ms. Oppenheimer makes them **elaborate** on their project.
   - (A) It is an **elaborate** undertaking, because Matthew and Heather have already gathered lots of data.
   - (B) It took them many hours to **elaborate** the project before they brought it to her, but the great effort will pay off.
   - (C) The complicated fifth step requires **elaborate** preparation.
   - (D) Matthew explains how the project will be set up, and then Heather begins to **elaborate** on the results they hope to get. Her detailed explanation impresses Ms. Oppenheimer.

EXERCISE 2 Word Analysis ✍

Prefixes

Directions. Read each numbered pair of words below. Then, circle the letter of the choice that best describes the meaning of the underlined prefix as it is used in each pair.

3. <u>co</u>incide <u>co</u>operate
   - (A) for
   - (B) together
   - (C) against
   - (D) between

4. <u>ap</u>proximate <u>ap</u>point
   - (A) to
   - (B) beyond
   - (C) across
   - (D) both

Suffixes

Directions. Read each numbered pair of words below. Then, circle the letter of the choice that best describes the meaning of the underlined suffix as it is used in each pair.

5. magni**tude**   alti**tude**
   - (A) state of being
   - (B) study of
   - (C) producing
   - (D) that which

6. radi**ate**   activ**ate**
   - (A) that which
   - (B) resembling
   - (C) to become
   - (D) pertaining to

Word Origins

Directions. Read each of the following sentences. Then, from the vocabulary list below, choose the word that best completes the sentence. Write the word in the blank.

abrupt	commit	infinite	probability
accord	confirm	kernel	radiate
approximate	debris	magnitude	random
chaos	elaborate	manual	repel
coincide	inert	mechanism	surplus

7. The Middle English word *cynel*, meaning "corn seed," became the Modern English
   word _____.

8. You may recognize the French word *debrisier*, meaning "to break to pieces," in our
   word _____.

9. It's easy to see the English word _____ in the Latin word *manualis*,
   meaning "pertaining to the hand."

10. The Latin word *probare*, meaning "to prove," is related in meaning to our word

    _____.

UNDERSTANDING NEW WORDS AND THEIR USES

Lesson 14 | CONTEXT: Change in Science and Technology

Making Decisions

EXERCISE 1 *Multimeaning*

Directions. Read each numbered sentence below. Then, circle the letter of the choice that uses the boldface word in the same way as it is used in the numbered sentence.

1. Whitney is discussing two ideas for a science project with her biology teacher; her final choice tends to **alternate** between the two.
   (A) She is taking chemistry as an **alternate** to general science next year.
   (B) She was an **alternate** delegate to the state science convention last year.
   (C) "I don't want to **alternate** back and forth," she says. "I want to make a decision as soon as possible."
   (D) Her teacher has an **alternate** proposal.

2. Ms. Oppenheimer **challenges** Whitney to take her suggestion.
   (A) The project Ms. Oppenheimer suggests will be a **challenge** to Whitney.
   (B) Whitney usually responds well to a **challenge**.
   (C) She **challenges** herself to do her best.
   (D) She takes Ms. Oppenheimer's suggestion as a **challenge**.

EXERCISE 2 *Word Analysis*

Prefixes

Directions. Read each numbered pair of words below. Then, circle the letter of the choice that best describes the meaning of the underlined prefix as it is used in each pair.

3. <u>in</u>credible   <u>in</u>secure
   (A) against
   (B) not
   (C) for
   (D) after

4. <u>un</u>predictable   <u>un</u>true
   (A) against
   (B) not
   (C) for
   (D) before

Suffixes

Directions. Read each numbered pair of words below. Then, circle the letter of the choice that best describes the meaning of the underlined suffix as it is used in each pair.

5. inquisit<u>ive</u>   destruct<u>ive</u>
   (A) becoming
   (B) tending to
   (C) resembling
   (D) somewhat

6. glob<u>al</u>   norm<u>al</u>
   (A) somewhat
   (B) pertaining to
   (C) study of
   (D) one who

Word Origins

Directions. Read each of the following sentences. Then, from the vocabulary list below, choose the word that best completes the sentence. Write the word in the blank.

aerial	ecosystem	glacial	tributary
alternate	effect	inquisitive	universal
barren	encounter	navigable	unpredictable
challenge	exotic	poach	via
diversity	geological	propel	vital

7. You may recognize the Old French word *encontrer*, meaning "to meet," in our word
   _____.

8. We get a hint of the meaning of the word _____ when we learn that the Latin word *via* means "road."

9. The Latin word *vita*, meaning "life," is closely related to our word
   _____.

10. You may recognize the Latin word *glacies*, meaning "ice," in our word
    _____.

UNDERSTANDING NEW WORDS AND THEIR USES

Lesson 15 | CONTEXT: Change in Science and Technology

Preparing the Presentation

EXERCISE 1 | *Multimeaning* ☞

Directions. Read each numbered sentence below. Then, circle the letter of the choice that uses the boldface word in the same way as it is used in the numbered sentence.

1. Douglas and Kate are **prompt** to arrive at the science fair.
   (A) As they make their presentation, they sometimes have to **prompt** each other.
   (B) Once Doug gave Kate the wrong **prompt,** and she jumped ahead in the presentation.
   (C) Kate was **prompt** to correct the error.
   (D) "Don't do that when we go to the state contest," Kate **prompts** Doug.

2. Kate thinks they should redesign some of their posters because the figures are out of **proportion**.
   (A) Doug reminds Kate that they need to **proportion** their time to cover what is important.
   (B) "The posters are only a small **proportion** of this project," warns Doug.
   (C) "What matters most is the **proportion** of the chemicals in our experiment."
   (D) "We have to **proportion** them carefully."

EXERCISE 2 | *Word Analysis* ☞

Prefixes

Directions. Read each numbered pair of words below. Then, circle the letter of the choice that best describes the meaning of the underlined prefix as it is used in each pair.

3. <u>pre</u>caution   <u>pre</u>dict
   (A) before
   (B) after
   (C) against
   (D) for

4. <u>in</u>voluntary   <u>in</u>valid
   (A) above
   (B) after
   (C) against
   (D) not

Suffixes

Directions. Read each numbered pair of words below. Then, circle the letter of the choice that best describes the meaning of the underlined suffix as it is used in each pair.

5. capac**ity**   pur**ity**
   (A) resembling
   (B) make
   (C) state of being
   (D) belief

6. prelimin**ary**   custom**ary**
   (A) relating to
   (B) full of
   (C) study of
   (D) resembling

Word Origins

Directions. Read each of the following sentences. Then, from the vocabulary list below, choose the word that best completes the sentence. Write the word in the blank.

capacity	intricate	precise	speculate
conifer	involuntary	preliminary	stability
digital	minimum	prompt	stationary
germinate	perpetual	proportion	submerge
intermediate	precaution	reception	

7. The Latin word *recipere*, meaning "to receive," is related to our word _____.

8. The Middle English word *stacionarye*, meaning "unmoving," became our Modern English word _____.

9. The French word *precis*, meaning "condensed," is related to our word _____.

10. We get a hint of the meaning of the word _____ when we learn that the Latin word *minimus* means "least."

Why We Practice Analogies

Practice with analogies builds logic skills. To answer analogy questions correctly, you think about two words and discover the relationship between them. Then you match that relationship with one shared by another pair of words. In addition, when you study analogies, you think about the precise meanings of words and fix these definitions in your memory.

Understanding Word Analogies

A word analogy is a comparison between two pairs of words. Here is how word analogies are written:

Example 1 FIND : LOCATE :: lose : misplace

The colon (:) stands for the phrase "is related to." Here is how to read the relationships in Example 1:

> FIND [is related to] LOCATE
> lose [is related to] misplace

The double colon [::] between the two pairs of words stands for the phrase "in the same way that." Here is how to read the complete analogy:

> FIND [is related to] LOCATE
> [in the same way that]
> lose [is related to] misplace

Here is another way:

> FIND is to LOCATE as lose is to misplace.

A properly constructed analogy, then, tells us that the relationship between the first pair of words is the same as the relationship between the second pair of words. In Example 1, *find* and *locate* are synonyms, just as *lose* and *misplace* are synonyms.

Let's look at another example:

Example 2 GIFT : JOY :: grief : tears

What is the relationship here? A *gift* causes *joy*, just as *grief* causes *tears*. These two pairs of words have the same relationship, a cause-and-effect relationship. The chart on page 156 will help you to identify analogy relationships. No chart could list all possible relationships between words, but the twelve relationships on the chart are the ones most often used. Also, they are the only relationships used in the analogy lessons.

TYPES OF ANALOGIES		
RELATIONSHIP	**EXAMPLE**	**EXPLANATION**
Synonym	DRY : ARID :: find : locate	*Dry* is similar in meaning to *arid*, just as *find* is similar in meaning to *locate*.
Antonym	KIND : CRUEL :: find : lose	A *kind* action is the opposite of a *cruel* action, just as to *find* something is the opposite of to *lose* it.
Cause and Effect	GIFT : JOY :: rain : flood	A *gift* can cause *joy*, just as *rain* can cause a *flood*.
Part and Whole	CHAPTER : BOOK :: fender : automobile	A *chapter* is a part of a *book*, just as a *fender* is a part of an *automobile*.
Classification	POLKA : DANCE :: frog : amphibian	A *polka* may be classified as a *dance*, just as a *frog* may be classified as an *amphibian*.
Characteristic Quality	PUPPIES : FURRY :: fish : slippery	*Puppies* are *furry*, just as *fish* are *slippery*.
Degree	CHUCKLE : LAUGH :: whimper : cry	A *chuckle* is a little *laugh*, just as a *whimper* is a little *cry*.
Function	KNIFE : CUT :: pen : write	The function of a *knife* is to *cut*, just as the function of a *pen* is to *write*.
Performer and Action	AUTHOR : WRITE :: chef : cook	You expect an *author* to *write*, just as you expect a *chef* to *cook*.
Performer and Object	CASHIER : CASH :: plumber : pipe	A *cashier* works with *cash*, just as a *plumber* works with *pipe*.
Action and Object	BOIL : EGG :: throw : ball	You *boil* an *egg*, just as you *throw* a *ball*.
Location	FISH : SEA :: moose : forest	A *fish* can be found in the *sea*, just as a *moose* can be found in a *forest*.

A Process for Solving Analogies

Your job in solving multiple-choice analogy questions is to identify the relationship between the first two words and then to find the pair of words that has the most similar relationship. Keep in mind that a word pair has the same relationship no matter in which order the two words appear. For example, both CHAPTER : BOOK and BOOK : CHAPTER have a part-and-whole relationship. Here is a hint for identifying relationships. Try using word pairs in the explanation sentences on the chart. When a word pair makes sense in the explanation sentence for a particular relationship, you have found the relationship that the two words have to each other.

Here is a process that will help you with analogy questions:

Answering Analogy Questions: A 4-Step Method

1. Identify the relationship between the capitalized pair of words.
2. Identify the relationship between the pair of words in each possible answer.
3. Eliminate answer choices that have relationships that do not match the relationship between the capitalized words.
4. Choose the remaining possible answer. This answer will have the same relationship as the capitalized pair.

Let's apply this pattern to a sample question.

Example 3

WRITE : PEN :: __*F*__   [*Function*]

(A) toe : foot __*PW*__   [*Part and Whole*—does not match]
(B) toss : salad __*AO*__   [*Action and Object*—does not match]
(C) gymnast : mat __*PO*__   [*Performer and Object*—does not match]
(D) sky : blue __*CQ*__   [*Characteristic Quality*—does not match]
(E) shine : sun __*F*__   [*Function*—does match]

None of relationships (A) through (D) match that of the capitalized pair. They can be eliminated. Choice E must be the correct answer. Notice that the words make sense in the explanation sentence: The function of a *pen* is to *write* just as the function of the *sun* is to *shine*.

A Final Word

Analogies are easier and more fun if you tackle them with a sense of adventure. Allow yourself to discover the relationship between the first pair of words and to explore the relationships between the words in the answer choices. Keep in mind that some words can represent more than one part of speech and that many words have several meanings. Remember, these little verbal puzzles call for flexibility as well as logic.

CONNECTING NEW WORDS AND PATTERNS

Lesson 1 | ANALOGIES

Directions. On each line, write the letter or letters that describe the type of relationship the words have to each other. Choose from the following types:

S synonym	**A** antonym	**PW** part and whole	**PA** performer and action
F function	**L** location	**CE** cause and effect	**PO** performer and object
D degree	**C** classification	**CQ** characteristic quality	**AO** action and object

Circle the letter of the pair of words that has the same relationship as the capitalized words. Each relationship is used no more than once in each numbered item.

1. ALIEN : FOREIGN :: ____
    (A) soap : clean ____
    (B) cushion : soft ____
    (C) ruby : gem ____
    (D) normal : usual ____
    (E) familiar : strange ____

2. DIPLOMATIC : TACTFUL :: ____
    (A) polite : well-mannered ____
    (B) bear : furry ____
    (C) mask : costume ____
    (D) increase : shrink ____
    (E) electrician : cable ____

3. GALAXY : STAR :: ____
    (A) German : language ____
    (B) bulb : lamp ____
    (C) thread : needle ____
    (D) accept : deny ____
    (E) secure : safe ____

4. GESTURE : EXPRESSIVE :: ____
    (A) dime : coin ____
    (B) lid : box ____
    (C) letter : written ____
    (D) piglet : farm ____
    (E) step : stomp ____

5. GHASTLY : UNPLEASANT :: ____
    (A) ballet dancer : costume ____
    (B) overpowering : strong ____
    (C) polish : silver ____
    (D) watch : wrist ____
    (E) lie : truth ____

6. LUMINOUS : STAR :: ____
    (A) winner : proud ____
    (B) injury : pain ____
    (C) pry : ask ____
    (D) page : book ____
    (E) bulldozer : push ____

7. OVERTURE : OPERA :: ____
    (A) purple : color ____
    (B) damage : repair ____
    (C) car : street ____
    (D) heal : cure ____
    (E) introduction : essay ____

8. PLANETARY : GLOBAL :: ____
    (A) strange : unfamiliar ____
    (B) caring : friend ____
    (C) tension : outburst ____
    (D) leg : table ____
    (E) cactus : desert ____

9. SATELLITE : MOON :: ____
    (A) hammer : nail ____
    (B) air conditioner : cool ____
    (C) criticize : praise ____
    (D) tailor : tape measure ____
    (E) star : sun ____

10. STELLAR : SUPERIOR :: ____
    (A) buckle : belt ____
    (B) dark : shadow ____
    (C) success : celebration ____
    (D) regular : ordinary ____
    (E) notice : ignore ____

CONNECTING NEW WORDS AND PATTERNS

Lesson 2 | ANALOGIES

Directions. On each line, write the letter or letters that describe the type of relationship the words have to each other. Choose from the following types:

S synonym	A antonym	PW part and whole	PA performer and action
F function	L location	CE cause and effect	PO performer and object
D degree	C classification	CQ characteristic quality	AO action and object

Circle the letter of the pair of words that has the same relationship as the capitalized words. Each relationship is used no more than once in each numbered item.

1. CONSEQUENCE : RESULT :: _____
   (A) swell : shrink _____
   (B) solution : answer _____
   (C) good : perfect _____
   (D) June : month _____
   (E) magician : wand _____

2. CONTROVERSIAL : POLITICS :: _____
   (A) patch : tear _____
   (B) remarkable : special _____
   (C) complicated : maze _____
   (D) satisfactory : excellent _____
   (E) practice : improvement _____

3. DEFIANT : COOPERATIVE :: _____
   (A) housekeeper : broom _____
   (B) hurtful : helpful _____
   (C) jump : leap _____
   (D) oil : hinge _____
   (E) puddle : muddy _____

4. DELIBERATE : PURPOSEFUL :: _____
   (A) blade : cut _____
   (B) instrument : flute _____
   (C) trotting : galloping _____
   (D) fortunate : lucky _____
   (E) attack : protect _____

5. DISTORT : TWIST :: _____
   (A) stingy : generous _____
   (B) orange : color _____
   (C) zebra : Africa _____
   (D) throw : toss _____
   (E) pharmacist : medicine _____

6. GROTESQUE : ODD :: _____
   (A) answer : question _____
   (B) day : year _____
   (C) dig : ditch _____
   (D) elementary : basic _____
   (E) deadly : harmful _____

7. INFERIOR : SUPERIOR :: _____
   (A) boring : interesting _____
   (B) debate : discuss _____
   (C) cold : freezing _____
   (D) bride : veil _____
   (E) tool : pliers _____

8. ORIGINALITY : FRESHNESS :: _____
   (A) polish : shoe _____
   (B) enthusiasm : eagerness _____
   (C) receiver : telephone _____
   (D) easy : difficult _____
   (E) lace : delicate _____

9. REALITY : FANTASY :: _____
   (A) fact : fiction _____
   (B) delegate : vote _____
   (C) rabbit : garden _____
   (D) injury : discomfort _____
   (E) squash : vegetable _____

10. RECOIL : RETREAT :: _____
    (A) begin : start _____
    (B) spinach : green _____
    (C) beginner : intermediate _____
    (D) ring : bell _____
    (E) ant : anthill _____

CONNECTING NEW WORDS AND PATTERNS

Lesson 3 | ANALOGIES

Directions. On each line, write the letter or letters that describe the type of relationship the words have to each other. Choose from the following types:

S synonym	A antonym	PW part and whole	PA performer and action
F function	L location	CE cause and effect	PO performer and object
D degree	C classification	CQ characteristic quality	AO action and object

Circle the letter of the pair of words that has the same relationship as the capitalized words. Each relationship is used no more than once in each numbered item.

1. CANDID : FRANK :: ____
   (A) lime : sour ____
   (B) sport : baseball ____
   (C) mouthpiece : trumpet ____
   (D) beautician : mirror ____
   (E) honest : truthful ____

2. DIAPHRAGM : MUSCLE :: ____
   (A) kickstand : bike ____
   (B) lawn mower : mow ____
   (C) seeing-eye dog : accompany ____
   (D) peach : fruit ____
   (E) annoyed : fuming ____

3. HAUNT : GHOST :: ____
   (A) touch : feel ____
   (B) optician : glasses ____
   (C) trick : leprechaun ____
   (D) orange : fruit ____
   (E) loudspeaker : stereo ____

4. HOVER : HUMMINGBIRD :: ____
   (A) concerned : alarmed ____
   (B) play : violin ____
   (C) scamper : squirrel ____
   (D) trip : stumble ____
   (E) grapes : vineyard ____

5. IDLE : BUSY :: ____
   (A) psychiatrist : couch ____
   (B) wheel : round ____
   (C) key : unlock ____
   (D) season : winter ____
   (E) serious : joking ____

6. IGNORANCE : KNOWLEDGE :: ____
   (A) raining : pouring ____
   (B) boil : water ____
   (C) eagle : soar ____
   (D) health : sickness ____
   (E) refrigerator : chill ____

7. LEASH : DOG TRAINER :: ____
   (A) wash : dishes ____
   (B) rooster : farm ____
   (C) balance beam : gymnast ____
   (D) ice : frozen ____
   (E) dentist : examine ____

8. LENIENT : STRICT :: ____
   (A) sweet : honey ____
   (B) sorrow : weep ____
   (C) viola : instrument ____
   (D) harsh : mild ____
   (E) slam : door ____

9. MODEST : VAIN :: ____
   (A) frisky : lively ____
   (B) fearless : afraid ____
   (C) eye : see ____
   (D) sticky : jelly ____
   (E) jig : dance ____

10. SUBTLE : OBVIOUS :: ____
    (A) clear : confused ____
    (B) salt : shaker ____
    (C) hate : emotion ____
    (D) bake : aroma ____
    (E) look : stare ____

CONNECTING NEW WORDS AND PATTERNS

Lesson 4 | ANALOGIES

Directions. On each line, write the letter or letters that describe the type of relationship the words have to each other. Choose from the following types:

S synonym	A antonym	PW part and whole	PA performer and action
F function	L location	CE cause and effect	PO performer and object
D degree	C classification	CQ characteristic quality	AO action and object

Circle the letter of the pair of words that has the same relationship as the capitalized words. Each relationship is used no more than once in each numbered item.

1. AGGRAVATE : IMPROVE :: ____
   (A) appreciation : gratitude ____
   (B) pen : write ____
   (C) damage : repair ____
   (D) paragraph : sentence ____
   (E) accountant : calculator ____

2. DASHING : STYLISH :: ____
   (A) late : early ____
   (B) house : window ____
   (C) barber : shave ____
   (D) lively : exciting ____
   (E) mixer : blend ____

3. DISMAL : CHEERFUL :: ____
   (A) disappointed : delighted ____
   (B) toss : ball ____
   (C) earthquake : chaos ____
   (D) cashier : cash register ____
   (E) game : entertain ____

4. FLAW : DEFECT :: ____
   (A) simmer : boil ____
   (B) siren : warn ____
   (C) error : mistake ____
   (D) leg : chair ____
   (E) table : furniture ____

5. FRAIL : STURDY :: ____
   (A) vain : conceited ____
   (B) danger : fear ____
   (C) wet : dry ____
   (D) month : July ____
   (E) card catalog : library ____

6. MAINTAIN : NEGLECT :: ____
   (A) waltz : dance ____
   (B) create : destroy ____
   (C) demolish : harm ____
   (D) car : engine ____
   (E) banker : money ____

7. OBLIGATION : DUTY :: ____
   (A) teacher : instruct ____
   (B) task : job ____
   (C) minute : hour ____
   (D) ruler : measure ____
   (E) pat : slap ____

8. PHASE : STAGE :: ____
   (A) zone : area ____
   (B) fort : protect ____
   (C) collar : shirt ____
   (D) smooth : mirror ____
   (E) subject : mathematics ____

9. SPONTANEOUS : LAUGHTER :: ____
   (A) speak : shout ____
   (B) clear : blurry ____
   (C) color : pink ____
   (D) joyous : celebration ____
   (E) garden : vegetables ____

10. TIRESOME : BORING :: ____
    (A) cut : bleed ____
    (B) row : boat ____
    (C) cherry : stem ____
    (D) bumpy : smooth ____
    (E) irritable : touchy ____

CONNECTING NEW WORDS AND PATTERNS

Lesson 5 ANALOGIES

Directions. On each line, write the letter or letters that describe the type of relationship the words have to each other. Choose from the following types:

S synonym   A antonym   PW part and whole   PA performer and action
F function   L location   CE cause and effect   PO performer and object
D degree   C classification   CQ characteristic quality   AO action and object

Circle the letter of the pair of words that has the same relationship as the capitalized words. Each relationship is used no more than once in each numbered item.

1. CONSISTENT : REGULAR :: ____
   (A) draw : picture ____
   (B) usual : ordinary ____
   (C) member : club ____
   (D) skyscraper : building ____
   (E) singer : microphone ____

2. CONTEMPLATE : CONSIDER :: ____
   (A) admit : confess ____
   (B) blender : appliance ____
   (C) study : look ____
   (D) snow : cold ____
   (E) lie : distrust ____

3. CRUCIAL : UNIMPORTANT :: ____
   (A) vacant : empty ____
   (B) underground : coal ____
   (C) rose : flower ____
   (D) robbery : loss ____
   (E) loud : silent ____

4. FORMAL : TUXEDO :: ____
   (A) goat : chew ____
   (B) beautiful : ugly ____
   (C) smooth : satin ____
   (D) sculpture : museum ____
   (E) steering wheel : car ____

5. INDISPENSABLE : ESSENTIAL :: ____
   (A) strike : match ____
   (B) basketball : sport ____
   (C) under : above ____
   (D) nice : pleasant ____
   (E) horse : trot ____

6. INTERPRET : SYMBOLS :: ____
   (A) assemble : gather ____
   (B) pasture : cow ____
   (C) peek : search ____
   (D) deliver : speech ____
   (E) squeal : pig ____

7. LEGENDARY : WELL KNOWN :: ____
   (A) demand : request ____
   (B) pass : test ____
   (C) major : minor ____
   (D) cowboy : hat ____
   (E) eggs : nest ____

8. MYTH : TRADITIONAL :: ____
   (A) gymnast : mat ____
   (B) polite : rude ____
   (C) newspaper : inform ____
   (D) feather : light ____
   (E) damp : soaked ____

9. MYTHOLOGY : LEGEND :: ____
   (A) wrinkled : smooth ____
   (B) cat : tail ____
   (C) flowers : greenhouse ____
   (D) lead : dense ____
   (E) traffic light : regulate ____

10. VIGOR : STRENGTH :: ____
    (A) delicateness : fragility ____
    (B) textbook : book ____
    (C) train : transport ____
    (D) shark : ocean ____
    (E) uncertainty : pause ____

CONNECTING NEW WORDS AND PATTERNS

Lesson 6 ANALOGIES

Directions. On each line, write the letter or letters that describe the type of relationship the words have to each other. Choose from the following types:

S synonym	A antonym	PW part and whole	PA performer and action
F function	L location	CE cause and effect	PO performer and object
D degree	C classification	CQ characteristic quality	AO action and object

Circle the letter of the pair of words that has the same relationship as the capitalized words. Each relationship is used no more than once in each numbered item.

1. GUARANTEE : PROMISE :: ____
    (A) sign : indication ____
    (B) transplant : tree ____
    (C) sailor : harbor ____
    (D) cover up : bury ____
    (E) desert : dry ____

2. HYPOCRITE : INSINCERE :: ____
    (A) pop : explode ____
    (B) caboose : train ____
    (C) thief : dishonest ____
    (D) enjoyable : pleasant ____
    (E) bouquet : bride ____

3. ILLUSTRIOUS : FAMOUS :: ____
    (A) saxophone : instrument ____
    (B) king : govern ____
    (C) full : overflowing ____
    (D) palace : queen ____
    (E) silly : foolish ____

4. INDEFINITE : CERTAIN :: ____
    (A) leap : dancer ____
    (B) confusing : clear ____
    (C) cockpit : plane ____
    (D) glove : protect ____
    (E) ending : conclusion ____

5. INITIAL : NAME :: ____
    (A) title : book ____
    (B) final : last ____
    (C) weaken : collapse ____
    (D) earn : salary ____
    (E) diamond : hard ____

6. MERIT : WORTH :: ____
    (A) keyboard : computer ____
    (B) electric blanket : heat ____
    (C) ability : skill ____
    (D) challenging : impossible ____
    (E) cheerleader : megaphone ____

7. MODERATE : MILD :: ____
    (A) starved : hungry ____
    (B) rudder : sailboat ____
    (C) easy : simple ____
    (D) nourishment : growth ____
    (E) fruit : pear ____

8. MOMENTARY : PERMANENT :: ____
    (A) photographer : camera ____
    (B) hot : flame ____
    (C) allowed : permitted ____
    (D) beach : shell ____
    (E) brief : endless ____

9. PARTIAL : UNFAIR :: ____
    (A) raw : uncooked ____
    (B) fair : stormy ____
    (C) sky : blue ____
    (D) violet : color ____
    (E) jungle : monkey ____

10. VETO : PROPOSAL :: ____
    (A) trickery : distrust ____
    (B) evergreen : tree ____
    (C) accept : invitation ____
    (D) scheme : plot ____
    (E) violinist : violin ____

CONNECTING NEW WORDS AND PATTERNS

Lesson 7 ANALOGIES

Directions. On each line, write the letter or letters that describe the type of relationship the words have to each other. Choose from the following types:

S synonym	A antonym	PW part and whole	PA performer and action
F function	L location	CE cause and effect	PO performer and object
D degree	C classification	CQ characteristic quality	AO action and object

Circle the letter of the pair of words that has the same relationship as the capitalized words. Each relationship is used no more than once in each numbered item.

1. CREDIBLE : BELIEVABLE :: _____
   (A) heart : organ _____
   (B) concert : auditorium _____
   (C) bright : blinding _____
   (D) loyal : faithful _____
   (E) nose : smell _____

2. FACULTY : TEACHER :: _____
   (A) planet : space _____
   (B) guppy : fish _____
   (C) sketch : draw _____
   (D) lifeguard : save _____
   (E) choir : singer _____

3. FORUM : PUBLIC :: _____
   (A) water : boil _____
   (B) soda : beverage _____
   (C) garbage : smelly _____
   (D) antenna : radio _____
   (E) doubt : believe _____

4. JOURNAL : DIARY :: _____
   (A) maple : tree _____
   (B) cabinet : shelf _____
   (C) tale : story _____
   (D) peanut butter : sticky _____
   (E) sunburn : pain _____

5. LEGIBLE : READABLE :: _____
   (A) gentle : tender _____
   (B) spade : dig _____
   (C) petal : flower _____
   (D) feather : soft _____
   (E) exercise : sweat _____

6. LITERARY : AUTHOR :: _____
   (A) radiator : heat _____
   (B) goat : mammal _____
   (C) food : kitchen _____
   (D) lens : glasses _____
   (E) scientific : chemist _____

7. MANUSCRIPT : WRITER :: _____
   (A) itch : scratch _____
   (B) recipe : chef _____
   (C) pendulum : clock _____
   (D) politician : speak _____
   (E) give : receive _____

8. MASTERY : PRACTICE :: _____
   (A) Dalmatian : dog _____
   (B) memorization : repetition _____
   (C) trail : highway _____
   (D) bake : bread _____
   (E) remember : forget _____

9. PERSUASION : OPINION :: _____
   (A) call : cab _____
   (B) crack : shatter _____
   (C) ice : slippery _____
   (D) thought : idea _____
   (E) easel : studio _____

10. TUTOR : TEACH :: _____
    (A) start : finish _____
    (B) chef : cook _____
    (C) performer : entertain _____
    (D) worry : despair _____
    (E) butcher : knife _____

CONNECTING NEW WORDS AND PATTERNS

Lesson 8 | ANALOGIES

Directions. On each line, write the letter or letters that describe the type of relationship the words have to each other. Choose from the following types:

S synonym   A antonym   PW part and whole   PA performer and action
F function   L location   CE cause and effect   PO performer and object
D degree   C classification   CQ characteristic quality   AO action and object

Circle the letter of the pair of words that has the same relationship as the capitalized words. Each relationship is used no more than once in each numbered item.

1. ADHERE : STICK :: _____
  (A) hint : suggest _____
  (B) zipper : close _____
  (C) giraffe : tall _____
  (D) painter : brush _____
  (E) bats : attic _____

2. EXPAND : CONTRACT :: _____
  (A) grouchy : crabby _____
  (B) banana : yellow _____
  (C) grow : wither _____
  (D) strange : outrageous _____
  (E) camels : desert _____

3. FATIGUE : EXHAUSTION :: _____
  (A) protect : bandage _____
  (B) boats : bay _____
  (C) windshield : car _____
  (D) energy : power _____
  (E) foolishness : annoyance _____

4. FORBIDDING : INVITING :: _____
  (A) finger : hand _____
  (B) wave : flag _____
  (C) joke : laughter _____
  (D) soggy : damp _____
  (E) opposite : identical _____

5. EXCEL : STUDENT :: _____
  (A) manual : instruct _____
  (B) separate : divide _____
  (C) build : carpenter _____
  (D) step : stairs _____
  (E) triangle : shape _____

6. HARDY : WEAK :: _____
  (A) odd : strange _____
  (B) apple : fruit _____
  (C) mischievous : wicked _____
  (D) chapter : novel _____
  (E) dry : moist _____

7. OPPONENT : TEAMMATE :: _____
  (A) circular : round _____
  (B) answer : telephone _____
  (C) butterfly : delicate _____
  (D) ferry : boat _____
  (E) enemy : friend _____

8. PURSUE : CHASE :: _____
  (A) sculptor : statue _____
  (B) start : begin _____
  (C) bushes : trim _____
  (D) mouse : small _____
  (E) ant : insect _____

9. RECOMMEND : ADVISE :: _____
  (A) handle : mug _____
  (B) plaid : kilt _____
  (C) gem : opal _____
  (D) order : command _____
  (E) tense : relax _____

10. SCHOLARSHIP : STUDENT :: _____
  (A) needless : necessary _____
  (B) stanza : poem _____
  (C) paycheck : employee _____
  (D) scissors : cut _____
  (E) jet : airport _____

CONNECTING NEW WORDS AND PATTERNS

Lesson 9 ANALOGIES

Directions. On each line, write the letter or letters that describe the type of relationship the words have to each other. Choose from the following types:

S	synonym	A	antonym	PW	part and whole	PA	performer and action
F	function	L	location	CE	cause and effect	PO	performer and object
D	degree	C	classification	CQ	characteristic quality	AO	action and object

Circle the letter of the pair of words that has the same relationship as the capitalized words. Each relationship is used no more than once in each numbered item.

1. ACUTE : SHARP :: _____
   (A) mound : hill _____
   (B) bees : hive _____
   (C) plain : simple _____
   (D) join : split _____
   (E) frost : white _____

2. ADOPT : PLAN :: _____
   (A) cat : scratch _____
   (B) dungeon : dark _____
   (C) borrow : book _____
   (D) farmer : crop _____
   (E) gill : fish _____

3. ANGUISH : AGONY :: _____
   (A) magician : entertain _____
   (B) sailboat : boat _____
   (C) hinge : door _____
   (D) happiness : joy _____
   (E) fan : breeze _____

4. HESITATION : UNCERTAINTY :: _____
   (A) electron : atom _____
   (B) oak : wood _____
   (C) ending : conclusion _____
   (D) lie : truth _____
   (E) damage : storm _____

5. HYSTERICAL : WILD :: _____
   (A) virus : common cold _____
   (B) tame : gentle _____
   (C) condemn : praise _____
   (D) wheels : car _____
   (E) pacifier : baby _____

6. IRRITABLE : CALM :: _____
   (A) crow : black _____
   (B) cotton : fabric _____
   (C) evil : good _____
   (D) cactus : desert _____
   (E) disturbing : troubling _____

7. RIDICULE : EMBARRASSMENT :: _____
   (A) illness : sickness _____
   (B) city : countryside _____
   (C) mechanic : repair _____
   (D) praise : confidence _____
   (E) climb : tree _____

8. TIMID : CONFIDENT :: _____
   (A) scene : play _____
   (B) gray : elephant _____
   (C) chickenpox : disease _____
   (D) attached : separated _____
   (E) corridor : hall _____

9. VAGUE : DEFINITE :: _____
   (A) overcast : clear _____
   (B) dissatisfied : miserable _____
   (C) elementary : simple _____
   (D) mumps : discomfort _____
   (E) duck : quack _____

10. WRETCHED : UNHAPPY :: _____
    (A) stylish : fashionable _____
    (B) work : weariness _____
    (C) neighborhood : park _____
    (D) excellent : adequate _____
    (E) sand : gritty _____

CONNECTING NEW WORDS AND PATTERNS

Lesson 10 ANALOGIES

Directions. On each line, write the letter or letters that describe the type of relationship the words have to each other. Choose from the following types:

S synonym   A antonym   PW part and whole   PA performer and action
F function   L location   CE cause and effect   PO performer and object
D degree   C classification   CQ characteristic quality   AO action and object

Circle the letter of the pair of words that has the same relationship as the capitalized words. Each relationship is used no more than once in each numbered item.

1. BARBAROUS : CRUEL :: _____
   (A) polite : well-mannered _____
   (B) lawn : green _____
   (C) polluted : pure _____
   (D) collar : coat _____
   (E) melon : fruit _____

2. BARON : NOBLEMAN :: _____
   (A) poorly : badly _____
   (B) acrobat : balance _____
   (C) muffler : car _____
   (D) truck : vehicle _____
   (E) football : rough _____

3. CULTURAL : EDUCATIONAL :: _____
   (A) story : tale _____
   (B) money : buy _____
   (C) outside : inside _____
   (D) bulldozer : construction site _____
   (E) trunk : tree _____

4. FORTRESS : PROTECT :: _____
   (A) microscope : laboratory _____
   (B) grow : shrink _____
   (C) weapon : harm _____
   (D) direct : instruct _____
   (E) mouthpiece : clarinet _____

5. GRANDEUR : MAGNIFICENCE :: _____
   (A) ball : round _____
   (B) checkers : game _____
   (C) oven : bake _____
   (D) carelessness : accident _____
   (E) courage : bravery _____

6. MONARCHY : GOVERNMENT :: _____
   (A) sickness : weakness _____
   (B) sweater : woolly _____
   (C) French : language _____
   (D) sharpen : pencil _____
   (E) mechanic : car _____

7. PERILOUS : SAFE :: _____
   (A) uneasy : calm _____
   (B) lint : fluff _____
   (C) pout : weep _____
   (D) litterbug : toss _____
   (E) oboe : instrument _____

8. TOIL : EXHAUSTION :: _____
   (A) abandoned : vacant _____
   (B) grubby : clean _____
   (C) popcorn : snack food _____
   (D) foot : bed _____
   (E) success : pride _____

9. TYRANT : UNJUST :: _____
   (A) winter : season _____
   (B) velvet : soft _____
   (C) crane : lift _____
   (D) teacher : instruct _____
   (E) whale : ocean _____

10. VENGEANCE : FORGIVENESS :: _____
    (A) hand : glove _____
    (B) jockey : saddle _____
    (C) cinnamon : spice _____
    (D) roughness : smoothness _____
    (E) row : boat _____

CONNECTING NEW WORDS AND PATTERNS

Lesson 11 ANALOGIES

Directions. On each line, write the letter or letters that describe the type of relationship the words have to each other. Choose from the following types:

S synonym	A antonym	PW part and whole	PA performer and action
F function	L location	CE cause and effect	PO performer and object
D degree	C classification	CQ characteristic quality	AO action and object

Circle the letter of the pair of words that has the same relationship as the capitalized words. Each relationship is used no more than once in each numbered item.

1. EDIBLE : POISONOUS :: ____
  (A) nasty : dirty ____
  (B) baby : bib ____
  (C) fresh : stale ____
  (D) milk : white ____
  (E) lifeguard : save ____

2. ENDURANCE : PATIENCE :: ____
  (A) librarian : book ____
  (B) second : minute ____
  (C) truthfulness : honesty ____
  (D) letter : mailbox ____
  (E) ketchup : red ____

3. GLUCOSE : SUGAR :: ____
  (A) sherbet : cold ____
  (B) spaghetti : food ____
  (C) untruth : lie ____
  (D) microscope : magnify ____
  (E) tiredness : yawn ____

4. HABITAT : NATURAL :: ____
  (A) ocean : deep ____
  (B) soiled : dirty ____
  (C) failure : disappointment ____
  (D) sweet : sour ____
  (E) fasten : nail ____

5. MAMMAL : WHALE :: ____
  (A) punishment : discomfort ____
  (B) insect : termite ____
  (C) driver : truck ____
  (D) pop : balloon ____
  (E) bump : crash ____

6. NATURALIST : TREE :: ____
  (A) racehorse : swift ____
  (B) peak : mountain ____
  (C) report : crime ____
  (D) counselor : advise ____
  (E) beautician : hair ____

7. NUTRITION : NOURISH :: ____
  (A) mustard : yellow ____
  (B) bread : sandwich ____
  (C) whisper : talk ____
  (D) exercise : strengthen ____
  (E) play : piano ____

8. ORGANISM : LIVING THING :: ____
  (A) organist : organ ____
  (B) cold : shiver ____
  (C) pants : trousers ____
  (D) injury : painful ____
  (E) blackboard : classroom ____

9. TEMPERATE : MILD :: ____
  (A) lamp : table ____
  (B) excited : thrilled ____
  (C) trout : fish ____
  (D) lettuce : salad ____
  (E) ride : bicycle ____

10. ZOOLOGY : SCIENCE :: ____
  (A) swift : slow ____
  (B) German : language ____
  (C) dietitian : meal ____
  (D) cemetery : graveyard ____
  (E) busy : frantic ____

CONNECTING NEW WORDS AND PATTERNS

Lesson 12 | ANALOGIES

Directions. On each line, write the letter or letters that describe the type of relationship the words have to each other. Choose from the following types:

S synonym	A antonym	PW part and whole	PA performer and action
F function	L location	CE cause and effect	PO performer and object
D degree	C classification	CQ characteristic quality	AO action and object

Circle the letter of the pair of words that has the same relationship as the capitalized words. Each relationship is used no more than once in each numbered item.

1. CANCEL : APPOINTMENT :: ____
   (A) diamond : gem ____
   (B) air conditioner : cool ____
   (C) plan : party ____
   (D) fern : forest ____
   (E) foundation : building ____

2. COMPETENT : EXCELLENT :: ____
   (A) metal : hard ____
   (B) lick : envelope ____
   (C) naughty : evil ____
   (D) foot : mile ____
   (E) red : color ____

3. EFFICIENCY : WASTEFULNESS :: ____
   (A) lily : plant life ____
   (B) child : toy ____
   (C) long : lengthy ____
   (D) tender : rough ____
   (E) overeating : bellyache ____

4. FUNDAMENTAL : BASIC :: ____
   (A) reader : skim ____
   (B) difficult : hard ____
   (C) train : transport ____
   (D) dry : wet ____
   (E) polar bear : Arctic ____

5. FUTILE : EFFECTIVE :: ____
   (A) toddler : walk ____
   (B) valuable : worthless ____
   (C) sweater : clothing ____
   (D) paint : house ____
   (E) keys : piano ____

6. LOGICAL : REASONABLE :: ____
   (A) practice : improvement ____
   (B) student : textbook ____
   (C) type : novelist ____
   (D) tail : kite ____
   (E) keen : sharp ____

7. MEMORANDUM : REMIND :: ____
   (A) inch : foot ____
   (B) carpenter : measure ____
   (C) night : dark ____
   (D) story : entertain ____
   (E) fold : clothes ____

8. RECOGNITION : PRIDE :: ____
   (A) beach : sandy ____
   (B) approval : pleasure ____
   (C) boxing : sport ____
   (D) baker : oven ____
   (E) hay : field ____

9. STATIONERY : DESK :: ____
   (A) staples : attach ____
   (B) folders : file cabinet ____
   (C) talk : yell ____
   (D) jungle : green ____
   (E) cellar : basement ____

10. UTILITY : ELECTRICITY :: ____
    (A) glass : juice ____
    (B) climb : tree ____
    (C) instrument : piano ____
    (D) stream : river ____
    (E) ear : hear ____

Name _____ Date _____ Class _____

CONNECTING NEW WORDS AND PATTERNS

Lesson 13 | ANALOGIES

Directions. On each line, write the letter or letters that describe the type of relationship the words have to each other. Choose from the following types:

S synonym   A antonym   PW part and whole   PA performer and action
F function L location   CE cause and effect   PO performer and object
D degree   C classification CQ characteristic quality AO action and object

Circle the letter of the pair of words that has the same relationship as the capitalized words. Each relationship is used no more than once in each numbered item.

1. ABRUPT : CLIFF :: ____
   (A) deck : ship ____
   (B) bell : alert ____
   (C) high : peak ____
   (D) enter : invade ____
   (E) member : join ____

2. DEBRIS : DESTRUCTION :: ____
   (A) effort : attempt ____
   (B) ashes : fire ____
   (C) apply : wallpaper ____
   (D) general : lead ____
   (E) branch : tree ____

3. DIVERSITY : VARIETY :: ____
   (A) break : repair ____
   (B) basketball : round ____
   (C) conductor : direct ____
   (D) sign : agreement ____
   (E) regular : everyday ____

4. ELABORATE : COMPLICATED :: ____
   (A) safety pin : fastener ____
   (B) cut : pain ____
   (C) tape : sticky ____
   (D) ornamented : decorated ____
   (E) fountain : park ____

5. INFINITE : LIMITED :: ____
   (A) soldier : uniform ____
   (B) shower : cleanse ____
   (C) dusk : twilight ____
   (D) lengthy : brief ____
   (E) dip : soak ____

6. KERNEL : CENTRAL :: ____
   (A) coin : toss ____
   (B) plate : circular ____
   (C) chair : furniture ____
   (D) seize : grab ____
   (E) release : capture ____

7. MANUAL : INSTRUCT :: ____
   (A) glance : stare ____
   (B) daisy : flower ____
   (C) wheelchair : transport ____
   (D) purchase : buy ____
   (E) bench : park ____

8. MECHANISM : CLOCK :: ____
   (A) tennis : sport ____
   (B) attract : magnet ____
   (C) genius : smart ____
   (D) skeleton : body ____
   (E) shut : slam ____

9. REPEL : ATTRACT :: ____
   (A) push : pull ____
   (B) jury : decide ____
   (C) table : flat ____
   (D) beg : ask ____
   (E) press : steam iron ____

10. SURPLUS : EXTRA :: ____
    (A) athlete : exercise ____
    (B) England : country ____
    (C) crooked : bent ____
    (D) lightning rod : roof ____
    (E) clown : shoes ____

170 CONNECTING NEW WORDS AND PATTERNS

Name _____ Date _____ Class _____

Lesson 14 ANALOGIES

Directions. On each line, write the letter or letters that describe the type of relationship the words have to each other. Choose from the following types:

S synonym	A antonym	PW part and whole	PA performer and action
F function	L location	CE cause and effect	PO performer and object
D degree	C classification	CQ characteristic quality	AO action and object

Circle the letter of the pair of words that has the same relationship as the capitalized words. Each relationship is used no more than once in each numbered item.

1. BARREN : FERTILE :: ____
   (A) shine : shoes ____
   (B) roof : cover ____
   (C) musician : instrument ____
   (D) poor : rich ____
   (E) flower : delicate ____

2. ENCOUNTER : UNEXPECTED :: ____
   (A) audience : clap ____
   (B) press : smash ____
   (C) volleyball : game ____
   (D) party : entertaining ____
   (E) clown : balloon ____

3. EXOTIC : FOREIGN :: ____
   (A) knee : leg ____
   (B) shaded : blackened ____
   (C) regular : ordinary ____
   (D) sleep : restful ____
   (E) cat : pounce ____

4. INQUISITIVE : CHIMPANZEE :: ____
   (A) August : month ____
   (B) stretch : elastic ____
   (C) comfort : luxury ____
   (D) slippery : eel ____
   (E) firehouse : firetruck ____

5. NAVIGABLE : OCEAN :: ____
   (A) comb : hair ____
   (B) shrill : whistle ____
   (C) high : highest ____
   (D) chrysanthemum : flower ____
   (E) mane : horse ____

6. POACH : HUNTER :: ____
   (A) doll : toy ____
   (B) polish : luster ____
   (C) gorgeous : attractive ____
   (D) heal : doctor ____
   (E) coins : round ____

7. PROPEL : PROPELLER :: ____
   (A) juggler : ball ____
   (B) laces : shoes ____
   (C) steer : rudder ____
   (D) delighted : satisfied ____
   (E) glass : breakable ____

8. TRIBUTARY : RIVER :: ____
   (A) scoutmaster : lead ____
   (B) crab : beach ____
   (C) rake : leaves ____
   (D) highway : road ____
   (E) fire : panic ____

9. UNPREDICTABLE : SURPRISE :: ____
   (A) hot : fire ____
   (B) bed : furniture ____
   (C) dishes : kitchen ____
   (D) stove : cook ____
   (E) joy : glee ____

10. VITAL : ESSENTIAL :: ____
    (A) riot : destruction ____
    (B) key : unlock ____
    (C) wanted : desired ____
    (D) soap : sink ____
    (E) door : cabinet ____

CONNECTING NEW WORDS AND PATTERNS

Lesson 15 ANALOGIES

Directions. On each line, write the letter or letters that describe the type of relationship the words have to each other. Choose from the following types:

S synonym	A antonym	PW part and whole	PA performer and action
F function	L location	CE cause and effect	PO performer and object
D degree	C classification	CQ characteristic quality	AO action and object

Circle the letter of the pair of words that has the same relationship as the capitalized words. Each relationship is used no more than once in each numbered item.

1. DISCRIMINATION : FAIRNESS :: _____
   - (A) golfer : golf ball _____
   - (B) finish : begin _____
   - (C) ice : cold _____
   - (D) wasp : insect _____
   - (E) poison ivy : itch _____

2. INTRICATE : SIMPLE :: _____
   - (A) lumberjack : chop _____
   - (B) horse : pasture _____
   - (C) fancy : plain _____
   - (D) knight : brave _____
   - (E) tooth : comb _____

3. INVOLUNTARY : HICCUP :: _____
   - (A) bighorn sheep : mountain _____
   - (B) tattered : ragged _____
   - (C) sweep : floor _____
   - (D) gardener : shrub _____
   - (E) voluntary : enlistment _____

4. PERPETUAL : ETERNAL :: _____
   - (A) challenging : impossible _____
   - (B) roots : plant _____
   - (C) death : sorrow _____
   - (D) raisin : sweet _____
   - (E) attached : joined _____

5. PRECAUTION : SAFETY :: _____
   - (A) shirt : clothing _____
   - (B) Cinderella : slipper _____
   - (C) kite : sky _____
   - (D) sleeplessness : tiredness _____
   - (E) flipper : whale _____

6. PROMPT : QUICK :: _____
   - (A) line : poem _____
   - (B) neat : spotless _____
   - (C) bomb : destruction _____
   - (D) safe : secure _____
   - (E) chess : game _____

7. RELINQUISH : SURRENDER :: _____
   - (A) pour : cement _____
   - (B) baby : cry _____
   - (C) antenna : receive _____
   - (D) arrive : leave _____
   - (E) clue : hint _____

8. SPECULATE : THINK :: _____
   - (A) ask : request _____
   - (B) page : book _____
   - (C) cards : amuse _____
   - (D) dancer : performer _____
   - (E) bake : potato _____

9. STATIONARY : MOVABLE :: _____
   - (A) shovel : dirt _____
   - (B) needle : sharp _____
   - (C) broken : fixed _____
   - (D) friction : heat _____
   - (E) helmet : protect _____

10. SUBMERGED : SUNKEN SHIP :: _____
    - (A) singer : microphone _____
    - (B) spinning : dizziness _____
    - (C) nightingale : bird _____
    - (D) buried : treasure _____
    - (E) clothing : closet _____

Why We Read Strategically

Reading is active. As you read, you step into the writer's world. When you come across a new idea, you usually look for a clue to help you determine the writer's meaning. You move ahead to see if the idea is explained, or you retrace your steps to look for any signs you missed.

You can use these same strategies to build your vocabulary. If you do not know the meaning of a word, you should look in the passage surrounding the word for hints. These hints are called context clues. The more you practice hunting for context clues, the better you become at reading new words, and the larger your vocabulary will grow. Remember, strengthening your vocabulary skills will help you to score higher on standardized vocabulary tests.

The following reading selection shows the kinds of context clues you will find in the Reading New Words in Context lessons.

Strategic Reading: An Example

Long, long ago, long before there were humans on Earth—much less humans who could record history—dinosaurs walked the earth. During these **prehistoric** times, strange and wonderful creatures ruled the entire earth. All in all, *this* **reign** lasted 135 million years.

Note that a *summary* indicates the meaning of **prehistoric**.

A *pronoun* (*this*) refers us to the meaning of **reign**.

The dinosaur was one **descendant** of the thecodonts, mighty reptiles whose *later generations* also included many other reptiles, as well as all of today's birds. One of these relatives was a huge flying reptile. Another was a creature with a body like that of a turtle but with a 25-foot-long neck. Like the dinosaurs, these unusual *and* **extraordinary** creatures became extinct. Any of these creatures has the power to *stun,* **astonish,** *and amaze* us, but it is the dinosaurs that most people find especially fascinating.

The meaning of **descendant** is made clear through *restatement,* that is, through saying the same thing in a different way.

A *coordinating conjunction* (*and*) provides a clue to the meaning of **extraordinary**. The words *but, or,* and *nor* are other coordinating conjunctions.

Note that a clue to the meaning of **astonish** is provided by using the word in a *series* of words that have similar meanings.

Some dinosaurs were **mammoth** creatures. *The euhelopus, for example, was 60 feet tall and weighed 50,000 pounds.* In contrast, the 20-foot, 7,000-pound stegosaurus seems almost small. Although enormous size *was* a **characteristic** of many dinosaurs, others were much, much smaller, no bigger than a chicken or a duck. Some of these smaller ones looked much like either the iguana or the komodo dragon, two reptiles that inhabit Earth today.

An *example* provides the key to understanding **mammoth**.

A form of the verb *to be* (*was*) links an example of a quality to the word **characteristic**.

Some of the dinosaurs were fierce, meat-eating creatures. Often, other *milder and gentler dinosaurs were unable to defend themselves from the more savage ones and thus became their* **victims**. Even the vegetarian dinosaurs who roamed about peacefully snacking on plants could be quite frightening to other species that shared the planet. A 55-ton brachiosaurus lumbering across the countryside would have presented a real **threat,** *a clear danger,* to any unsuspecting creature who got in its way. The huge Triceratops had frightening horns on its nose and over both of its eyes. The sight of this 10-ton animal bounding along at 30 miles per hour certainly scared the newly emerging mammals that had to scurry out of its way. Nevertheless, it was also a threat to any other dinosaur that tried to attack it.

Although groups of dinosaurs might be in **competition** with each other, *cooperation within a group was also common.* Members of a species might travel in a herd, eat and nest together, share responsibility for the young, and present a united defense against enemies.

Scientists are still debating about why the dinosaurs disappeared. We do not know for sure. All we know is that **twilight** *arrived for these creatures at the same time all across the earth. Then, in a twinkling, it was night,* and the dinosaurs were gone.

In a *cause-and-effect* relationship, one thing causes another thing to happen. The meaning of **victims** is established through a cause-and-effect relationship. *Thus* is a cause-and-effect clue word.

An *appositive phrase* contains a noun or pronoun that explains the noun or pronoun beside it. An appositive phrase indicates the meaning of **threat**.

Note that the meaning of **competition** is established through *contrast,* the placement of opposites near each other to point out their difference. The word *although* indicates contrast.

The meaning of **twilight** is established through *figurative language*. Figurative language is language that imaginatively describes one thing by comparing it to something else.

A Final Note

How can you learn strategic reading? Practice is a great way to improve your skill. The following lessons will help you learn the different context clues a writer uses. As you complete each lesson, you will become a more effective reader.

READING NEW WORDS IN CONTEXT

Lesson 1 | CONTEXT: Change in Arts and Literature

Introduction. What science fiction films have you seen? Have you seen any of the great ones? In the following story, a mother tells her daughter about some of the great science fiction classics.

The story gives you an opportunity to expand your vocabulary. Below are twenty vocabulary words that are used in the passage and in the exercise that follows it.

alien	diplomatic	gesture	luminous	satellite
ally	fascinate	ghastly	mortal	stellar
avert	fugitive	humane	overture	tranquil
destiny	galaxy	invade	planetary	velocity

They Came from Outer Space

Teresa sat at the kitchen table, twisting a strand of her hair, a **gesture** (1) that indicated she was bothered about something. She stared out the window and made a face, as though something troublesome were going on outside. However, the moon was especially **luminous** (2) tonight, and she could clearly see that the backyard was **tranquil** (3), only the leaves stirring slightly in the gentle breeze.

Teresa stirred when she heard the front door. Mom was home. Time to set the table.

"Hi, Manuel! How was your day? Where's your sister?" Teresa heard her mother ask her brother.

"Okay. Teresa's in the kitchen. She said she had homework, but I think she went in there to stare out the window."

Teresa wondered for a moment why it was her **destiny** (4) to have such a pest for a younger brother. "Fate," she muttered, "could have been kinder." Actually, she didn't feel all that irritated with Manuel, but she rattled the silverware and clanged the plates anyway.

"What's up, Teresa? Give me a hug." Teresa's mom plopped a bag of groceries down on the counter and gave her daughter a quick hug. "What are your plans for tonight?"

"I guess I'm going to Kim's to watch a science fiction film festival on TV tonight," said Teresa, wrinkling her nose.

Manuel began to fake a heart attack. He staggered around the table. "Oh, the horror! How terrible! How **ghastly** (5)! How will you survive the evening?" Teresa thought her brother was being especially annoying.

A Closet Sci-Fi Fan

"Hush, Manuel," her mother said. "Here's a better question—how did I wind up with a daughter who doesn't like science fiction? A good sci-fi film or book never fails to **fascinate** (6) me. It's fun. It's interesting."

"Oh, come on, Mom. You don't really like that stuff, do you?"

"Sweetie, I love it—when it's good. I've been a fan ever since high school. That's when I first saw the science fiction film classic *Forbidden Planet*."

"Let me guess," Teresa said sarcastically. "A bunch of **aliens** (7) come from another **galaxy** (8) and **invade** (9) Earth. These outer-space creatures from another group of stars take over the planet by turning into giant plants."

"Teresa, I said I liked *good* science fiction. Although you have a good idea for a spoof of a science fiction film." Manuel rolled his eyes.

"Okay, Mom, so what does happen in *Forbidden Planet*?" Teresa asked.

"I'm not going to tell you. Maybe it is on TV tonight. I will tell you that the film has some things that have become a part of most science fiction films. And there's a spaceship that can travel at a **velocity** (10) faster than the speed of light. There's a lovable robot. And there's a moment when human beings realize that they are mere **mortals** (11) and should not try to behave as though they are gods."

"Yeah, it's pretty good," Manuel added. "You can see how it led to later science fiction like *Star Trek* and *Star Wars*, but there's a movie I like better."

"Wait a minute," Teresa interrupted. "Are you saying that people have copied *Forbidden Planet*?"

An Outer-Space Saga as Old as the Hills

Teresa's mom answered. "Well, sort of, but the people who made *Forbidden Planet* copied, too. They borrowed the story from William Shakespeare's *The Tempest*, a **stellar** (12) play. See, if a story is truly outstanding, people use it again and again."

"Let me tell you about my favorite old science fiction movie," Manuel said. "It's a **planetary** (13) tale called *The Day the Earth Stood Still*. This guy Klaatu comes to Earth from another planet on a **diplomatic** (14) mission to gain our trust and friendship. He represents this group of **aliens**. He says he comes in peace, and he makes **overtures** (15) of friendship. By making these friendly offers, he wants the people of Earth to **ally** (16) themselves with this group of **aliens**. But the people in Washington don't want to join forces with the **aliens**. They are afraid of Klaatu. So they shoot him, but he doesn't die. They put him in a hospital, but he escapes, and so everybody thinks Klaatu's a dangerous **fugitive** (17) on the run from the law."

"Then what happens?" Teresa was becoming interested.

"You'll have to watch it!" Manuel teased. "Maybe it will be on tonight. It's got a great ending, though. Humanity is saved! Disaster is **averted** (18), but questions remain. Have human beings learned a lesson? Will they become more **humane** (19), or will they continue to be mean and cruel?"

"Mom, where did you get him? He must be the product of **aliens** from outer space."

"If I'm from outer space," Manuel responded, "then so are you. At least I know enough to like science fiction. There's this one old film in which the government launches a communications **satellite** (20). As the craft orbits Earth, it runs into an **alien** spaceship that—hey! Where are you going?"

Teresa had stood up. "Over to Kim's. Now that I have heard about every science fiction movie ever made, I might as well watch them."

EXERCISE *Reading Strategically* ☞

Directions. Answer each of the following items by circling the letter of the correct answer. You may need to refer to the story as you answer the items. The numbers of the items are the same as the numbers of the boldface vocabulary words in the story.

1. Which of the following is an example of a **gesture** that appears in the story?
(A) Teresa twists her hair.
(B) The backyard seems tranquil.
(C) Something strange is going on.
(D) Teresa has to set the table.

2. The writer tells us that the moon seemed especially **luminous**. Here, **luminous** means
(A) dim
(B) full
(C) clear
(D) glowing

3. All of the following are good definitions of **tranquil** *except*

   (A) quiet
   (B) peaceful
   (C) dull
   (D) calm

4. You can tell from the story that
destiny means

   (A) fate
   (B) calling
   (C) knowledge
   (D) destination

5. Manuel teases Teresa by suggesting
that watching science fiction films is
terrible and **ghastly**. Here, **ghastly**
means

   (A) ghostlike
   (B) horrible
   (C) silly
   (D) staggering

6. You can tell from the story that
fascinate means

   (A) barely entertain
   (B) strongly interest
   (C) completely bore
   (D) slightly attract

7. To give a clue to the meaning of
aliens, the writer

   (A) tells us they come in bunches
   (B) hints that they are imaginary
       creatures
   (C) treats them humorously
   (D) tells us they come from another
       group of stars

8. Teresa sarcastically says that "A
bunch of aliens come from another
galaxy and invade Earth." Here,
galaxy means

   (A) foreign country
   (B) group of planets
   (C) system of stars
   (D) time zone

9. The writer gives us a clue to the meaning of **invade**. What is the clue?

   (A) The writer says that Teresa is
       guessing.
   (B) The writer shows us how Teresa
       responds to her mother.
   (C) Teresa guesses that the aliens take
       over Earth.
   (D) The writer tells us that Teresa
       doesn't like science fiction.

10. Teresa's mother says, "There's a
spaceship that can travel at a **velocity**
faster than the speed of light." Here,
velocity means

   (A) fast
   (B) light
   (C) speed
   (D) travel

11. The writer says that the human beings
in *Forbidden Planet* realize they are
mortals. Here, **mortals** means

   (A) godlike beings
   (B) alien beings
   (C) robots
   (D) human beings

12. Teresa's mom considers William
Shakespeare's *The Tempest* a **stellar**
play. Here **stellar** means

   (A) borrowed
   (B) outstanding
   (C) interesting
   (D) long-lasting

13. The writer tells us that *The Day the
Earth Stood Still* is a **planetary** tale.
Here, **planetary** means

   (A) coming to Earth
   (B) having to do with planets
   (C) traveling with a group of aliens
   (D) science fiction

14. Which of the following is the most likely reason that Klaatu comes to Earth on a **diplomatic** mission?

(A) Klaatu wants to gain the friendship of humans.

(B) Klaatu doesn't die when shot.

(C) The people of Washington don't trust Klaatu because he is an **alien**.

(D) Klaatu is from outer space.

15. In this story, **overtures** means

(A) offers

(B) songs

(C) gifts

(D) threats

16. You can tell from the story that **ally** means

(A) forget

(B) join

(C) fight

(D) understand

17. To give a clue to the meaning of **fugitive,** the writer

(A) hints that Klaatu is armed and probably dangerous

(B) refers to Klaatu by name

(C) tells us that people think Klaatu is on the run from the law

(D) reminds us that Klaatu is an alien

18. To let us know that **averted** means "avoided," the writer

(A) says that Manuel asks if human beings have learned a lesson

(B) hints that Teresa would enjoy the movie

(C) hints that aliens cause disasters

(D) tells us that Manuel says that humanity is saved

19. To let us know that **humane** means "kind and sympathetic," the writer

(A) associates **humane** with the word *lesson*

(B) contrasts **humane** with the words *mean* and *cruel*

(C) links **humane** with human beings

(D) uses **humane** with the word *more*

20. In this story, the word **satellite** means

(A) the moon

(B) a government program that sends people into space

(C) an object that orbits another object

(D) the plot of a movie

READING NEW WORDS IN CONTEXT

Lesson 2   CONTEXT: Change in Arts and Literature

Introduction. People have always had mixed feelings about art because art is always changing. However, no change has been greater in the world of painting than the move away from tradition that took place in the early twentieth century.

The following essay gives you an opportunity to expand your vocabulary. Below are twenty vocabulary words that are used in the essay and in the exercise that follows it.

abstract	controversial	eventual	inferior	originality
absurd	defiant	excess	mere	reality
conform	deliberate	grotesque	obsolete	recoil
consequence	distort	impact	offend	technique

Changing Times, Changing Tastes

Almost every change seems to be **controversial** (1). Some people will welcome the change, while other people will fight it. This has been especially true of changes in painting.

Changes in Painting

People's tastes have always changed over time, and so have styles of painting. As times change, some styles become **obsolete** (2) and others take their place. For example, paintings from Europe's Baroque period, which fell mainly in the seventeenth century, were once very popular. Later generations, however, believed that there was an **excess** (3) of detail in these pictures. They felt that Baroque artists overcrowded their paintings with figures and action. As a result, new and simpler styles of art came to replace Baroque art.

Of course, these new movements in art also caused **controversy**. In the mid-nineteenth century, for example, many people disliked a movement in art called Realism, which pictured things as people thought they were in **reality** (4). The idea that art should show things as they actually are was considered by many to be ridiculous,

outrageous, and downright **absurd** (5).

A New Style of Painting

Today, many people continue to have difficulty accepting **abstract** (6) painting, even though it has been around for over one hundred years. An artist making an **abstract** painting doesn't try to represent a subject the way a photograph would represent it. Instead, the artist focuses on line, shape, and color. The person or thing that inspired the painting may not even be visible in the finished work. This type of painting does not **conform** (7) to many people's idea of what a painting should be. They think that all paintings should be something they can recognize, just like a photograph. So they stand in front of the **abstract** painting and ask, "What is it supposed to be?" They may **deliberate** (8) on this question for quite some time, but in spite of their pondering, many people will never find an answer.

Some people who oppose **abstract** painting call the works of the great Russian artist Wassily Kandinsky (1866–1944) **mere** (9) scribblings, nothing more than doodles. They simply do not understand the **technique** (10) of this painter, who was a highly skilled artist with well-thought-out methods.

The Armory Show

The most misunderstood paintings may be some that were created at the beginning of the twentieth century. These paintings were by important European artists such as Kandinsky, Constantin Brancuşi (1876–1957), Georges Braque (1882–1963), Aristide Maillol (1861–1944), Marcel Duchamp (1887–1968), Henri Matisse (1869–1954), and Pablo Picasso (1881–1973).

The works of these and other artists were presented at the Armory Show in New York City in 1913. The Armory Show had a major **impact** (11) on art in the United States. The art world was never quite the same again.

Several of the artists had been greatly influenced by African art. They had experimented with shape, line, and color. The artists considered their work to be creative and interesting, but many of the critics called it weird to the point of being **grotesque** (12). These paintings **offended** (13)

many people, who thought the works were inappropriate. Several of the painters had painted people and things as basic geometric forms such as triangles, circles, and squares. Many people thought that these artists had **distorted** (14) their subjects. Of course, not all critics believed that the art was **inferior** (15); many people thought the art was excellent. They did not **recoil** (16) from the new styles, but instead they welcomed them.

Fortunately, the artists themselves were **defiant** (17). They were not about to let critics tell them what kind of art to create. They knew that their **originality** (18) and creativity had led to something that was new and different. Time would prove them right. The European works that hung in the Armory Show **eventually** (19) were to become classics. Within fifty years, they were recognized as masterpieces throughout the world.

The Armory Show had major **consequences** (20) for art in the United States. The main result was that it brought modern art to this country. Like other changes in art, the changes brought by the Armory Show were **controversial**. But such **controversy** is a normal part of the world of art.

EXERCISE *Reading Strategically* ☞

Directions. Answer each of the following items by circling the letter of the correct answer. You may need to refer to the essay as you answer the items. The numbers of the items are the same as the numbers of the boldface vocabulary words in the essay.

1. To give a clue to the meaning of **controversial,** the writer
   (A) tells us that change will occur whether or not people want it to
   (B) tells us that things do not stay the same
   (C) tells us that some people welcome change and others fight it
   (D) tells us that there have been changes in painting

2. To give a clue to the meaning of **obsolete,** the writer
   (A) tells us that styles of painting change and are replaced by new styles
   (B) tells us that Baroque paintings were very popular
   (C) tells us that some people thought there was too much going on in Baroque art
   (D) tells us the century of the Baroque period in Europe

3. To let us know that **excess** means "too much," the writer
  (A) tells us that Baroque artists over-crowded their paintings
  (B) associates **excess** with painting
  (C) associates **excess** with change
  (D) tells us that, in time, new styles of art came to replace Baroque art

4. In the third paragraph of this essay, **reality** means
  (A) Baroque
  (B) a perfect world
  (C) the actual world
  (D) ridiculousness

5. The writer tells us that the idea that art might show things as they are was once considered **absurd**. Here, **absurd** means
  (A) old-fashioned
  (B) idealistic
  (C) considered
  (D) ridiculous

6. **Abstract,** in the world of art, means
  (A) lasting for a long time
  (B) painted
  (C) not representational
  (D) accepted

7. Which of the following is the most likely reason that **abstract** painting does not **conform** to the ideas some people have about art?
  (A) People think art should last a long time.
  (B) People think **abstract** painting has been around too long.
  (C) People don't like lines, shapes, and colors.
  (D) People think that art should be more like a photograph.

8. The writer states that people may **deliberate** on a question for quite some time. Here, **deliberate** means
  (A) ponder
  (B) answer
  (C) avoid
  (D) ask

9. In the fifth paragraph of this essay, **mere** means
  (A) mirror
  (B) only
  (C) fantastic
  (D) simple

10. You can tell from the essay that **technique** means
  (A) doodle
  (B) art
  (C) method
  (D) understanding

11. The author writes, "The Armory Show had a major **impact** on art in the United States." Here, **impact** means
  (A) threat
  (B) hit
  (C) attraction
  (D) effect

12. All of the following are good definitions of **grotesque** *except*
  (A) bizarre
  (B) strange
  (C) absurd
  (D) humorous

13. The author writes, "These paintings **offended** many people, who thought the works were inappropriate." Here, **offended** means
  (A) upset
  (B) explained
  (C) created
  (D) attracted

14. To give a clue to the meaning of **distorted,** the writer
   (A) tells us that some basic geometric forms are triangles, circles, and squares
   (B) tells us that painters had painted people and things as basic geometric forms
   (C) tells us that the artists painted people and things
   (D) tells us that some people thought the new art was inappropriate

15. The writer tells us that not all critics believed the art to be **inferior.** Here, **inferior** means
   (A) not realistic
   (B) unusual
   (C) of poor quality
   (D) similar

16. To let us know that **recoil** means "to back away from," the writer
   (A) associates **recoil** with new styles
   (B) contrasts **recoil** with the word *welcomed*
   (C) tells us that many people thought the art was excellent
   (D) lets us know that critics **recoil**

17. To give a clue to the meaning of **defiant,** the writer
   (A) tells us that the artists were creative
   (B) tells us that the artists refused to let critics tell them what to create
   (C) tells us that some people welcomed the new styles in art, and others criticized them
   (D) tells us the Armory Show is important in the history of art for a number of reasons

18. The author writes, "They knew that their **originality** and creativity had led to something that was new and different" in the history of art. Here, **originality** means
   (A) the ability to make something new and different
   (B) the knowledge of an important act
   (C) the first artists
   (D) the determination not to be different

19. In the next to the last paragraph, the word **eventually** means
   (A) in the future
   (B) second to last
   (C) possibly
   (D) recognizably

20. Which of the following is an example of the major **consequences** of the Armory Show?
   (A) Some people still opposed **abstract** art.
   (B) Art shows were held in this country.
   (C) Modern art came to the United States.
   (D) There are masterpieces still unrecognized in some parts of the world.

READING NEW WORDS IN CONTEXT

Lesson 3 | CONTEXT: Change in Arts and Literature

Introduction. Are the movies you watch today much different from those your parents and grandparents watched at your age? The author of the following article tells us something about the history of movies for and about teens.

The article gives you an opportunity to expand your vocabulary. Below are twenty vocabulary words that are used in the article and in the exercise that follows it.

audible	diaphragm	ignorance	maturity	signify
candid	haunt	leash	modest	subtle
congregate	hover	lenient	motive	supervise
conspicuous	idle	loiter	notorious	threshold

Getting Better: A Brief History of Movies for Teenagers

Teenagers have long been important people to filmmakers. Since the 1930s, Hollywood has produced thousands of films especially for teenagers. In some of these films adults have only minor roles. They are secondary characters who **hover** (1) in the background and hang around to speak only a few familiar lines—lines like "Have you finished your homework?" and "Don't stay out too late" and "You're grounded."

In other films, the relationships between teens and adults are seriously explored. These movies may focus on whether the adults are responsible and caring people. Do they **supervise** (2) the teenagers they take care of, or do they let the teenagers have total freedom? Are they too **lenient** (3)—or are they too strict? Do they respect teenagers as individual human beings? Such movies can make teenagers think seriously about their own relationships with adults.

Some movies about teenagers are about important issues, and some are meant only to entertain. Yet, if you look at a group of films about teens from one time period, the films will indicate a great deal about what people felt or believed dur-

ing that period. In other words, the films will **signify** (4) the attitudes of the time.

Films of the 1930s

Andy Hardy, a teenager played by Mickey Rooney, was probably the most popular adolescent in the films of the 1930s. During this time, the nation was in the middle of a terrible economic crisis, the Great Depression, and millions of people were losing their jobs and their homes. Andy Hardy's world, however, was filled with large homes and happy people. No one was **idle** (5) because no one was jobless, although few people seemed to have to work very hard. People had time to **loiter** (6) on lawns or linger to chat on front porch steps. The family dog did not have to be kept on a **leash** (7) and frolicked freely in the yard.

The conflicts between teenagers and adults were minor. Perhaps Mom insisted that Andy clean his room before the big game, or maybe Dad asked Andy to wash the car. The music teacher might demand that the teenager practice the song one more time ("This time, breathe correctly and use the proper muscle, your **diaphragm** (8)"). The problems in Andy Hardy's world were small, and they were always solved by the end of the movie.

Maybe these films were popular because times were so tough in the real world. Teenagers and parents alike needed to see a movie world in which problems were minor and everything came out all right in the end.

Films of the 1940s and 1950s
Films about teenagers in the 1940s were not all that much different from those of the 1930s. People who relied on the movies to find the solutions to serious problems remained in **ignorance** (9); films did not inform them in any way. Movies did sometimes focus on the problems of young people on the **threshold** (10) of adulthood. These problems concerning life at the edge of adulthood, however, tended to be treated lightly. The most popular movies were comedies such as *The Bachelor and the Bobby Soxer,* starring a teenage Shirley Temple.

In the 1950s, Hollywood began to take a serious look at the problems facing teenagers in films such as *Blackboard Jungle* and *Rebel Without a Cause.* These sophisticated films tried to be **candid** (11), or honest, in their portrayal of adolescent life. The movies had **subtle** (12) themes that required some serious thought on the part of the audience.

In contrast, teenagers also played major roles in science fiction and horror films of the decade. Because of their silly plots and cheap special effects, many of these movies became **notorious** (13), that is, they were well known for being bad. Perhaps the worst of this batch was *Teenagers from Outerspace,* a movie about alien teenagers who want to conquer Earth to use it as grazing land for their food supply—which seems to consist of giant lobsters!

Rock and roll arrived in the 1950s, and Hollywood was quick to use it in films as a reason for teens to see movies. In fact, a primary **motive** (14) for making movies like *Rock Pretty Baby, Rock Around the Clock,* and *Rock, Rock, Rock* seemed to be to attract teens to the theaters. The plots for movies like these were usually weak, but the music was certainly **audible** (15). Adults, for the most part, hated these loud musicals—but teenagers flocked to see them.

Films of the 1960s and 1970s
Many of the films about adolescents in the 1960s were **conspicuous** (16) for their brainlessness. Beach movies are a good example of such noticeably silly films. Teens in the films of the past had gathered at the local malt shop; now it seemed that every teen in American had decided to **congregate** (17) at the beach. The craze for beach movies started in 1959 with *Gidget,* a film that cashed in on the surfing craze. Popular beach movies of the early 1960s included *Beach Party, Bikini Beach,* and *Beach Blanket Bingo*. All of these featured the wholesome antics of teen idols Frankie Avalon and Annette Funicello. These films were produced on fairly **modest** (18) budgets, and so they did not need to be blockbuster hits to make profits. Most teens enjoyed them for what they were: mindless entertainment.

Hollywood took teens more seriously in the 1970s. One of the best films of the decade was *Breaking Away,* a coming-of-age story. *American Graffiti* was made in the 1970s but was set in an earlier time. It told a story about teenagers in the early 1960s, prior to the change and turmoil of the second half of the decade.

The Films of the 1980s and 1990s
Movies for and about teenagers finally reached their **maturity** (19) in the 1980s. By then, filmmakers like John Hughes had done a lot to bring teenage films to their full development. Among Hughes's best films were *The Breakfast Club* and *Sixteen Candles*. Other popular teen films included *Ferris Bueller's Day Off, The Karate Kid,* and *Dead Poets' Society*. That film, directed by Australian filmmaker Peter Weir, contains many memorable, visually stunning scenes that continue to **haunt** (20) viewers even after they leave the theater.

Quality movies for teenagers were a bit scarcer in the 1990s, but filmmakers continued to take teenagers seriously. And if nothing at the box office appealed to teenage viewers, they could turn on the TV and catch an old movie—and catch the waves with Frankie and Annette.

EXERCISE   *Reading Strategically* ✍

Directions. Answer each of the following items by circling the letter of the correct answer. You may need to refer to the article as you answer the items. The numbers of the items are the same as the numbers of the boldface vocabulary words in the article.

1. You can tell that **hover** means
   (A) secondary
   (B) joke around
   (C) adult
   (D) hang around

2. All of the following are good definitions of **supervise** *except*
   (A) take care of
   (B) look after
   (C) reward
   (D) oversee

3. To give a clue to the meaning of **lenient,** the writer
   (A) contrasts **lenient** with the word *strict*
   (B) asks if the adult film characters truly respect teenagers
   (C) uses the word *individual*
   (D) uses the word *hinder*

4. To give a clue to the meaning of **signify,** the writer
   (A) suggests we look at films from one time period
   (B) tells us that films indicate what people believe
   (C) uses the word *attitudes*
   (D) suggests that attitudes may change over time

5. The writer says that no one was **idle** in Andy Hardy films. Here, **idle** means
   (A) very active
   (B) pointless
   (C) not busy
   (D) wasted

6. The author writes, "People had time to **loiter** on lawns or linger to chat on front porch steps." Here, **loiter** means
   (A) cook
   (B) mow
   (C) practice
   (D) linger

7. You can tell from the essay that **leash** means
   (A) porch
   (B) lawn
   (C) pen
   (D) strap

8. In this article, **diaphragm** means
   (A) a music instructor
   (B) an instrument
   (C) abdominal muscle
   (D) a song

9. To let us know that **ignorance** means "a state of unawareness," the writer
   (A) lets us know that the movies did not inform their audiences about solutions to problems
   (B) tells us that films from the 1940s did not differ from films of the 1930s
   (C) lets us know that people did not realize that movies about teens could be serious
   (D) links **ignorance** to the word *relied*

10. In this article, **threshold** means
    (A) window sill
    (B) edge
    (C) wrong side
    (D) adulthood

11. The author writes, "These sophisti-
cated films tried to be **candid** . . . in
their portrayal of adolescent life."
Here, **candid** means
(A) popular
(B) blunt
(C) honest
(D) modern

12. To let us know that **subtle** means "re-
quiring mental sharpness," the writer
(A) links **subtle** to the need for honesty in films' portrayals
(B) tells us that **subtle** themes
required serious thought
(C) reminds us that the films were
serious
(D) gives an example of a **subtle**
theme

13. Which of the following is the most
likely reason that many of the science
fiction and horror films of the 1950s
were **notorious**?
(A) Many were very good.
(B) Many were very bad.
(C) Many were about teenagers.
(D) Many were very popular.

14. You can tell from the essay that
motive means
(A) effect
(B) example
(C) weakness
(D) reason

15. The writer says that the rock music in
the movies was certainly **audible**.
Here, **audible** means
(A) able to be heard
(B) excellent
(C) able to be recorded
(D) containing well-written lyrics

16. The writer indicates that some films
were **conspicuous** for their brainless-
ness. Here, **conspicuous** means
(A) marvelous
(B) noticeable
(C) admired
(D) avoided

17. To give a clue to the meaning of **congregate,** the writer
(A) tells us that it is something teenagers did
(B) tells us that teens of the past gathered at the malt shop
(C) indicates that people only **congregate** at beaches
(D) suggests that teenagers no longer
congregate

18. To let us know that **modest** means
"reasonable," the writer
(A) tells us that beach movies were
popular
(B) tells us that the films did not need
to be smash hits to make profits
(C) says that teenagers enjoyed the
movies in spite of their weak plots
(D) reminds us that beach movies
were mindless entertainment,
much like malt-shop movies of
earlier years

19. The author writes, "Movies for and
about teenagers finally reached their
maturity in the 1980s." Here, **maturity**
means
(A) adolescence
(B) adulthood
(C) full development
(D) lowest point

20. At the end of the article, the word
haunt means to
(A) frighten
(B) study carefully
(C) change
(D) occupy the thoughts of

READING NEW WORDS IN CONTEXT

Lesson 4   CONTEXT: Change in Arts and Literature

Introduction. Most of us have probably heard or read stories about the fabulous adventures of young boys who fight dragons, explore strange lands, and finally triumph over great odds. Many of us have wondered, why aren't we reading about girls having these same wonderful adventures? Fortunately, today we can read about courageous girls who test their strength and find that they can handle as much adventure as any male hero.

The following article gives you an opportunity to meet some of these female heroes and to expand your vocabulary. Below are twenty vocabulary words that are used in the article and in the exercise that follows it.

aggravate	dismal	frail	obstinate	porcelain
anticipate	distract	fulfill	optional	principally
caliber	eloquent	maintain	phase	spontaneous
dashing	flaw	obligation	placid	tiresome

Long Overdue: The Female Hero

Not long ago, female characters in literature were almost never referred to as heroes. This was true even if the character was strong and brave and had interesting adventures. Then, she might be referred to as a heroine. But to most people, a heroine was a **frail** (1) and helpless creature. They thought of a heroine as a female who resembled a fragile, **porcelain** (2) figurine more than a real, live, flesh-and-blood female.

Of course, there were some strong female characters in literature. Some stories featured young girls who were rowdy and mischievous, who were "tomboys." However, older female characters were usually **placid** (3) creatures—quiet, gentle souls who didn't have adventures for fear it would rumple their dresses, make them late for tea, and upset their boyfriends. Any young women who did have adventures often needed **dashing** (4) young men to ride boldly to their rescue.

Some people saw nothing wrong with these stories. In fact, they enjoyed them. Girls who longed to have adventures of their own, though, found such stories **tiresome** (5). Boys also often found the stories boring and irritating. To discover that he is expected to rush about rescuing these helpless women from disasters is enough to **aggravate** (6) even the most romantic young man.

In recent years, we have left that **phase** (7) of storytelling behind us and begun a new period. Today, almost no one **maintains** (8), or insists, that the hero of an adventure book must be a male. In fact, the sex of the hero is **optional** (9). As a result, many writers of modern books for young readers choose girls as their heroes.

The Modern Hero
Of course, having a girl as a hero is no guarantee that a book will be a good one. Some of these books are of a higher **caliber** (10) than others. Some of these particularly good adventure stories are fantasy or science fiction. Among the best are Anne MacCaffrey's *Dragonsong* and

Dragonsinger, Patricia McKillip's *The Forgotten Beasts of Eld,* Robin McKinley's *The Hero and the Crown* and *The Blue Sword,* and Robert Heinlein's *The Star Beast.*

The female hero in each of these books **fulfills** (11), or satisfies, all the expectations we have of a hero. She has great qualities of strength and courage, but she also has **flaws** (12). She may be **obstinate** (13), stubbornly refusing to listen to reason. She may be thoughtless or too quick to judge others. Of course the heroes are not all alike. One hero may be **spontaneous** (14) in her approach to life, while another may be cautious and careful.

A Writer of Songs

One of the most interesting of these heroes is Menolly, the hero of *Dragonsong.* Before she discovers her mission, Menolly leads a rather **dismal** (15) existence. She spends her days cleaning fish and caring for the other members of her household. Menolly is silent in her home by day, but at night she is **eloquent** (16) in her true calling as an expressive writer of songs. Although Menolly has many interesting adventures, she is most heroic in her determination to find and become herself.

The Dragonslayer

Aerin is the hero of *The Hero and the Crown.* Because she is the hero of the story, the reader is able to **anticipate** (17) that in the future she will succeed in her quest and reach maturity. The question is, how?

Aerin's struggle is a difficult one, but she succeeds **principally** (18), or chiefly, because she is courageous. She kills the Black Dragon that threatens the countryside, recovers the crown that will save her country, and leads an army into battle. Eventually, she becomes mature enough to assume the duties and **obligations** (19) of a queen.

These two tales are very different, but they do have important things in common. Both have interesting male characters who play major roles in the stories, and both have animal characters interesting enough to **distract** (20) readers from the adventures of the human beings. They both are excellent examples of good literature in which the hero is a female.

EXERCISE *Reading Strategically* ☞

Directions. Answer each of the following items by circling the letter of the correct answer. You may need to refer to the article as you answer the items. The numbers of the items are the same as the numbers of the boldface vocabulary words in the article.

1. The writer describes the heroines of some novels as **frail**. Here, **frail** means
   (A) fragile
   (B) pitiful
   (C) strong
   (D) realistic

2. You can tell from the article that a **porcelain** doll is
   (A) fragile
   (B) frail
   (C) helpless
   (D) flesh-and-blood

3. To give a clue to the meaning of the word **placid,** the writer
(A) uses **placid** to describe creatures
(B) reminds us that **placid** is an old-fashioned word
(C) tells that young women had adventures
(D) tells us that female characters were usually quiet and gentle

4. The writer tells us that in some stories young women were rescued by **dashing** young men who came to their rescue. Here, **dashing** means
(A) bold
(B) young
(C) kind
(D) interesting

5. To give a clue to the meaning of the word **tiresome,** the writer
(A) tells us that people enjoyed the stories
(B) tells us that some girls wanted to have adventures
(C) tells us that boys also often found the stories boring and irritating
(D) refers to men rescuing women

6. All of the following are good definitions of **aggravate** *except*
(A) displease
(B) please
(C) annoy
(D) irritate

7. How does the writer let us know that the word **phase** means "stage"?
(A) The writer refers to recent years.
(B) The writer tells us that storytelling has entered a new period.
(C) The writer focuses on the present.
(D) The writer mentions a romantic young man.

8. The author writes, "Today, almost no one **maintains** . . . that the hero of an adventure book must be a male." Here, **maintains** means
(A) keeps up
(B) argues
(C) takes care of
(D) insists

9. In the fourth paragraph, the word **optional** means
(A) already chosen
(B) female
(C) unimportant
(D) left to choice

10. To give a clue to the meaning of **caliber,** the writer
(A) links **caliber** to the word *guarantee*
(B) reminds us that a girl can be a hero
(C) tells us that some adventure stories are also fantasy or science fiction stories
(D) indicates that some adventure stories are particularly good

11. The author writes, "The female hero in each of these books **fulfills** . . . all the expectations we have of a hero." Here, **fulfills** means
(A) has
(B) enters
(C) expects
(D) satisfies

12. Which of the following is an example of a **flaw** that is mentioned in the article?
(A) strength
(B) courage
(C) quickness
(D) stubbornness

13. The author writes, "She may be **obstinate**, stubbornly refusing to listen to reason." Here, **obstinate** means
   (A) heroic
   (B) flaw
   (C) stubborn
   (D) courageous

14. To let us know that **spontaneous** means "open and impulsive," the writer
   (A) tells us that not all heroes are alike
   (B) contrasts **spontaneous** with *cautious* and *careful*.
   (C) uses **spontaneous** to describe a hero
   (D) claims that some heroes have flaws

15. Which of the following is a likely reason that Menolly's existence is **dismal**?
   (A) She is a hero.
   (B) She spends her days cleaning fish.
   (C) She writes songs.
   (D) She has interesting adventures.

16. The author writes, "Menolly is silent in her home by day, but at night she is **eloquent** in her true calling as a writer of songs." Here, **eloquent** means
   (A) expressive
   (B) silent
   (C) true
   (D) heroic

17. Which of the following is the most likely reason that the reader is able to **anticipate** that Aerin will succeed?
   (A) Aerin is a minor character in the story.
   (B) Aerin is already completely mature.
   (C) A black dragon threatens the countryside.
   (D) Aerin is the hero of the novel.

18. In this article, the word **principally** means
   (A) partly
   (B) usually
   (C) chiefly
   (D) only

19. The writer tells us that Aerin matures enough to assume the **obligations** of a queen. Here, **obligations** means
   (A) promises
   (B) privileges
   (C) services
   (D) responsibilities

20. In the last paragraph of the article, the word **distract** means
   (A) to draw away
   (B) to lose
   (C) to borrow
   (D) to manage

READING NEW WORDS IN CONTEXT

Lesson 5 | CONTEXT: Change in Arts and Literature

Introduction. You've probably studied legends and myths in school, and you may think of them as stories about long-ago times, but the author of the following article claims that we create folklore every day.

The article gives you an opportunity to expand your vocabulary. Below are twenty vocabulary words that are used in the article and in the exercise that follows it.

authentic	contemplate	formal	interpret	profound
cherish	crucial	gratify	legendary	resolve
comparable	designate	immortal	myth	versatile
consistent	dual	indispensable	mythology	vigor

Once Upon A Time, Maybe Last Week

Lupe Morales' seventh-grade class is studying **mythology** (1). For two weeks, the class studied the myths of the Greeks and stories about the ancient Greek and Roman gods. Then, they studied tales and legends from Africa, Asia, Europe, and Latin America. Some of the students particularly liked the **myths** (2) that explain how things began. Others enjoyed the legends that were told over the years about the adventures of heroic men and women. In fact, the students thought that these **legendary** (3) heroes were very useful. They found that they could use the information they learned in class to **interpret** (4), or explain the meaning of, many movies and comic books in a new way. They could look at the modern heroes and see how modern heroes were **comparable** (5) to those heroes of the old tales. It was surprising to find how often they were alike.

The Uses of Folklore

Ms. Morales explained to her class that folklore, including **myths,** legends, and fairy tales, is very **versatile** (6) literature. It can be used for different purposes. It is entertaining, so it can be read just for fun. It also reveals **profound** (7) truths about human beings, so it is worth careful study. Ms. Morales then made a claim that surprised her students. She said that folklore is **indispensable** (8) —that people can't get along without it.

Her students disagreed. "It's fun," they said, "but we can live without this old stuff."

"Maybe," Ms. Morales replied, "just maybe, you think you can get along without the old stuff, but I wouldn't want to. It seems important to me to **cherish** (9) and protect our heritage, but that's not what I'm getting at. I'm talking about the new stuff, the folklore that we pass on every day."

The students were confused. Latisha raised her hand. "Excuse me, Ms. Morales, but how can folklore be real if it was just made up yesterday?"

Ms. Morales replied that some people do think that the only **authentic** (10) folklore is the tales and legends from the past. However, she said that there were several stories that she had overheard students telling that she would **designate** (11) as folklore.

Folklore Today

"For example," she said, "remember yesterday before class when Allison was telling Shiu Chiu about the woman in white who wanders around Blue Mountain Lake? Well, that is folklore. And that story reminds me of a story we tell in my community. Most Mexican Americans have heard the story of La Llorona, a woman in white. Like the woman of Blue Mountain Lake, she appears to be **immortal** (12). She lives forever as a ghost. She walks the streets at night and looks for children who are out past their bedtimes. The White Lady of Blue Mountain Lake walks the roads around the lake at night and frightens teenagers. What do you think these stories are for?"

Ms. Morales gave the students time to **contemplate** (13) her question. Then, she asked them what they thought. Hassan raised his hand. "The stories are used to frighten us so that we won't do things that are dangerous. Is that it?"

"Exactly," said Ms. Morales. "It is **crucial** (14) that you remember that often the stories are told for a reason. It is also very important for you to remember that these stories reflect the values of the group that tells them. In other words, they have a **dual** (15) purpose—to warn or to explain and to pass on values. Let's try to keep both of those purposes in mind while we think some more

about folklore. Who has heard stories about large animals living in sewers?"

Several students raised their hands. One told the story of giant alligators living underneath the streets in Chicago. Another told about giant blind rats that scurried through the sewers of Detroit. Many students had heard almost the same stories, stories that were **consistent** (16) with these two stories except for one or two details.

"I heard about the alligators," Natalie said, "except I heard that they were in New York City. Which is true?"

"Neither one," Ms. Morales said gently. "Both stories are folklore. Now, think about other stories you have heard that are probably folklore."

Ms. Morales divided the class into small groups and asked each group to make a list of all the folklore they could think of. The groups had a lot of energy and enthusiasm. Ms. Morales was pleased by the **vigor** (17) with which they approached their task. She was also **gratified** (18) by the results of each group.

As a result of their casual discussions, the students decided that they wanted to explore modern folklore in a more **formal** (19) way. The students **resolved** (20) to do their research projects on folklore, and Ms. Morales decided to make folklore a class project every year.

EXERCISE *Reading Strategically* 👆

Directions. Answer each of the following items by circling the letter of the correct answer. You may need to refer to the article as you answer the items. The numbers of the items are the same as the numbers of the boldface vocabulary words in the article.

1. Examples of **mythology** that are mentioned in the passage include
   (A) stories about the ancient Greek and Roman gods
   (B) Lupe Morales' seventh-grade class
   (C) the fact that some students like to read comic books
   (D) the fact that the students studied it for two weeks

2. To give a clue to the meaning of **myths,** the writer
   (A) says that the **myths** come from the world over
   (B) links **myths** to the word *legends*
   (C) tells us that students explained the **myths**
   (D) lets us know that some students liked **myths**

3. The writer tells us that the students found **legendary** men and women interesting. Here, **legendary** means

(A) forgotten
(B) Greek
(C) heroic
(D) interesting

4. The writer tells us that the students used what they learned to **interpret** movies and comic books. Here, **interpret** means

(A) read aloud
(B) draw
(C) compose
(D) explain

5. To give a clue to the meaning of **comparable**, the writer

(A) tells us that the students looked at comic-book heroes to discover things
(B) tells us that yesterday's heroes and today's heroes are often alike
(C) tells us that the students used the information
(D) compares the attitudes of the student and the teacher

6. To give a clue to the meaning of **versatile**, the writer

(A) tells us that Ms. Morales explained things to her class
(B) mentions entertainment
(C) lets us know that folklore can be used for different purposes
(D) mentions myths, legends, and fairy tales

7. The writer tells us that folklore can be studied seriously because it contains **profound** truths about human beings. Here, **profound** means

(A) lost
(B) favorable
(C) funny
(D) deep

8. The author writes, "She said that folklore is **indispensable**—that people couldn't get along without it." Here, **indispensable** means

(A) absolutely necessary
(B) recyclable
(C) soon to be outdated
(D) completely useless

9. The writer reports that Ms. Morales said, "It seems important to me to **cherish** and protect our heritage." Here, **cherish** means

(A) hide
(B) discover
(C) hold dear
(D) understand

10. The author writes, "Ms. Morales replied that some people do think that the only **authentic** folklore is the tales and legends from the past." Here, **authentic** means

(A) living
(B) real
(C) past
(D) dead

11. All of the following are good definitions of **designate** *except*

(A) call
(B) name
(C) refer to
(D) design

12. Which of the following is the most likely reason that Ms. Morales describes La Llorona as **immortal**?

(A) La Llorona lives forever.
(B) La Llorona wears white.
(C) La Llorona appears at night.
(D) La Llorona looks for children.

13. You can tell that **contemplate** means

(A) to ignore
(B) to rephrase
(C) to think about
(D) to answer back

14. The writer has Ms. Morales give us a clue to the meaning of **crucial**. What is the clue?
(A) She says that the stories are told for a reason.
(B) She says that it is important that groups tells stories and pass them on to the next generation.
(C) She says that it is also very important to remember that the stories reflect values and attitudes.
(D) She says that the students should keep things in mind.

15. In this article, **dual** means
(A) important
(B) second
(C) twofold
(D) unimportant

16. To let us know that **consistent** means "in agreement," the writer
(A) hints that the stories are very different
(B) lets us know that the students did not agree with the stories
(C) indicates that the rats and alligators get along
(D) indicates that the stories were the same except for one or two details

17. In this article, the word **vigor** means
(A) organization
(B) thought
(C) energy
(D) fun

18. To give a clue to the meaning of **gratified**, the writer
(A) links **gratified** to the word *pleased*
(B) tells us that the students shared examples
(C) tells us to learn at home
(D) tells us that the students were enthusiastic

19. The writer states that the students wanted to explore folklore in a **formal** way. Here, **formal** means
(A) stiff
(B) modern
(C) old-fashioned
(D) orderly

20. The author writes, "The students **resolved** to do their research projects on folklore." Here, **resolved** means
(A) solved again
(B) decided
(C) forgot over time
(D) explored a possibility

READING NEW WORDS IN CONTEXT

Lesson 6 | CONTEXT: Change in Individuals and Communities

Introduction. Some of the most important changes in American society have happened in the area of civil rights. In the time since the Civil War, Americans have made slow but steady progress toward equal rights for all citizens.

The following article gives you an opportunity to learn about the civil rights movement and to expand your vocabulary. Below are twenty vocabulary words that are used in the article and in the exercise that follows it.

constitution	hypocrite	initial	moderate	prudent
discrimination	illustrious	judicial	moral	segregation
elective	indefinite	legitimate	notable	unison
guarantee	indirect	merit	partial	veto

Changing America: The Civil Rights Movement

Following the Civil War, Congress took actions to **guarantee** (1) that African Americans would become free and equal citizens. These actions included changing the government's **constitution** (2) by passing three amendments between 1865 and 1870. Within twenty years, however, the Supreme Court had made decisions that made those earlier promises meaningless. These **judicial** (3) decisions, for example, made it legal to build separate schools for African American children. In effect, the Supreme Court had made the **segregation** (4), or separation, of African Americans legal.

Individuals and Organization

African Americans thus began a long and difficult struggle to regain their civil rights. Many **illustrious** (5) African American individuals participated in these efforts, including noted writer and educator Alice Dunbar-Nelson (1875–1935), renowned sociologist W.E.B. DuBois (1868–1963), and the famous scientist George Washington Carver (1864?–1943). Many organizations were also **notable** (6) for their civil rights activities. Perhaps the two best known groups are the National Association for the Advancement of Colored People (NAACP), founded in 1909, and the National Urban League, organized in 1910. The idea behind these groups was that African Americans could achieve more by working in **unison** (7) than they could through the efforts of individuals. However, even though many groups and individuals worked heroically, little changed for African Americans during the first half of the twentieth century. Many citizens of the United States were not ready to accept the idea that people should be judged by their **merit** (8), that is, by the worth of their words and deeds, instead of by the color of their skin.

A major breakthrough occurred in 1954, when the Supreme Court ruled in a case called *Brown* v. *Board of Education of Topeka* that school segregation violated the Constitution. The nation's public school systems were required to desegregate, that is, to allow the enrollment of African American students in mostly white schools. The **initial** (9) attempts at desegregation were strongly opposed. These first attempts at desegregation are among some of the uglier events in United States history.

The Civil Rights Movement

After the decision of *Brown* v. *Board of Education of Topeka,* the struggle for equal rights grew even stronger. This struggle has come to be known as the civil rights movement. Those who supported the civil rights movement were disappointed with the United States government, which they believed had not done enough to protect African Americans' rights. By the early 1960s, the civil rights movement was in full swing. Many people had joined the cause out of a sense of honor. They did not want to feel like **hypocrites** (10) when they said the words "with liberty and justice for all." It was hard to repeat and to believe these words when so many citizens were denied their civil rights. Many gave **indirect** (11) support. For example, instead of marching in demonstrations, they voted for candidates who supported civil rights.

Two Civil Rights Acts

In the 1960s, millions of U.S. citizens recognized that support of the civil rights movement was the only **moral** (12), or decent, course of action. Many agreed that it was time for **discrimination** (13) to come to an end. Others, however, opposed equal rights and fair treatment for all, and some people were **indefinite** (14), or uncertain, about their position. The time for change was long overdue, and a historic law, the Civil Rights Act, was passed in 1964.

The Voting Rights Act of 1965 protected African Americans' right to vote, thus providing them a better opportunity to hold **elective** (15) offices. The result was that more African Americans were elected to the government. Still, their success seemed only temporary as, in the long run, new legislation proved hard to enforce or failed to achieve its goals. Some civil rights activists came to believe that extreme action would be necessary for African Americans to achieve justice. Even some **moderate** (16) leaders, who normally rejected extreme actions, felt they understood the anger of those who supported violence. They felt that perhaps strong action was needed to bring about the **legitimate** (17), or reasonable, rights of African Americans. The success of the civil rights acts had been only **partial** (18) at best, not nearly complete, because racism and discrimination were still very much a part of life in the United States.

However, a great leader of the civil rights movement, Dr. Martin Luther King, Jr. (1929–1968), opposed violent action. He didn't think it was **prudent** (19) to follow the violent course that some frustrated activists favored. He believed it was wiser to practice peaceful protest instead. Dr. King always **vetoed** (20) violence and force as methods for change. The cowardly murder of this great man contrasts dramatically with his and his followers' bravery. Inequality still exists in the U.S., but the determined civil rights workers of the past provide the inspiration we need to achieve equality in the future.

EXERCISE *Reading Strategically* ✍

Directions. Answer each of the following items by circling the letter of the correct answer. You may need to refer to the article as you answer the items. The numbers of the items are the same as the numbers of the boldface vocabulary words in the article.

1. In the first paragraph of this article, to **guarantee** means
   (A) to decide
   (B) to become equal
   (C) to become free
   (D) to promise

2. The writer states that the government's **constitution** was changed by three amendments passed between 1865 and 1870. Here, **constitution** means
   (A) laws of the courts
   (B) Congress
   (C) document of principles and laws
   (D) Civil Rights Act

3. In the first paragraph, **judicial** means
  (A) having to do with wisdom
  (B) having to do with schools
  (C) meaningless
  (D) having to do with courts

4. Which of the following is an example of **segregation** that appears in the article?
  (A) The Supreme Court decided to **desegregate** schools.
  (B) African American children attended separate schools.
  (C) African Americans received the right to vote.
  (D) The Congress **guaranteed** equality to African Americans.

5. How does the writer let us know that **illustrious** means "very distinguished"?
  (A) The writer mentions three famous African Americans.
  (B) The writer associates **illustrious** with a long and difficult struggle.
  (C) The writer mentions different civil rights organizations.
  (D) The writer associates **illustrious** with activity and struggle.

6. You can tell from the article that **notable** means
  (A) organized
  (B) daring
  (C) outstanding
  (D) unfurnished

7. The writer indicates that African Americans felt they could achieve the most by acting in **unison**. Here, **unison** means
  (A) individually
  (B) effort
  (C) achievement
  (D) together

8. To give a clue to the meaning of **merit**, the writer
  (A) hints that **merit** has something to do with skin color
  (B) suggests that most U.S. citizens disapproved of **merits**
  (C) says that there were no **merits** during the first half of the century
  (D) links **merit** to the word *worth*

9. All of the following are good definitions of **initial** *except*
  (A) beginning
  (B) first
  (C) later
  (D) original

10. You can tell from the passage that **hypocrites** are
  (A) people who say one thing but believe or do another
  (B) people who are overly critical of others
  (C) people who always tell the truth
  (D) people who are against change

11. To give a clue to the meaning of **indirect**, the writer
  (A) indicates that a demonstration is an **indirect** action
  (B) indicates that *direct* and **indirect** can sometimes be synonyms
  (C) indicates that an **indirect** approach like demonstrating is often the most effective one
  (D) indicates that voting is an example of **indirect** action

12. The author writes, "In the 1960s, millions of U.S. citizens recognized that support of the civil rights movement was the only **moral** . . . course of action." Here, **moral** means
  (A) truthful
  (B) popular
  (C) historical
  (D) right

13. In the article, all of the following are likely reasons that **discrimination** needed to end *except*

(A) it was time for a change
(B) it was the decent course of action
(C) people shouldn't be judged by the color of their skin
(D) more African Americans were elected to the government

14. The writer claims that "some people were **indefinite** . . . about their position." Here, **indefinite** means

(A) uncertain
(B) indifferent
(C) uneasy
(D) determined

15. The writer tells us that the Voting Rights Act of 1965 gave African Americans a better chance of holding **elective** offices. Here, **elective** means

(A) appointed by the president
(B) optional
(C) decided by chance
(D) chosen by vote

16. To give a clue to the meaning of **moderate,** the writer

(A) tells us that some activists come to support extreme action
(B) tells us that the civil rights movement did not achieve all its goals
(C) tells us that **moderate** leaders normally rejected extreme actions
(D) associates **moderate** with the word *justice*

17. The word **legitimate** in this article means

(A) reasonable
(B) unimportant
(C) extreme
(D) successful

18. Which of the following is the most likely reason that the writer calls the civil rights acts a **partial** success?

(A) Dr. Martin Luther King, Jr., was a great leader of the civil rights movement.
(B) Some leaders still rejected extreme actions.
(C) Racism and discrimination had all but disappeared.
(D) Racism and discrimination had not completely ended.

19. The author writes, "He didn't think it was **prudent** to follow the violent course that some frustrated activists favored." Here, the word **prudent** means

(A) prudish
(B) economical
(C) moral
(D) wise

20. In the last paragraph of this article, the word **vetoed** means

(A) violated
(B) regarded
(C) rejected
(D) accepted

READING NEW WORDS IN CONTEXT

Lesson 7 CONTEXT: Change in Individuals and Communities

Introduction. Education has changed a lot in the past few decades. In recent years, schools have shifted from an emphasis on memorizing dry facts and figures to learning that actively involves the student. More and more, teachers are trying to show students how to teach themselves—and other students.

In the following essay, a student talks about the differences between her English class and her mother's. The essay gives you an opportunity to expand your vocabulary. Below are twenty vocabulary words that are used in the essay and in the exercise that follows it.

credible	forum	literary	participate	revise
dialogue	grammatical	manuscript	persuasion	symbolic
editorial	journal	mastery	prose	tutor
faculty	legible	narration	refrain	usage

Learning in Communities

My mother didn't like English when she was in school. She's glad that I do, but it is really hard for her to understand why. She doesn't realize how much schools have changed. For example, the English **faculty** (1) at our school believe in cooperative learning. That means that the teachers encourage us to get together to share our ideas and thoughts. It really is true that two heads are better than one, but the English teachers in my mother's school thought that students should sit in straight rows and never take part in group discussion. In my class, on the other hand, everybody **participates** (2) in some kind of class or group discussion every day. Our classroom is really a **forum** (3), because in it everyone's ideas can be heard and discussed.

Something Old, Something New

We still study some of the things my mom studied. For example, we spend some time on **literary** (4) works, and we have even read some of the same stories and poems that she did. Sometimes we talk about the elements of literature, like characters and plots. We discuss what's **symbolic** (5) and what's not. My mom didn't get to do that. The teacher just told the students which things stood for something else. We enjoy figuring it out for ourselves.

We get to add our own ideas to a literary work sometimes. For example, we might write a **dialogue** (6) between two characters that takes place ten or twenty years after the story ends. It really is fun to think about what they might say to each other. We get to use our imaginations, but we have to think critically, too. The dialogue has to be **credible** (7). It's easy to be imaginative, but it's not always easy to be believable.

A lot of our writing assignments are harder than the ones my mother had. Her teacher just asked that the handwriting be **legible** (8) and that students avoid **grammatical** (9) mistakes. My mom says that as long as the paper was easy to read, and as long as there weren't problems with subject-verb agreement and stuff like that, she never had to rewrite a paper, even if her paper didn't say anything interesting.

Getting Writing Right

Our class is really different. We treat each writing assignment as if we were professional writers getting our **manuscripts** (10) ready to be published. The first draft is never the last. We **revise** (11) and **revise**, and we always keep in mind our audience and our purpose for writing. This means we make changes in content and in tone. We add stuff, we take stuff out, we move stuff around. All my mother did was edit for mechanics, grammar, and **usage** (12). We care about that, too, but it's the last thing we do. Actually, I'm pretty good at grammar and mechanics, but I have some trouble using words like *specially* and *especially*. I'm specially—oops!—especially prone to mixing them up. That's one reason I like working in groups. Sometimes a couple of the other kids can help me understand something that's not clear. Usually I can return the favor and **tutor** (13) them in something they don't understand very well. That way we can show our **mastery** (14) of language skills on the tests our teacher gives us. Our high scores on these tests show we are experts at language skills.

At the beginning of the year we spent a few weeks on poetry, but now we are writing mainly **prose** (15)—mostly stories and essays. Last week we all wrote **editorials** (16). I gave my opinion when I wrote that the school board ought to provide funds for more soccer equipment at our school. I think it may be published in Thursday's school paper. We are working on longer pieces of **persuasion** (17) this week. The purpose of my essay will be to convince the city council to start a local recycling program.

Our next paper will require us to use **narration** (18). That just means each of us will have to tell a story. I think I'm going to write about the day we had a funeral for my sister Angela's pet frog.

I use writing a lot now as a way to explore how I feel and what I think. I really got into that habit because we have to keep a **journal** (19) for class. I write in mine almost every day now. I use it like a diary to sort out my feelings, thoughts, and memories.

My mother is amazed to see me write in it so often. She is proud to have a good English student in the house, and she says, "I can't believe it. I can't believe it," over and over like a **refrain** (20) in a song. I think she is beginning to realize that it's not too late to learn to like to write or to learn to use writing in her life. "You know, Mom," I tell her, "it's never too late to change."

EXERCISE *Reading Strategically* ☛

Directions. Answer each of the following items by circling the letter of the correct answer. You may need to refer to the essay as you answer the items. The numbers of the items are the same as the numbers of the boldface vocabulary words in the essay.

1. In the first paragraph of the essay, **faculty** means
  (A) teachers
  (B) classes
  (C) thinkers
  (D) students

2. The writer says that "everybody **participates** in some kind of class or group discussion every day." Here, **participates** means
  (A) divides
  (B) enjoys with
  (C) argues
  (D) takes part

3. Which of the following is the most likely reason that the writer says her classroom is a **forum**?
(A) The classroom is like a law court.
(B) The classroom is a place for public discussion.
(C) Group discussions cannot take place in the classroom.
(D) The students are required to sit in straight rows and stay silent.

4. To give a clue to the meaning of **literary,** the writer
(A) uses the word *works*
(B) tells us that the class reads stories and poems
(C) refers to time
(D) says her mother has read some of these works

5. To give a clue to the meaning of **symbolic,** the writer
(A) refers to characters and plots
(B) refers to class discussions
(C) says that her mom was never permitted to participate in any sort of class discussion
(D) tells us that her mother's teacher told students which things stood for something else

6. All of the following are good definitions for **dialogue** except
(A) conversation
(B) discussion
(C) command
(D) exchange

7. The writer says that the **dialogue** should be **credible**. Here, **credible** means
(A) imaginative
(B) critical
(C) thoughtful
(D) believable

8. In the fourth paragraph, **legible** means
(A) free of error
(B) mistaken
(C) easy to read
(D) difficult to understand

9. To let us know that **grammatical** means "following the rules of standard English," the writer
(A) reminds us that papers should be neat
(B) uses the example of subject-verb agreement
(C) reminds us that problems should be avoided
(D) suggests that papers should be interesting

10. The writer indicates that she treats each writing assignment as if she were preparing a **manuscript** to submit for publication. Here, **manuscript** means
(A) a work prepared by a writer for publication
(B) a published work of literature
(C) a typical writing assignment
(D) writing not expected to be seen by anyone except for the author

11. To give a clue to the meaning of **revise,** the writer
(A) says that the class members keep audience and purpose in mind
(B) uses the word *stuff*
(C) says that the class members make changes in their writing
(D) repeats herself

12. Which of the following items is an example of a rule of **usage** that is revealed indirectly in the essay?
  (A) Ask other students for help.
  (B) Place an exclamation point at the end of *oops*.
  (C) Work in groups.
  (D) Do not use the word *specially* to mean *especially*.

13. The author writes, "Usually I can return the favor and **tutor** them in something they don't understand very well." Here, **tutor** means
  (A) confuse
  (B) instruct individually
  (C) thank
  (D) organize thoroughly

14. You can tell from the essay that **mastery** means
  (A) expert skill or knowledge
  (B) general confusion
  (C) a teacher
  (D) complete lack of understanding

15. The writer states that she and her classmates write different kinds of **prose.** Here, **prose** means
  (A) writing that is not poetry
  (B) stories and essays only
  (C) writing that will be published
  (D) editorials only

16. In this essay, **editorials** means
  (A) essays
  (B) written opinions
  (C) any writing other than prose
  (D) all forms of prose

17. To give a clue to the meaning of **persuasion,** the writer
  (A) says she is working on an essay
  (B) refers to the length of her paper
  (C) tells us the purpose of her essay is to convince
  (D) indicates she supports a local recycling plan

18. To provide a clue to the meaning of **narration,** the writer
  (A) associates **narration** with paper
  (B) hints that she will write a humorous essay
  (C) hints that **narration** is about nature
  (D) says the students will have to tell stories

19. You can tell that **journal** means
  (A) a writing assignment
  (B) a newspaper or magazine
  (C) a record of personal thoughts
  (D) a class project

20. You can tell that **refrain** means
  (A) an expression of disbelief
  (B) something that only occurs once
  (C) something that is repeated
  (D) a realization

READING NEW WORDS IN CONTEXT

| Lesson 8 | **CONTEXT:** Change in Individuals and Communities

Introduction. Are you a football fan? If not, you probably know someone who is. Since the first college football game in the United States, the game has gone through many changes to become football as we know it today.

The following article describes the highlights of the history of football and gives you an opportunity to expand your vocabulary. Below are twenty vocabulary words that are used in the article and in the exercise that follows it.

adhere	forbidding	minority	opposition	recommend
excel	hardy	obstacle	participant	scholarship
expand	intellect	officially	penetrate	tactics
fatigue	maneuver	opponent	pursue	yield

Changing the Rules: The Development of College Football

The first college football game in the United States was played in 1869 between Rutgers and Princeton. Rutgers beat its **opponent** (1) by two goals. In those days, however, football was very different from the game it is today. The rules were almost the same as those for soccer. The **tactics** (2) that the players used were very similar to those that soccer players use today. A player could move the ball only with his feet, his head, or his shoulders.

Different Rules
In the early days of the game, different schools played by different rules. Eventually, Columbia and Yale, two big football schools, agreed to play by the same rules. But Harvard was different. For example, Harvard allowed the team to **maneuver** (3) the ball by having a player pick it up and run with it. Since Harvard wanted to stick with its own rules rather than **adhere** (4) to the rules set down by Columbia and Yale, Harvard had to look elsewhere for teams to play.

Harvard found McGill, a university in Montreal, Canada. The schools agreed to play two games. The first game used Harvard rules, and Harvard won easily. The second game was played by McGill's rules, the rules of rugby. The McGill team provided Harvard with stiff **opposition** (5), but Harvard's resistance was also strong, and the game ended in a tie. However, McGill won in a way because the Harvard team enjoyed the McGill approach to football. They ended up adopting McGill's egg-shaped ball and most of the rules of rugby.

A Truly American Game
Eventually Yale, Rutgers, Princeton, and Columbia adopted the Harvard style of play, and the first intercollegiate football association was established. By 1880, a truly American game of football had been developed.

In those early years, football was an extremely rough game. There were few rules to protect **participants** (6). It was okay to kick, to punch, and to poke other players on the field. At that time, the goal was to advance the ball five yards in three downs. If the team did not make the five yards, it had to **yield** (7) the ball by giving it to the other team.

Since a player was likely to play on both offense and defense and no substitutions were allowed, football players had to be **hardy** (8). Also, teams sometimes played more than one game per week. Naturally, players were tired, but **fatigue** (9) was the least of their problems. The game seemed to become rougher, more brutal, and more **forbidding** (10) each year. After several deaths and many serious injuries, parents and many faculty members began to **recommend** (11) that colleges no longer have football teams.

Changing the Rules

Instead of following this suggestion that colleges ban the game, representatives of the colleges decided to find ways to make the game safer. Rather than completely stop the game, representatives from several teams met at a conference called by President Theodore Roosevelt. They designed new rules and regulations. These rules were formally adopted and **officially** (12) went into effect at the beginning of the 1906 football season. The new rules made the game safer and more interesting. One significant change made the forward pass legal.

Further rule changes occurred in 1912. One change **expanded** (13) the area of the field in which a pass could be caught. This increase in playing space allowed for catches ten yards behind the goal line. In addition, teams were allowed four downs to move the ball ten yards, and a touchdown became worth six points.

The new rules also opened up the running game, and a new kind of player was added to the team—the running back. These backs, who carried the ball, had to be fast because they were chased by the opposing team. They also had to be able to do some fancy cutting and running while being **pursued** (14) down the field.

The Two-Squad System

Football remained much the same game for thirty years. Then, in 1945, Michigan coach Fritz Crisler sprung a surprise at the Michigan-Army game.

The Army team was strong, and Crisler knew only one way to keep his team in the game. He divided his team into two squads. One squad played offense, and the other played defense. This kept his players from becoming too tired. His team didn't win, but at least it was able to play a strong game. Crisler's two-squad system was legal because of a rule change that had occurred in 1941. No one else had thought of how to take advantage of it.

Soon most schools adopted the practice of using two separate squads, an offense and a defense. Schools using the single-squad approach were so few that they were in the **minority** (15). However, the two-squad system was not without its problems. Recruiting and maintaining two squads was so expensive that colleges began to think of the two-squad system as an **obstacle** (16) to running an efficient team. The two-squad system was banned in 1953. However, primarily for the sake of the health and safety of the players, the system was restored in the early 1960s. In the meantime, another important rule change had been made. Beginning in 1958, a team could make two points after a touchdown if a runner could **penetrate** (17) the defense by pushing through it to cross the goal line or if a receiver could catch the ball behind the goal line.

Changing Attitudes

No major changes have been made in the game in many years, but colleges have begun to make some changes in their treatment of football players. Schools have traditionally offered **scholarships** (18) to good football players. A lot of young men who received those scholarships probably could not have afforded college without them. However, players were often treated as though only their ability to play football mattered. They weren't expected to **excel** (19), or even be very good, in their studies, because athletic ability was valued over **intellect** (20). Often the player flunked many of his classes, and, when his playing days were over, he had no real education to rely on in the workplace. Today, more and more universities are recognizing their duty to educate the football players who make Saturday and Sunday afternoons so exciting and memorable for their fans.

EXERCISE   *Reading Strategically* ☞

Directions. Answer each of the following items by circling the letter of the correct answer. You may need to refer to the article as you answer the items. The numbers of the items are the same as the numbers of the boldface vocabulary words in the article.

1. All of the following are good definitions of **opponent** *except*
   (A) foe
   (B) rival
   (C) defense
   (D) enemy

2. To let us know that **tactics** means "methods or techniques" the writer
   (A) compares football to soccer
   (B) reminds us that the game requires rules
   (C) provides examples of methods that players could use
   (D) suggests that soccer and football are different

3. Which of the following is an example mentioned in the article of a way football teams may **maneuver**?
   (A) Harvard was different.
   (B) A player may run with the ball.
   (C) Columbia and Yale were two big football schools.
   (D) Columbia, Yale, and Harvard could not agree on the rules.

4. The writer states that Harvard did not want to **adhere** to the rules that the other teams had established. Here, **adhere** means
   (A) hear out
   (B) overcome
   (C) stick to
   (D) set down

5. You can tell from the article that **opposition** means
   (A) resistance
   (B) rules
   (C) opponent
   (D) hostility

6. You can tell from the article that **participants** means
   (A) early football was especially rough
   (B) players in the game
   (C) few rules in the game
   (D) the goal was to advance the ball

7. The author writes, "If the team did not make the five yards, it had to **yield** the ball by giving it to the other team." Here, **yield** means
   (A) kick
   (B) give up
   (C) throw
   (D) advance

8. The most likely reason a football player had to be **hardy** was that
   (A) players often had to give the ball to the other team
   (B) players were often tired
   (C) players had to play on both offense and defense
   (D) players were members of a team

9. The author writes, "Naturally, players were tired, but **fatigue** was the least of their problems." Here, **fatigue** means
   (A) football
   (B) tiredness
   (C) clothing
   (D) roughness

10. To give a clue to the meaning of **forbidding,** the writer
   (A) uses it with the words *rougher* and *brutal*
   (B) states that some recommended an end to college football teams
   (C) lets us know the players were tired
   (D) tells us fatigue was a problem

11. The writer indicates that people began
to **recommend** that colleges eliminate
football. Here, **recommend** means
- (A) argue
- (B) agree
- (C) suggest
- (D) understand

12. The writer indicates that the new rules
were formally adopted and **officially**
went into effect in 1906. Here, **offi-
cially** means
- (A) effectively
- (B) completely
- (C) ceremoniously
- (D) formally

13. You can tell from the article that
expanded means
- (A) increased
- (B) surrounded
- (C) explained
- (D) indicated

14. The writer tells us that running backs
were **pursued** down the field. Here,
pursued means
- (A) caught
- (B) ran
- (C) scored
- (D) chased

15. To give a clue to the meaning of
minority, the writer
- (A) reminds us that one squad played
offense and the other squad
played defense
- (B) lets us know that the two-squad
system had problems
- (C) tells us that only a few schools
used the single-squad system
- (D) uses the word to
describe two-squad schools

16. Another meaning for **obstacle** is
- (A) something that defends
- (B) something that tackles
- (C) something that brings good luck
- (D) something that gets in the way

17. The writer reports that beginning in
1958, a team could make two points
after a touchdown if a runner could
penetrate the defense and cross the
goal line. Here, **penetrate** means
- (A) push through
- (B) pass over
- (C) charm
- (D) throw a pass

18. To let us know that **scholarships** are
gifts of money used to help students
pay for school, the writer
- (A) tells us that only good players got
scholarships
- (B) tell us that many football players
needed **scholarships** to afford
college
- (C) tells us that players were often
treated as if only their football
skills mattered
- (D) reminds us that the football
players were students

19. You can tell from the selection that
excel means
- (A) not to play athletics
- (B) to get an education
- (C) to try very hard
- (D) to be superior

20. In the last paragraph, **intellect** means
- (A) memory
- (B) emotions
- (C) mental ability
- (D) physical agility

Name _____ Date _____ Class _____

| Lesson 9 | **CONTEXT: Change in Individuals and Communities**

Introduction. One of the biggest challenges that we face in growing up is accepting change. In the following excerpt from a story, you will read about a group of young people who face that challenge.

The excerpt gives you an opportunity to expand your vocabulary. Below are twenty vocabulary words that are used in the passage and in the exercise that follows it.

acute	crisis	inhabit	ridicule	timid
adopt	hesitation	intolerable	rival	turmoil
anguish	hysterical	irritable	self-conscious	vague
blemish	immature	maternal	tendency	wretched

Going Their Separate Ways

Carmen, Anna, Jennifer, Roberto, and Brad have known each other almost all their lives. They've gone to the same school since preschool. Twice, they've all been in the same class. Only a few groups of friends get anywhere near their level of closeness. Almost none can **rival** (1) it.

In the Beginning
They are a little **vague** (2) about how they first met. No one remembers for sure.

"I think I met Anna when our moms parked us in strollers in front of Lou Capello's fruit stand," offers Brad.

"Yeah," giggles Carmen, "and Anna probably tried to wipe the drool from your chin and comb your hair." The group jokes often about Anna's **maternal** (3) instincts, and they call her Little Mother.

"Jen and Carmen were born two days apart at St. Anthony's," says Roberto. "We think they probably met in the nursery and plotted then and there to take over the neighborhood. Jen, how did you two first get together with Anna?"

"Who knows?" says Jen, "We've been in and out of each other's houses ever since I can remember. We **adopted** (4) each other as sisters and the guys as brothers a long time ago. We had a **tendency** (5) to always be together. That natural leaning became a habit. I guess that's why it's so hard to deal with what will happen this fall."

It's a sunny warm Saturday afternoon in late August, and the group is gathered on Jen's front steps. September is going to bring big changes for the Grant Heights kids. The members of this close-knit group are about to lose much of what they have taken for granted. As a result, these teens are experiencing the worst emotional **turmoil** (6) of their young lives.

"We're all pretty stressed out," says Brad. "Everybody is a little **hysterical** (7) from time to time. Yesterday I told Anna a joke. One minute she was laughing, the next she was crying."

The group falls silent. Brad fidgets. He grows more and more uncomfortable with the unbearable silence. Finally, it becomes **intolerable** (8) for him. "Have you heard the joke? It's the one about the grizzly bear who moves to Atlantic City—"

Roberto moans. Anna covers her ears.

"Stop him, somebody, before he tells it again, and we all cry," Carmen shrieks. Roberto fakes strangling Brad. "He is the world's worst joke teller. It's a **blemish** (9) on his otherwise perfect character, the flaw in an otherwise charming personality. Actually it's only one of several flaws. If you'd like a list . . ."

"Go ahead. **Ridicule** (10) me. Mock me. Laugh and point. You'll see. One night ten years from now, you'll turn on *The Tonight Show* and there I'll be. You'll say, 'I used to know him in the old neighborhood.'" Suddenly Brad stops and looks away.

Anna's Reaction

"Nothing will ever be the same." There is **anguish** (11) in Anna's voice, and tears well up in her eyes. She points down the street to the sign indicating that Carmen's house has been sold. Then she points across the street to the For Sale sign on Roberto's.

"I hate this. I hate it. I hate it!" The group considers Anna the shy one, but there is nothing **timid** (12) about her today. She expresses her frustration and pain openly and readily without **hesitation** (13).

"My dad keeps saying you have to accept change. Try to be more adult about it. I don't care if it is **immature** (14), though. I don't want to accept it. I want my friends here with me. I want things to be the way they've always been."

Roberto skillfully moves his wheelchair next to Anna and puts a comforting arm around her shoulders. "At least you and Jen will still have each other, and Brad will still be in the neighborhood. I can take the bus from Eastside. Carmen can come back on holidays." He is trying to cheer everyone up, but the look of **acute** (15) despair on his friends' faces tells him he has failed miserably.

"I know it's better than nothing, but with Carmen in Florida and you an hour and a half away, and Brad at Performing Arts instead of St. Thomas's . . . It's not the same. Sometimes my parents act like I'm being a spoiled child. I'm not some little kid who is **irritable** (16) because she didn't get her nap. I'm losing something big here." Anna's voice has gotten louder and louder. She realizes that she is drawing attention to herself and becomes **self-conscious** (17).

Jen speaks. "It's what my Aunt Maggie would call a **wretched** (18) state of affairs. It's miserable for all of us. It's a **crisis** (19), a major turning point in our lives, but, hey, guys, don't you know? We may not all live in the same neighborhood, but as long as we **inhabit** (20) the same planet, nothing can really keep us apart."

EXERCISE *Reading Strategically* ☞

Directions. Answer each of the following items by circling the letter of the correct answer. You may need to refer to the excerpt as you answer the items. The numbers of the items are the same as the numbers of the boldface vocabulary words in the story.

1. The author tells us that few friends reach the level of closeness that this group has and that none **rival** it. Here, **rival** means

(A) fight
(B) equal
(C) level
(D) make fun of

2. All of the following are good definitions of **vague** *except*

(A) uncertain
(B) unclear
(C) unbelievable
(D) general

3. To give a clue to the meaning of **maternal,** the writer
(A) tells us that the group calls Anna *Little Mother*
(B) tells us that Carmen giggles about Anna
(C) tells us that Jen and Anna were born two days apart
(D) hints that Anna should be less cautious

4. To let us know that **adopted** means "to take in as a family member," the writer
(A) lets us know that the group goes in and out of each other's houses
(B) shows that the members of the group have an easy relationship with one another
(C) lets us know that the group thinks of themselves as brothers and sisters
(D) hints that a change will occur in the fall

5. You can tell from the story that **tendency** means
(A) tenderness
(B) a natural leaning
(C) forgetfulness
(D) a dreamlike state

6. The author tells us that the group is experiencing emotional **turmoil**. Here, **turmoil** means
(A) change
(B) confusion
(C) closeness
(D) acceptance

7. Which of the following is an example of **hysterical** behavior that occurs in the story?
(A) The group falls silent after Brad speaks.
(B) Brad tells jokes to try to cheer up the others.
(C) Brad blames everyone for being stressed out.
(D) Anna laughs one minute and cries the next.

8. The writer tells us that silence became **intolerable** for Brad. Here, **intolerable** means
(A) slightly uncomfortable
(B) unlikeable
(C) unbearable
(D) completely unnecessary

9. The writer of this story gives a clue to the meaning of **blemish**. What is the clue?
(A) Carmen shouts.
(B) Roberto pretends to strangle Brad as punishment for being such a bad joke teller.
(C) All the characters are teenagers.
(D) Carmen links a character **blemish** to a personality flaw.

10. The writer reports that Brad says, "**Ridicule** me. Mock me. Laugh and point." Here, **ridicule** means
(A) hurt
(B) watch eagerly
(C) make fun of
(D) doubt the truth of

11. You can tell from the story that **anguish** means
(A) pain
(B) tears
(C) embarrassment
(D) pity

12. To give a clue to the meaning of **timid,** the writer
(A) tells us that Anna points down the street
(B) tells us that the group thinks of Anna as the shy one
(C) tells us that Anna is frustrated
(D) tells us that Carmen's house has been sold

13. The author writes, "She expresses her frustration and pain openly and readily without **hesitation**." Here, **hesitation** means
   (A) arguing
   (B) pause
   (C) anger
   (D) fear

14. The author reports that Anna says, "I don't care if it is **immature,** though. I don't want to accept it." Here, **immature** means
   (A) childish
   (B) adult
   (C) overly emotional
   (D) silly

15. The writer reports that Roberto realizes he has failed to cheer his friends up when he sees the **acute** despair on their faces. Here, **acute** means
   (A) pretty
   (B) simple
   (C) severe
   (D) unnatural

16. How does the writer of this story let us know that **irritable** means "cranky or easily upset"?
   (A) Anna says she is losing something important and deserves to have her feeling respected.
   (B) Anna says that she wants more than anything in the world to take a nap.
   (C) Anna is speaking to her friends.
   (D) Anna refers to the way a small child feels when she doesn't get enough rest.

17. Which of the following is the most likely reason that Anna becomes **self-conscious**?
   (A) She has been talking about her family.
   (B) She realizes that she is drawing attention to herself.
   (C) She feels her loss deeply.
   (D) She thinks that things will never be the same after Carmen and Roberto move away.

18. In the story, Jen says, "It's what my Aunt Maggie would call a **wretched** state of affairs." Here, **wretched** means
   (A) miserable
   (B) important
   (C) twisted
   (D) ungrateful

19. In the last paragraph, **crisis** means
   (A) state of affairs
   (B) minor problem
   (C) a turning point
   (D) uncomfortable

20. In the last paragraph, **inhabit** means
   (A) wear
   (B) run away to
   (C) live on or in
   (D) agree

Name _____ Date _____ Class _____

| Lesson 10 | **CONTEXT: Change in Individuals and Communities**

Introduction. Historians and history teachers usually are fascinated by change and the past. The selection you are about to read will tell you about a group of students who share their teacher's enthusiasm.

The story gives you an opportunity to expand your vocabulary. Below are twenty vocabulary words that are used in the selection and in the exercise that follows it.

absolute	cultural	illusion	perilous	toil
banish	era	lure	proclamation	tyrant
barbarous	fortress	monarchy	serf	valiant
baron	grandeur	pageant	status	vengeance

In the Good Old Days

The students in Mr. Washington's history class are just finishing a unit on the Middle Ages (A.D. 476–1450). They have learned a lot. They know, for example, that historians consider the fall of Rome in the fifth century the end of the Roman period and the beginning of a new **era** (1). They can also tell you that historians usually describe the people who overthrew Rome as **barbarous** (2)—harsh, brutal, and oppressive—and as true **tyrants** (3), or cruel masters. To gain protection from these absolute rulers, many peasants in Europe bound themselves to wealthy landowners. These laborers, known as **serfs** (4), were tied to the land and could not leave without their lords' permission.

All of the students are doing reports and will explain that the rulers were not totally uncivilized. Caroline is studying **monarchy** (5), government by kings and queens, and how it developed in the Middle Ages. She is especially interested in one of the most important of the early monarchs, Charlemagne. Charlemagne was king of the Franks. In 800 A.D. he was crowned emperor of the West.

Caroline is also interested in the fact that the monarchy that developed in England was not an **absolute** (6) monarchy. This means that the English rulers were important, but their power was not unlimited. To rule completely, they needed the help of the **barons** (7) and other members of the nobility. The power of the kings was further restricted when the barons forced King John to sign the Magna Carta in 1215. This document paved the way for the development of more democratic governments and proved to be one of the most important **cultural** (8) advancements of the time.

The Crusades
Emile has been especially interested in the crusades, a series of attempts by Christians and Muslims to capture the Holy Land in the Middle East. A crusade involved taking a long and **perilous** (9) journey. One might die of disease, drown at sea, or be killed or captured. Some people made the journey and braved the terrible conditions because of their religious beliefs. Emile, however, is most interested in the servants who went because they had no choice.

For them, the journey involved hard work. They **toiled** (10) to build camps, make food, and haul heavy loads. Of course, some other people went because they could not resist the **lure** (11) of adventure, the call to danger and excitement.

The Tournaments

Kirsten and Suni are working together on a report on a tournament tradition begun in the tenth century. Before a tournament was held, a **proclamation** (12) was issued by a king or a great lord. Such an announcement could only be made by people of very high **status** (13), people of high rank and importance.

The tournaments were spectacular events, **pageants** (14) of color, noise, and excitement. The stands for the wealthier spectators were decorated, and everyone dressed in their best clothes.

Knights in the Middle Ages were expected to be **valiant** (15). Bravery, however, was not the only requirement for knighthood. Tournaments were open only to honorable knights. A knight accused of wrongdoing was questioned by tournament officials. If they believed he was guilty, they could **banish** (16) him from the tournament. To be sent away in this way was a terrible disgrace.

The knights battled each other on horseback. Usually, the fights were not serious; they were more or less games. Sometimes, however, a knight would take the opportunity to get his **vengeance** (17) on a fellow knight whom he felt had wronged him. In any case, each knight carried something that belonged to his chosen lady when he went onto the field. It might be a ribbon or a scarf. The colors indicated that he was her protector and was sworn to fight for her.

Castles

Arnold and Hoa are both interested in the castles of the period. Castles were not just homes for the nobility. They were also sturdy **fortresses** (18), buildings designed to withstand attacks. Arnold and Hoa say that most of their ideas about ancient castles have proved to be **illusions** (19), false images that have little to do with fact.

Castles in the Middle Ages were not luxurious places. In fact, they weren't even comfortable. They were dark, drafty, and dirty. Nevertheless, there was a certain **grandeur** (20) about them. They may have been uncomfortable, but they were magnificent buildings with high towers and grand halls. Many of these castles still stand today throughout Europe, and most are now museums and tourist attractions. These castles, like the knights, the tournaments, and the crusades, help guide students like Arnold and Hoa to a new understanding of what life was really like in the Middle Ages.

Mr. Washington's students are learning a great deal about history and change, but the most important change may be the change that is occurring inside them—they love their history class.

EXERCISE *Reading Strategically* ✍

Directions. Answer each of the following items by circling the letter of the correct answer. You may need to refer to the selection as you answer the items. The numbers of the items are the same as the numbers of the vocabulary words in the selection.

1. In the first paragraph of the selection, **era** means
   (A) a period of history
   (B) the fifth century
   (C) history
   (D) a lot of facts

2. All of the following are good definitions of **barbarous** *except*
   (A) harsh
   (B) overthrown
   (C) brutal
   (D) uncivilized

3. You can tell from the selection that **tyrants** means all of the following *except*
   (A) absolute rulers
   (B) cruel masters
   (C) knights
   (D) dictators

4. In the first paragraph, **serfs** means
   (A) people called by the lure of excitement
   (B) brutal invaders who overthrew Rome
   (C) laborers bound to their masters' land
   (D) people punished for their religious beliefs

5. The writer tells us that Caroline is studying the development of **monarchy**. Here, **monarchy** means
   (A) the development of government
   (B) a special branch of historical studies
   (C) government by a king, queen, or emperor
   (D) only the government of England

6. To give a clue to the meaning of **absolute,** the writer
   (A) tells us that Caroline is also interested in English **monarchs**
   (B) tells us that Caroline is aware of the importance of the Magna Carta
   (C) tells us that King John signed the Magna Carta
   (D) tells us that the power of the **monarch** was not unlimited

7. You can tell from the selection that **barons** means
   (A) emperors of the West
   (B) **monarchs**
   (C) people who hold complete power
   (D) members of the nobility

8. You can tell from the selection that **cultural** means pertaining to
   (A) improvements of a given period
   (B) restriction of power
   (C) an important event
   (D) more democratic governments

9. The author writes, "A crusade involved taking a long and **perilous** journey." Here, **perilous** means
   (A) lengthy
   (B) make-believe
   (C) dangerous
   (D) holy

10. Which of the following is an example of how some people **toiled** on the journey?
   (A) They were forced to go.
   (B) They attracted Emile's interest.
   (C) They built camps and moved heavy loads.
   (D) They lost their heavy loads.

11. The writer says that some people went on crusades because they could not resist "the **lure** of adventure." Here, **lure** means
   (A) danger
   (B) thought
   (C) temptation
   (D) journey

12. To give a clue to the meaning of **proclamation,** the writer
   (A) links **proclamation** to the word *announcement*
   (B) tells us that tournaments began in the tenth century
   (C) tells us that knights came to the town where the tournament was to be held
   (D) tells us that entertainers came to tournaments

13. How does the writer let us know that **status** means "rank"?
    (A) The writer tells us that the **proclamations** were only issued by people of high rank.
    (B) The writer tells us that knights accepted the invitations.
    (C) The writer hints that tournaments did not rank very highly in the tenth century.
    (D) The writer hints that no one could refuse the offer.

14. The author writes, "The tournaments were spectacular events, **pageants** of color, noise, and excitement." Here, **pageants** means
    (A) excitement
    (B) stands for wealthy spectators
    (C) tapestries and flags
    (D) spectacular events

15. To give a clue to the meaning of **valiant,** the writer
    (A) states that knights were expected to be honorable
    (B) indicates that knights could be questioned by tournament officials
    (C) links **valiant** to wrongdoing
    (D) links **valiant** to bravery

16. The writer states that officials could **banish** a knight from a tournament. Here, **banish** means
    (A) polish
    (B) judge
    (C) send away
    (D) laugh him out of

17. The writer indicates that a knight might use the tournament for purposes of **vengeance**. Here, **vengeance** means
    (A) making money
    (B) anger
    (C) opportunity
    (D) revenge

18. The author writes that castles were "**fortresses,** buildings designed to withstand attack." Here, **fortresses** means
    (A) museums
    (B) forts
    (C) homes
    (D) castles

19. The author writes, "Arnold and Hoa say that most of their ideas about ancient castles have proved to be **illusions**." Here, **illusions** means
    (A) magic tricks
    (B) false images
    (C) luxuries
    (D) old

20. The author writes that there is a certain **grandeur** about old castles. Here, **grandeur** means
    (A) uncomfortableness
    (B) magnificence
    (C) darkness
    (D) grimness

READING NEW WORDS IN CONTEXT

Lesson 11 | CONTEXT: Change in Science and Technology

Introduction. What do people who major in science do with their lives? Do they all go to medical school or into the space program? In the following dialogue, you'll discover some of their other options.

The dialogue gives you an opportunity to expand your vocabulary. Below are twenty vocabulary words that are used in the dialogue and in the exercise that follows it.

antiseptic	glucose	naturalist	organism	seasonal
camouflage	habitat	nocturnal	parasite	temperate
edible	immune	nutrition	pigment	undergrowth
endurance	mammal	optical	preservation	zoology

At Work in the World of Science

Renata Klein and Damien Green both like their science classes. They are thinking about pursuing careers in science, but they aren't certain.

Damien: My mom seems to think I should try to go to medical school, but the truth is I can't stand that **antiseptic** (1) smell that hospitals have. I know they have to be really clean, but it makes me gag.

Renata: I've thought about being an optometrist—you know, the person who does glasses and contact lenses. By the time I graduate from college, though, things may have changed so much that **optical** (2) problems are corrected in whole new ways.

Damien: Yeah, it's hard to plan ahead in a rapidly changing world, but biochemistry seems really exciting. I was interested in that lecture on the **immune** (3) system the other day. Finding ways for the body to build up a good healthy defense against diseases interests me more than finding ways to cure them.

Renata: Discovering cures for diseases could be exciting, too. I knew someone once who studied some **parasite** (4) that caused a terrible disease in people who live in . . . Oh, I forget where. Anyway, this bug lived on the human liver.

Damien: Didn't this woman study how to break its life cycle? It really was a small **organism** (5), wasn't it? A living creature that was almost invisible?

Renata: Yes, and one of her friends was researching the causes of skin cancer. The experiment had something to do with changing the **pigment** (6) in the skin of mice. He made some mice darker-skinned than others.

Damien: I don't think I'd want to do research using laboratory animals.

Renata: Well, maybe you could deal with **nutrition** (7) studies, though. You know, like feeding one group of mice vegetables and fruits and the others junk food. Maybe you'd try to make one group of mice overweight so that they develop diabetes. Then you'd run a **glucose** (8) test to check the level of sugar in their blood, or maybe you'd test their physical **endurance** (9) by having them run on little treadmills.

Damien: I don't know. I have a hard time seeing animals in cages. I have to admit, though, today's wildlife parks do a good job of making the animals' enclosures seem like their natural **habitats** (10). Some of the landscaping is so natural that you have to look carefully to see the animals. The last time I went to our wildlife park, there was this one little fawn that I almost missed because it was in the **undergrowth** (11) at the back of the enclosure. It was under a bush, and its coat was spotted the same colors as the plants and bushes, so it served as **camouflage** (12). You had to look really closely to see the fawn.

Renata: Since you like animals so much, you might want to work toward the **preservation** (13) of an endangered species. It would be great to help save the panda, don't you think? You know, you might even want to do something like Dian Fossey. You know, she's the one who observed mountain gorillas. That would be really interesting. She learned that if you hang around long enough, the animals will accept you as one of their own. I think that may mean that you have to eat whatever the animals think is **edible** (14)! Maybe you could fake it if they were eating something really disgusting. . . .

Damien: That would be interesting. I wonder, is it just primates like apes and chimpanzees who will accept humans, or would other **mammals** (15)?

I think maybe a lion or a tiger would just look at me and say to itself, "Dinner."

Renata: You have a point. I guess it's best to watch certain animals from a distance.

Damien: Yeah, and it's also probably best not to pick a **nocturnal** (16) animal. It would just be up all night, and you'd never get any sleep.

Renata: You would also want to pick an animal that lives in a **temperate** (17) climate. Can you imagine hanging out at the South Pole with penguins or in the desert with the Gila monster? Not for me, thank you.

Damien: I'll bet it's not **seasonal** (18) work either. If you worked in Alaska, I have a feeling you wouldn't be able to hang out and watch only during the summer and then take off in the winter for Acapulco. Maybe I should just study the plants of this area. On the other hand, I could study all the plants and animals in one area, and become an all-around **naturalist** (19).

Renata: Or we could become veterinarians. Then we would have to major in the study of animals in college. What do you call that?

Damien: **Zoology** (20). Let's think about that. We could open a clinic here after we graduate.

Renata: But what about the **antiseptic** smell? Animal hospitals have it, too.

Damien: Maybe I'll get used to it.

EXERCISE: *Reading Strategically*

Directions. Answer each of the following items by circling the letter of the correct answer. You may need to refer to the dialogue as you answer the items. The numbers of the items are the same as the numbers of the boldface vocabulary words in the dialogue.

1. Which is the most likely reason that hospitals have an **antiseptic** smell?
   (A) There are many medications in hospitals.
   (B) Hospitals are cleaned with disinfectants.
   (C) Hospitals need to be very clean.
   (D) Hospitals keep the windows closed.

2. To give a clue to the meaning of **optical,** the writer
   (A) lets us know that **optical** problems are a branch of biochemistry
   (B) associates **optical** with change
   (C) hints that **optical** problems are particularly interesting
   (D) links glasses and contact lenses to the correction of **optical** problems

3. To let us know that **immune** means "protected against disease," the writer
   (A) mentions finding ways to cure diseases
   (B) hints that there is more than one way to cure a disease
   (C) uses the phrase "a good healthy defense against diseases."
   (D) says that there is no defense for not protecting oneself against diseases

4. An example of a **parasite** that is mentioned in the dialogue is
   (A) a buglike creature that lives on the human liver
   (B) a terrible disease
   (C) someone who studies diseases, especially of the liver
   (D) breaking the life cycles of a tiny bug

5. Damien says, "It really was a small **organism**, wasn't it?" Here, **organism** means
   (A) a liver disease
   (B) a life cycle
   (C) a living thing
   (D) the study of **parasites**

6. To give a clue to the meaning of **pigment**, the writer
   (A) tells us that the researcher was a friend of the woman who studied **parasites**
   (B) tells us that the researcher made the skin of some mice darker
   (C) hints that Damien should not plan to work with animals
   (D) encourages us to avoid skin cancer

7. The writer indicates that Renata is interested in **nutrition** studies involving laboratory animals. Here, **nutrition** means
   (A) fruits and vegetables only
   (B) the study of diet
   (C) the study of skin cancer
   (D) studying in groups

8. You can tell from the dialogue that **glucose** means
   (A) treadmill
   (B) test
   (C) arteries
   (D) sugar

9. The writer indicates that to test their physical **endurance,** mice might run on treadmills. Here, **endurance** means
   (A) the ability to withstand hard work
   (B) the veins that carry blood to the heart
   (C) the level of sugar in the blood
   (D) the love of animals

10. All of the following are good definitions of **habitats** *except*
    (A) treadmills
    (B) environments
    (C) dwelling places
    (D) surroundings

11. The writer mentions a fawn that was hidden in the **undergrowth**. Here, **undergrowth** means
    (A) undercoat
    (B) not big enough
    (C) underbrush
    (D) invisible part

12. The writer indicates that the fawn's coat served as **camouflage**. Here, **camouflage** means
    (A) color
    (B) bushes
    (C) a disguise
    (D) a closer look

13. Renata says, "Since you like animals so much, you might want to work toward the **preservation** of an endangered species." Here, **preservation** means
    (A) hunting
    (B) infection
    (C) working
    (D) protection

14. You can tell from the dialogue that **edible** means
(A) poison
(B) fit to eat
(C) disgusting
(D) what animals eat

15. An example of a **mammal** that is mentioned in the dialogue is
(A) a lion
(B) a cave
(C) a point
(D) a distance

16. Damien says, "Yeah, and it's also probably best not to pick a **nocturnal** animal. It would just be up all night, and you'd never get any sleep." Here, **nocturnal** means
(A) nasty
(B) loud
(C) sleeping soundly at night
(D) moving about at night

17. Renata says, "You would also want to pick an animal that lives in a **temperate** climate." Here, **temperate** means
(A) very hot all year round
(B) cold all year round, as in the South Pole
(C) desert-like
(D) neither too hot nor too cold

18. To let us know that **seasonal** means "having to do with the times of the year," the writer
(A) refers to Acapulco
(B) hints that Christmas vacation is coming
(C) says the weather is good
(D) mentions winter and summer

19. The writer indicates that by studying all the plants and animals in an area, one could become a **naturalist**. Here, **naturalist** means
(A) a person who has been to college
(B) a person who lives in a particular area
(C) a person who studies plants and animals
(D) a special kind of veterinarian

20. Damien suggests that he and Renata should think about majoring in **zoology**. Here, **zoology** means
(A) a special kind of veterinarian
(B) the study of medicine
(C) the study of animals
(D) animal hospital

READING NEW WORDS IN CONTEXT

Lesson 12 | CONTEXT: Change in Science and Technology

Introduction. As we get older, we think a bit more seriously about what we want to do with our lives. As technology changes, so does the job market. Those of us entering the marketplace will have to adjust to those changes. The writer of the following essay reveals what she learned while searching for an answer to the question, "What do you want to be?"

The essay gives you an opportunity to expand your vocabulary. Below are twenty vocabulary words that are used in the essay and in the exercise that follows it.

cancel	economical	fundamental	metropolitan	relinquish
compensate	efficiency	futile	percentage	stationery
competent	exceed	logical	prestige	substantial
compute	financial	memorandum	recognition	utility

What Do You Want to Be When You Grow Up?

My first answer was Billy the Kid. Okay, so it was dumb, but I was only four. I didn't know that Billy the Kid was a bad guy. I didn't consider the fact that he was male and I was female. I was not concerned that my career choice did not seem reasonable. I wasn't interested in being **logical** (1) when I was four.

The truth is I'm still a little angry that my family laughed at me. Four-year-olds should be allowed to believe that they can achieve anything they want to achieve. They don't need to be told that their dreams are **futile** (2) and that they have to **relinquish** (3) them. My father, however, made me face the hard facts: It was useless—I was never going to be Billy the Kid, and I might as well let it go.

Finding My Calling—and Falling

The **recognition** (4) of my mistaken reality didn't force me into being aware of more realistic career goals. When I was four and a half, I decided I would learn to fly. I wanted to be a sort of human carrier pigeon and carry messages from one place to another. At first my parents thought I meant that I wanted to fly an airplane, so they left me alone. It was only when they caught me practicing the **fundamentals** (5) of flying that they realized their mistake.

I had a grasp of the basic elements because I had been watching the sparrows and cardinals in the birdbath. First, perch, then leap slightly forward while flapping your wings (arms, of course, in my case) and keeping your body parallel to the ground. I was using the porch railing for practice. I figured I had to stand on something high to **compensate** (6) for the fact that I was a lot bigger than a bird and that my wings were pretty scrawny. You'll have to admit, it makes sense to try to make up for not having feathers. I was not a totally unreasonable child.

I perched and leapt and perched and leapt and perched and leapt. Finally, Mom did her what-are-you-doing-out-there-you'll-break-your-neck-and-little-girls-can't-fly-anyway routine. There went my second career. So far, I had failed at a large **percentage** (7) of my career goals. In fact, I had failed 100 percent, but that did not keep me from trying more new ideas.

I had other answers to the question over the next year or so. I wanted to drive a stagecoach, to tend the gates to the Emerald City of Oz, and to be a garbage collector. Clearly, I was not concerned with **prestige** (8). I didn't care about power or fame or money. Like most kids, I had a limited grasp of the **financial** (9) element of career choices. I mean, I thought five dollars was an amazing sum of money.

At age five, I was also beginning to become a bit impatient with my parents. They didn't seem to think that I was able to do anything. I suspected that they thought I would never be **competent** (10) enough to do anything I wanted to do. True, my first goals were not very **substantial** (11) ones. But even if they were not very stable or solid, at least they were my own ideas. Now, I see some things in them that I think are very important.

Preparing Now for Future Work

First of all, as a child I was willing to pursue some very different goals because I had a variety of interests. In this respect, I was ahead of my time. Today, the job market is changing rapidly. We will all need a mixture of skills to survive.

Secondly, I was imaginative. The people who will be the most successful are the people who can think creatively. It will not be enough to see things clearly—we will have to go beyond that and be able to use things in new ways. In other words, we will have to **exceed** (12) the qualifications of the workers of the past.

Yes, we still need a work force that can read and write. A computer can make writing an office **memorandum** (13) much easier, but it won't tell us what message to write, and it can't tell us how to best get the point across to our fellow workers. We won't be able to just feed a piece of **stationery** (14) into the printer and get back a printed letter.

We'll need mathematics as well. Electronic devices can help us, but the machines can only **compute** (15) the information we give them. They don't tell us how to enter the information or tell us whether we need to add, multiply, divide, or find the square root. We have to know what to do with figures and data so that we can decide if our approach to a problem is **economical** (16)—considering costs is always an important concern in the world of work. A worker who goes into the boss with a set a figures that are wrong because the worker punched the divide button instead of the multiply button is a worker who will soon be out of a job.

As I said before, we will have to be able to do much more work in much less time, but **efficiency** (17) alone is not enough. We will have to be flexible thinkers, creative and adaptable. It's a matter of survival, because the odds are that each of us will change careers at least six times in our lives. We may begin as Billy the Kid and wind up as the gatekeeper in Oz. Okay, **cancel** (18) that idea. Drop it and substitute this instead: A person might graduate from college and work as a copyeditor for a publishing company and then become a teacher of English as a Second Language and then open her own toy store. Or, she might be an assistant to a research scientist, a financial planner, and then a grant writer.

These kinds of changes are likely for all of us whether we live in a rural farm area or in the **metropolitan** (19) area of a major city, whether we begin our working lives after high school or after eight years of college. My point is this: Everything you learn will count. It all has a certain **utility** (20)—creative writing or history can be just as useful as algebra. You have to use your imagination. Think about it this way—you are always trying to find X, when X might be anything, even a carrier pigeon or Billy the Kid.

EXERCISE Reading Strategically

Directions. Answer each of the following items by circling the letter of the correct answer. You may need to refer to the selection as you answer the items. The numbers of the items are the same as the numbers of the boldface vocabulary words in the selection.

1. To give a clue to the meaning of **logical**, the writer
(A) claims that Billy the Kid was a bad guy
(B) associates the word **logical** with career choices
(C) gives an example of unreasonable thinking
(D) says that the truth made her angry

2. The author writes that four-year-olds should not be told that their dreams are **futile**. Here, **futile** means
(A) silly
(B) useless
(C) difficult
(D) about to come true

3. In this essay, **relinquish** means
(A) go beyond
(B) give up
(C) understand
(D) redesign

4. All of the following are good definitions of **recognition** *except*
(A) realization
(B) approval
(C) fact
(D) awareness

5. To let us know that **fundamentals** means "basic elements," the writer
(A) tells us that her parents realized their mistake
(B) tells us that her parents misunderstood her
(C) tells us that she practiced alone
(D) gives us examples of what the child considered to be the basics of flying

6. The writer says that she felt that she had to **compensate** for her size. Here, to **compensate** means to
(A) make up for
(B) spend money
(C) pay back
(D) lie about

7. The author writes, "So far, I had failed at a large **percentage** of my career goals." Here, **percentage** means
(A) beginning
(B) part of one hundred
(C) favorable odd
(D) career choice

8. To give a clue to the meaning of **prestige**, the writer
(A) tells us that she didn't care about money, power, or fame
(B) tells us that she was like most kids
(C) tells us that her understanding of reality was limited
(D) associates the word with concern.

9. In this essay, **financial** means
(A) related to power
(B) famous
(C) related to money
(D) fantastic

10. The writer says that her parents didn't think she was **competent**. Here, **competent** means
(A) complete
(B) unqualified
(C) realistic
(D) able

11. You can tell from the essay that **substantial** means
(A) imaginative
(B) solid
(C) honest
(D) forceful

12. The author writes, "In other words, we will have to **exceed** the qualifications of the workers of the past." Here, **exceed** means
(A) grab
(B) go beyond
(C) review
(D) give up

13. To let us know that **memorandum** means "something written for other workers in the office," the writer
(A) states that the computer will make the work easier
(B) indicates that the computer can't tell us how to get our point across to other workers
(C) says to use stationery
(D) says the workforce must be able to read and write

14. You can tell from the essay that **stationery** means
(A) printed letters
(B) **memorandum**
(C) special paper for writing letters
(D) a floppy disk for the computer

15. The writer indicates that some electronic devices **compute** information. Here, **compute** means
(A) calculate
(B) inform
(C) divide
(D) confuse

16. The writer indicates that it is important to determine whether the solution to a problem is **economical**. Here, **economical** means
(A) spending too much money
(B) granting wishes
(C) useful
(D) spending money carefully

17. According to the essay, ____ is an example of **efficiency**.
(A) reading carefully
(B) doing more work in less time
(C) avoiding change
(D) dividing instead of multiplying

18. The author writes, "Okay, **cancel** that idea." Here, **cancel** means
(A) keep thinking about
(B) come back to
(C) do away with
(D) stamp

19. To give a clue to the meaning of **metropolitan,** the writer
(A) notes that a **metropolitan** area is a major city
(B) associates **metropolitan** with change in rural farm areas
(C) associates **metropolitan** with career choices
(D) tells us that change is likely

20. You can tell from the essay that **utility** means
(A) electricity
(B) creativity
(C) helplessness
(D) usefulness

READING NEW WORDS IN CONTEXT

| Lesson 13 | **CONTEXT:** Change in Science and Technology

Introduction. Science is a complex and constantly changing field. Just what is a scientist, and what does a scientist do? Is being a scientist the job for you?

The following article may help you answer these questions. The article also gives you an opportunity to expand your vocabulary. Below are twenty vocabulary words that are used in the article and in the exercise that follows it.

abrupt	coincide	elaborate	magnitude	radiate
accord	commit	inert	manual	random
approximate	confirm	infinite	mechanism	repel
chaos	debris	kernel	probability	surplus

Science: Asking Questions to Explain Our World

Most people know that scientists have improved the quality of our lives. For example, the work of scientists has helped to eliminate some **manual** (1) labor. Machines and computers do much of the work that human beings once did by hand. It is rare, though, for a person on the street to be able to describe accurately the work of a scientist. In general, however, we can say that scientists try to explain things. The scientist asks "Why do bees behave this way?" or "What causes volcanoes?" The best answers to these questions and the countless others that scientists ask are the ones that **coincide** (2), or agree, with all the known facts.

Scientists may study the entire universe or the life of a tiny cell. The scientist looking at the **mechanism** (3) of the universe and the scientist looking at the workings of a single cell approach their tasks in similar ways. In their searches, they rely on observation, experimentation, and study.

Scientific Answers Lead to More Questions

Each question answered by scientists leads to more unanswered ones, and there are many things that scientists cannot know for certain. Instead of referring to what definitely exists, scientists talk about what is most likely. For example, several decades ago scientists proposed that all matter may be composed of tiny particles called *quarks.* These particles seemed to be the **kernel** (4), the core, of matter.

Most scientists accept the **probability** (5) that quarks exist because quarks offer the best explanation of certain observed facts. Scientific probability is very different from what we mean when we say "maybe" or "possibly." The members of the scientific community are more exact than most people. They do not **commit** (6) themselves to saying something is likely unless they have enough evidence. In other words, they do not stand behind a theory unless it is clearly the most logical explanation. Scientists usually do not speak out about new theories or ideas on their own, but wait to see if the scientific community is in **accord** (7). In fact, it is only after scientists agree about a possibility that it becomes a **probability** or an accepted theory.

As much as scientists prefer hard and fast answers, some things simply cannot be known exactly. For example, how many subatomic particles are there in the universe? Since no one could possibly count all the particles, the number can't be **confirmed** (8). The answer has to be **approximate** (9). Scientists guess that there are 22 quinvigintillion particles in the universe (that's 22,000,000,000,000,000,000,000,000,000,000, 000,000,000,000,000,000,000,000,000,000,000,000, 000,000).

Science Is a Very Broad Field

It sometimes seems to many people that scientists have created a **surplus** (10) of information—so now we have more information than we know how to handle. No one person could understand it all—not even a scientist. That is why scientists specialize, to bring order out of what appears to be **chaos** (11).

For example, an astronomer might devote her entire career to the study of comets. She may further specialize in trying to identify the **debris** (12) that forms the tails of comets. Such study of the bits and pieces of comets may seem to have little **magnitude** (13) to most people. But this scientist's work, in combination with the work of other scientists, is actually very important because it will help us understand the universe. The knowledge she gains will **radiate** (14) like the spokes of a wheel and lend useful

information to other branches of science, such as physical chemistry, molecular biology, and nuclear physics.

A Career in Science

Does the idea of being a scientist attract you, or does it **repel** (15) you? Science is certainly not the career for the mentally **inert** (16), but if you have an active mind and enjoy solving problems, science may be the career for you. Remember, there are millions of things you could study. In fact, since scientists seek to explain the universe, and the universe seems to be without end, your choices are **infinite** (17)!

Most scientists carefully choose what to study. They do not choose their subjects at **random** (18). Once they've chosen their subjects, they examine them carefully. More complicated subjects require more in-depth, **elaborate** (19) study.

Your decision to become a scientist may be **abrupt** (20), or it may develop over a long period of time, but if you do choose to become a scientist, you will have a fascinating career. Like the scientist who studies comets, you will have to specialize in a field of study, but you will take satisfaction in knowing that the work you do will add to the knowledge of our constantly changing universe.

EXERCISE · Reading Strategically ☞

Directions. Answer each of the following items by circling the letter of the correct answer. You may need to refer to the article as you answer the items. The numbers of the items are the same as the numbers of the boldface vocabulary words in the article.

1. The writer of this article indicates that science has helped to eliminate some **manual** labor. Here, **manual** means

(A) done by hand
(B) done thoughtfully
(C) done by machine
(D) scientific

2. In this article, **coincide** means

(A) explain
(B) understand
(C) argue
(D) agree

3. To give a clue to the meaning of **mechanism**, the writer
   (A) indicates that a single cell is not a **mechanism**
   (B) indicates that the universe is like a cell
   (C) links looking at a **mechanism** to looking at the workings
   (D) tells us that different scientists approach their work in similar ways

4. The writer says that tiny particles called *quarks* may be the **kernel** of matter. Here, **kernel** means
   (A) subatomic
   (B) core
   (C) quark
   (D) existence

5. In this article, **probability** means
   (A) likelihood
   (B) slight possibility
   (C) definite proof
   (D) explanation

6. To give a clue to the meaning of **commit**, the writer
   (A) indicates that scientists will **commit** even to small possibilities
   (B) links **commit** to the phrase "stand behind"
   (C) says that explanations are logical
   (D) hints that truly cautious scientists gladly make **commitments**

7. Which is the most likely reason that scientists are usually in **accord** about scientific **probabilities**?
   (A) A scientific possibility is something that all scientists agree on.
   (B) Scientists hardly ever agree about a **probability**.
   (C) Scientists must generally agree about a possibility before it is called a **probability**.
   (D) Scientists reject all explanations that cannot be proven to be true.

8. Which of the following is the most likely reason that the number of particles can't be **confirmed**?
   (A) The number has already been carefully counted.
   (B) Scientists don't like to guess.
   (C) Some things can be known exactly.
   (D) No one can count them all.

9. To let us know that **approximate** means "estimated," the writer
   (A) indicates that scientists prefer facts
   (B) points out that the universe is made of particles
   (C) tells us that the scientists guess at the number of particles
   (D) says that there are 22 quinvigintillion particles in the universe

10. To give a clue to the meaning of **surplus**, the writer
    (A) indicates that the **surplus** occurs sometimes
    (B) indicates that a **surplus** is something scientists create
    (C) uses the phrase "more information than we know how to handle"
    (D) suggests that **surplus** is characteristic of information

11. You can tell from the article that **chaos** means
    (A) observations
    (B) scientific facts
    (C) organic matter
    (D) confusion

12. In this article, the word **debris** means
    (A) tails
    (B) unbroken materials
    (C) specialization
    (D) bits and pieces

13. The author writes, "Such study . . . may seem to have little **magnitude** to most people." Here, **magnitude** means

(A) importance
(B) brightness
(C) intelligence
(D) astronomy

14. In the article, the astronomer's knowledge about comets is said to **radiate** to other branches of science like

(A) the tail of a comet
(B) the rays of the sun
(C) the spokes of a wheel
(D) the understanding of the universe

15. To let us know that to **repel** means "to push away or drive off," the writer

(A) contrasts **repel** with the word *attract*
(B) gives a specific example
(C) says a scientist should enjoy solving problems
(D) associates **repel** with science

16. All of the following are good definitions of **inert** *except*

(A) slow
(B) dull
(C) mentally inactive
(D) intelligent

17. The writer suggests that a scientist's choices for study are **infinite**. Here, **infinite** means

(A) limitless
(B) intelligent
(C) limited
(D) probable

18. The author writes, "They do not choose their subjects at **random**." Here, **random** means

(A) carefully
(B) by chance
(C) by choice
(D) scientifically

19. The writer tells us that complicated subjects require in-depth, **elaborate** study. Here, **elaborate** means

(A) complex
(B) scientific
(C) chosen
(D) factual

20. The writer tells us that a decision to become a scientist may be **abrupt**. Here, **abrupt** means

(A) bound to happen
(B) frequent
(C) hard to make
(D) sudden

READING NEW WORDS IN CONTEXT

Lesson 14 | CONTEXT: Change in Science and Technology

Introduction. Some people answer questions without ever leaving their homes or offices. They do research in books, talk about their questions with associates, and spend a lot of time in deep thought. Other people have a different style of facing challenges. They go abroad, under the sea, even into outer space to find answers to their questions. Both ways of finding answers are valuable.

The following article tells you about some of the people whose curiosity sent them into the unknown. The article gives you an opportunity to expand your vocabulary. Below are twenty vocabulary words that are used in the article and in the exercise that follows it.

aerial	diversity	exotic	navigable	universal
alternate	ecosystem	geological	poach	unpredictable
barren	effect	glacial	propel	via
challenge	encounter	inquisitive	tributary	vital

Exploring, Discovering, and Changing

The desire to know more about our world is **universal** (1) among human beings. Maybe that's because humans everywhere are **inquisitive** (2) and always have been. Our earliest ancestors wanted to know what lay over the hill, beyond the mountains, and across the sea. Our curiosity even goes beyond this planet; we wonder what lies in space.

Not everyone who has wondered about the world has been brave enough to face the **challenge** (3) of exploring. To leave the safety of the world we know and go into uncharted territory is a demanding task. Many of us who will hike through a nearby park don't want to explore the frozen, **glacial** (4) regions near the poles or to fly over the Amazon doing **aerial** (5) surveys of the rain forest.

Yet, we are grateful to those who do explore. What explorers discover and learn has always had a profound **effect** (6) on the rest of us. Not only does it teach us about the **ecosystem** (7),

that important balance of nature, it also shapes and changes our understanding of the world. What makes someone want to explore, though?

Seeking New and Different Worlds

Different explorers have had a **diversity** (8) of reasons for their adventures. Of the many different reasons, the most common is an interest in the **exotic** (9), in that which seems strange or different. Of course, this is a matter of perspective. Cheng Ho (c. 1371–c. 1433), the great Chinese sailor, arrived in Zanzibar off the African coast in the early fifteenth century. He and his crew undoubtedly found the Africans there **exotic**, but Africans surely thought the Chinese **exotic** as well. What is strange to one culture may seem ordinary to another. Every culture has customs that seem strange to other cultures. Perhaps the explorers who have helped us most are those who have helped us to discover and respect our differences.

Exploring for Profit

Some explorers have hoped their missions would lead to financial gain. For example, in the fifteenth century, Europeans could no longer travel to Asia **via** (10) the old land routes. As a result, explorers set out to find new ways to get to China and Japan. They hoped to profit from trade. The search for other, **alternate** (11), routes led the Europeans to the Americas.

Explorers began to sail up streams in a search for a **navigable** (12) route across the land mass. While they looked for a waterway that would let them sail across the continent, these explorers **encountered** (13) more and more people in this "new" world. However, the American Indians whom the Europeans met thought of their world as the old one—it was the explorers who were new and **poaching** (14), or intruding, on their territory.

Seeking Adventure

No matter what other motives they have, all explorers seem to have one thing in common—a sense of adventure. If Mary Kingsley (1862–1900) had wanted an ordinary life, she would never have left England in the 1890s. Kingsley wanted a life that was exciting and **unpredictable** (15), so she paddled her way along the main river and the **tributaries** (16) of the Niger Delta in Africa. There she found beauty in the dignity of the peoples she met and in the awesome rivers and forests of West Africa.

Preparing for the Journey

Although explorers may be adventurous, they are seldom impulsive. They know that it is **vital** (17) to prepare carefully for their journeys. Proper preparation can make the difference between life and death. An explorer who enters a cave to learn more about its **geological** (18) formations takes good lights, the proper ropes, and other supplies. A scientist who explores the desert for signs of ancient civilizations does not start to cross the dry, **barren** (19) sand without enough water. Before river explorers will **propel** (20) a canoe through swift waters, they make sure their supplies will remain dry. Such preparation does not take away any of the sense of adventure in exploring. It does, however, help make sure explorers return safely to tell of the adventures they had.

EXERCISE *Reading Strategically* ☞

Directions. Answer each of the following items by circling the letter of the correct answer. You may need to refer to the article as you answer the items. The numbers of the items are the same as the numbers of the boldface vocabulary words in the article.

1. You can from the article tell that **universal** means
   (A) limited or restricted
   (B) throughout time
   (C) occurring everywhere
   (D) important to

2. To let us know that **inquisitive** means "curious," the writer
   (A) uses **inquisitive** to describe people
   (B) refers to our earliest ancestors as **inquisitive** people
   (C) provides examples of what people have wondered about
   (D) uses the phrase "always have been"

3. The word **challenge** in this article means
  (A) a demanding task
  (B) an unanswerable question
  (C) scientific exploration
  (D) a hike

4. The writer describes the earth's poles as frozen and **glacial**. Here, **glacial** means
  (A) icy
  (B) unfriendly
  (C) slow
  (D) warming

5. The author writes that many of us "don't want to . . . fly over the Amazon doing **aerial** surveys of the rain forest." Here, **aerial** means
  (A) dangerous
  (B) with equipment
  (C) scientific
  (D) from the air

6. Which of the following is an example mentioned in the article of an **effect** that explorers can have on us?
  (A) We should be grateful to explorers.
  (B) Explorers have a number of reasons for exploring.
  (C) Explorers can change our understanding of the world.
  (D) No one knows what makes certain people want to be explorers.

7. To let us know that **ecosystem** means "a community of plants and animals together with their environment," the writer
  (A) refers to explorers that fly over the rain forest
  (B) tells us that explorers change our understanding of the world
  (C) refers to a balance of nature
  (D) mentions the profound effect that explorers have on us

8. All of the following are good definitions for **diversity** *except*
  (A) different
  (B) various
  (C) assorted
  (D) similar

9. To give us a clue to the meaning of **exotic**, the writer
  (A) tells us that **exotic** is a matter of perspective
  (B) links **exotic** to the words *strange or different*
  (C) hints that explorers have different reasons for their adventures
  (D) uses the word to describe the fifteenth century

10. How does the writer let us know that **via** means "by the way of"?
  (A) The writer indicates that there was a way to profit from trade.
  (B) The writer tells us that explorers set out to find new ways.
  (C) The writer refers to a search.
  (D) The writer discusses the nations of Asia.

11. The author writes, "The search for . . . **alternate** routes led the Europeans to the Americas." Here, the word **alternate** means
  (A) discoverable
  (B) lost
  (C) substitute
  (D) American

12. The writer reports that explorers searched for a **navigable** route. Here, **navigable** means
  (A) water
  (B) newfound
  (C) passable
  (D) short

13. Another good word for **encountered** is
(A) introduced
(B) fought
(C) counted
(D) met

14. The word **poaching** in this article means
(A) traveling with
(B) taking over
(C) intruding
(D) foreigners

15. All of the following are good definitions of **unpredictable** *except*
(A) commonplace
(B) uncertain
(C) changeable
(D) not predictable

16. The writer tells us that Mary Kingsley traveled on a river and on its **tributaries**. Here, **tributaries** means
(A) people who pay tribute to a ruler
(B) supplies
(C) currents
(D) streams that flow into a river

17. The author writes, "They know that it is **vital** to prepare carefully for their journeys." Here, **vital** means
(A) full of life
(B) deadly
(C) careful
(D) necessary

18. To give a clue to the meaning of **geological**, the writer
(A) reminds us that preparation is important when exploring caves
(B) indicates that it is important to study caves
(C) contrasts **geological** with the word *proper*
(D) links **geological** to formations in caves

19. In the last paragraph, **barren** means
(A) old
(B) empty
(C) uncivilized
(D) thirsty

20. You can tell from the article that **propel** means
(A) to fly
(B) to throw
(C) to push
(D) to jump

READING NEW WORDS IN CONTEXT

Lesson 15 | **CONTEXT: Change in Science and Technology**

Introduction. We have come to realize how important plants are to our life-support system on planet Earth, and that they have to be protected. After almost 60 percent of the earth's rain forests have been destroyed, faster than any other natural group, conservationists and businesses are beginning to join together to find ways to make the rain forests more profitable standing than chopped down.

The following dialogue gives you an opportunity to expand your vocabulary. Below are twenty vocabulary words that are used in the dialogue and in the exercise that follows it.

capacity	intermediate	perpetual	preliminary	speculate
conifer	intricate	photosynthesis	prompt	stability
digital	involuntary	precaution	proportion	stationary
germinate	minimum	precise	reception	submerged

Rain Forests: Working to Save Them

The students in Mr. Jefferson's seventh-grade class have been assigned science projects. Five of the students—Charlene, Amy, Max, Dan, and Tara—are working together to research what is happening to prevent further loss of the rain forests. They have just completed some **preliminary** (1) research and are meeting to compare notes from their first trip to the library.

Max: I found that there are three types of forests, and it depends on the climate as to which trees grow where. Up north, close to the tundra, are generally evergreen **conifers** (2), cone-bearing trees such as spruces and firs. Farther south, hardwoods such as hickories and oaks grow, and there are a **minimum** (3) of thirty types of rain forests closer to the equator. There are probably even more than that.

Amy: Did you know that even though rain forests only cover about seven percent of the earth's land surface, about one half of the earth's species live there? There is no **precise** (4) number, but scientists think there are at least five million kinds of plants and animals on the planet. That fact alone should **prompt** (5) us to save the forests. The situation is not **stationary** (6); it is deteriorating rapidly. Where will these species live as the forests continue to be destroyed?

Charlene: I already knew that the rain forests were important, but I didn't really understand why. You know, we studied **photosynthesis** (7) and how plants **germinate** (8) last year, but evidently there's a lot more to plants than how they make food and sprout. A number of plants in the rain forests have chemicals with the **capacity** (9) to fight cancer—actually a higher **proportion** (10) of plants with that capability are found there than have been found anywhere else. Scientists can only **speculate** (11) as to the actual number of helpful chemicals that are there. Who can possibly guess?

Dan: We've all heard about the **perpetual** (12) battle, lasting for years, to stop further destruction of the rain forests, so I was glad to find that some businesses are working to find ways to make money from the forests without chopping them down. These ideas are getting a warm **reception** (13) from many conservationists. They are pleased to get any help to save trees.

Tara: I found that, too. Ecotourism is becoming very profitable. Some investors buy up sections of a rain forest and charge fees for people to come and see them. Businesspeople consider tourism a good way to make money while keeping the forests safe.

Amy: And there are rain forest products that are valuable, like chicle for gum and allspice for cooking. Can you imagine what our world would be like without such rain forest products as coffee or rubber?

Charlene: Did you know that forests supply water? There is an **intricate** (14), or involved, system of roots, layers of old leaves, and soil that works together to hold the water. And forests have lakes and rivers that provide water for a lot of people.

Dan: I've read that some companies are taking

the **precaution** (15) of trying to balance their industrial plants' output of carbon dioxide into the atmosphere by preserving some part of a rain forest. They buy part of a rain forest and take care to keep it from being destroyed because it can absorb the same amount of carbon dioxide that their factory produces. This strategy is only an **intermediate** (16) step, somewhere between total destruction and total protection.

Max: I think that the knowledge has been **submerged** (17), you know, kept from us, that more trees are damaged by loggers than are actually chopped down or damaged by **involuntary** (18) means, such as accidental burning.

Amy: You know, it will be very sad if we can't maintain the **stability** (19) of the forests for future generations. Not only are they beautiful and necessary to keep the earth in balance, but I think that keeping and protecting them is just the right thing to do.

Tara: Oh, the **digital** (20) clock says it is 2:28:05, so we had better save the rest for class tomorrow.

EXERCISE *Reading Strategically* ☜

Directions. Answer each of the following items by circling the letter of the correct answer. You may need to refer to the story as you answer the items. The numbers of the items are the same as the numbers of the boldface vocabulary words in the story.

1. The writer indicates that the five students have done some **preliminary** work. Here, **preliminary** means
   (A) difficult
   (B) beforehand
   (C) indefinite
   (D) later

2. You can tell from the dialogue that **conifers** means
   (A) fruit-bearing trees
   (B) evergreens
   (C) cone-bearing trees
   (D) tundras

3. To give a clue to the meaning of **minimum**, the writer
   (A) tells us that there are thirty types of rain forests
   (B) tells us that hickories and oaks grow farther south
   (C) tells us that there are at least thirty types of rain forests
   (D) tells us that rain forests only cover about seven percent of earth's land

4. The writer reports that there is no **precise** number of the earth's species. Here, **precise** means all the following *except*

(A) accurate
(B) correct
(C) approximate
(D) exact

5. Amy states, "That fact alone should **prompt** us to save the forests." Here, **prompt** means

(A) a reminder
(B) on time
(C) urge to action
(D) desire to change

6. You can tell from the dialogue that **stationary** means

(A) all in one place
(B) staying the same
(C) safe from harm
(D) destroyed

7. You can tell from Charlene's statement that **photosynthesis** means

(A) green plants
(B) growing plants
(C) a process to make food
(D) a process to make flowers

8. In this dialogue, **germinate** means to

(A) make chlorophyll
(B) make seed
(C) make food
(D) grow

9. The writer reports that a number of plants in the rain forests have chemicals with the **capacity** to fight cancer. Here, **capacity** means

(A) able to hold
(B) large number
(C) ability
(D) knowledge

10. All of the following are good definitions for **proportion** *except*

(A) a part of the whole
(B) a definite number
(C) to make balanced
(D) ratio

11. To give a clue to the meaning of **speculate**, the writer

(A) tells us that some plants have helpful chemicals
(B) hints that the actual number of plants is only a guess
(C) tells us that some plants have chemicals that might prevent cancer
(D) tells us about the plants in the rain forest

12. In the dialogue, the word **perpetual** means

(A) temporary
(B) fighting
(C) occasionally
(D) continual

13. Dan tells us that businesses working to save forests are getting a warm **reception** from many conservationists. Here, **reception** means

(A) response
(B) refusal
(C) enthusiasm
(D) feeling

14. Charlene tells us that forests have an **intricate** system for holding water. Here, **intricate** means

(A) complicated
(B) fascinating
(C) storage
(D) refreshing

15. To give a clue to the meaning of **precaution**, the writer
  (A) tells us that some companies buy up rain forests
  (B) tells us that some company plants discharge carbon dioxide
  (C) tells us that some companies are taking care to keep a portion of a rain forest safe
  (D) tells us that forests provide water

16. You can tell from the dialogue that **intermediate** means
  (A) a step
  (B) in the middle
  (C) a beginning
  (D) a result

17. In this dialogue, **submerged** means
  (A) flooded
  (B) available
  (C) hidden
  (D) sunken

18. In this dialogue, **involuntary** means all of the following *except*
  (A) accidental
  (B) not intentional
  (C) on purpose
  (D) automatic

19. Amy tells us it will be sad if we can't maintain the **stability** of the forests. Here, **stability** means
  (A) beauty
  (B) unchanging in condition
  (C) resources
  (D) keeping it solid

20. To give a clue as to the meaning of **digital**, the writer
  (A) refers to a clock
  (B) gives us specific numbers
  (C) lets us know that the class is ending for the day
  (D) tells us that we have to finish tomorrow

Vocabulary Words

abrupt
absolute
abstract
absurd
accord
acute
adhere
adopt
aerial
aggravate
alien
ally
alternate
anguish
anticipate
antiseptic
approximate
audible
authentic
avert

banish
barbarous
baron
barren
blemish

caliber
camouflage
cancel
candid
capacity
challenge
chaos
cherish
coincide
commit
comparable
compensate
competent
compute
confirm
conform
congregate
conifer
consequence
consistent

conspicuous
constitution
contemplate
controversial
credible
crisis
crucial
cultural

dashing
debris
defiant
deliberate
designate
destiny
dialogue
diaphragm
digital
diplomatic
discrimination
dismal
distort
distract
diversity
dual

economical
ecosystem
edible
editorial
effect
efficiency
elaborate
elective
eloquent
encounter
endurance
era
eventual
exceed
excel
excess
exotic
expand

faculty
fascinate

fatigue
financial
flaw
forbidding
formal
fortress
forum
frail
fugitive
fulfill
fundamental
futile

galaxy
geological
germinate
gesture
ghastly
glacial
glucose
grammatical
grandeur
gratify
grotesque
guarantee

habitat
hardy
haunt
hesitation
hover
humane
hypocrite
hysterical

idle
ignorance
illusion
illustrious
immature
immortal
immune
impact
indefinite
indirect
indispensable
inert

inferior
infinite
inhabit
initial
inquisitive
intellect
intermediate
interpret
intolerable
intricate
invade
involuntary
irritable

journal
judicial

kernel

leash
legendary
legible
legitimate
lenient
literary
logical
loiter
luminous
lure

magnitude
maintain
mammal
maneuver
manual
manuscript
mastery
maternal
maturity
mechanism
memorandum
mere
merit
metropolitan
minimum
minority
moderate

modest
monarchy
moral
mortal
motive
myth
mythology

narration
naturalist
navigable
nocturnal
notable
notorious
nutrition

obligation
obsolete
obstacle
obstinate
offend
officially
opponent
opposition
optical
optional
organism
originality
overture

pageant
parasite
partial
participant

participate
penetrate
percentage
perilous
perpetual
persuasion
phase
photosynthesis
pigment
placid
planetary
poach
porcelain
precaution
precise
preliminary
preservation
prestige
principally
probability
proclamation
profound
prompt
propel
proportion
prose
prudent
pursue

radiate
random
reality
reception
recognition

recoil
recommend
refrain
relinquish
repel
resolve
revise
ridicule
rival

satellite
scholarship
seasonal
segregation
self-conscious
serf
signify
speculate
spontaneous
stability
stationary
stationery
status
stellar
submerged
substantial
subtle
supervise
surplus
symbolic

tactics
technique
temperate

tendency
threshold
timid
tiresome
toil
tranquil
tributary
turmoil
tutor
tyrant

undergrowth
unison
universal
unpredictable
usage
utility

vague
valiant
velocity
vengeance
versatile
veto
via
vigor
vital

wretched

yield

zoology

NOTES

NOTES

NOTES

NOTES